W9-DBQ-782

Safe Eyes

A Story of Healing

——◆◆◆——

Dr. Deborah Hall Berkley

Safe Eyes: A Story of Healing

© 2001
Deborah Hall Berkley

No portion of this book may be reproduced
without the written permission of the author.

ISBN 1-890306-31-2

Library of Congress Catalog Card Number: 2001092234

A MADELINE CENTER BOOK
The Madeline Center
18679 Forest Road
Lynchburg, Virginia 24502
(434) 239-0003
www.madelinecenter.com

Chapter Divider Photographs by: Amy Moore (1, 2, 3, 5),
Bill Moore (6, 8), Sylviane P. Bellamy (4), and Deborah Berkley (7).

Warwick House

Publishing
720 Court Street
Lynchburg, VA 24504

DEDICATION

When I was lost, wandering aimlessly in the darkness of a compelling and seemingly endless project, Dr. Charles O. Matthews of The College of William and Mary in Williamsburg, Virginia, told me: "Deborah, in twenty-five years of teaching at the college level, I have never encountered a doctoral dissertation that had the power to change peoples' lives. I know you're frustrated, but hang in there!"

I will always be grateful to him for opening my eyes, for expanding my consciousness to the world of the transpersonal, a world of *lived spirituality*.

Jon Winder, Lavinia Garbee and Stacey Barbour kindly offered editorial comments that served to strengthen the work, and I am deeply indebted to them for their time and patience. Joyce Abbott, our on-site redeemer, supplied the massage and Reiki treatments that kept me grounded. My dear friend of many years, JoAnn Chrysanthus, offered her own special brand of assistance. She fed me *chocolate*—lots and lots of chocolate! ("Deborah, you look stuck! Would some chocolate help?") While the Hershey's Crunch Bars seemed to be an answer to prayer at the time, I reconsider their value daily now as I wrestle with my once attractive wardrobe.

When overwhelmed, as I frequently was, it was these folks who reminded me that it was not *my right, but my responsibility,* to share the story of Grace Ann Hughes. In doing so, they, I'm sure unbeknownst to them, furnished the ballast that steadied me and ultimately legitimized my struggle.

In addition, it would be difficult, if not impossible, to undertake such a daunting task, first a doctoral dissertation, and then a book, without the support of family. They have paid by far the biggest price. These guys have not even once in more than five years so much as hinted that I abandon the work. So to Karl, your belief in me, when I had little faith in myself, has sustained me throughout this process. A special thanks to you for creating and maintaining The Madeline Center's idyllic gardens, a haven not only for our clients, but for the therapists as well. To Jason, the *real* writer in the family, be kind to yourself. Joy is but one heartbeat away. It, as Grace Ann has shown us all, can only be found by turning within. To Justin, my budding entrepreneur, I pray I have taught you to fish!

To Mom and Dad, Madeline and Bob Hall, my deepest gratitude for guiding me, in your own way, to the light.

I also offer this book to you, the reader, and honor your willingness and *courage* as you walk these pages with Grace Ann Hughes. I have been in awe of the written word for most of my life. On those days when I allowed myself to dream the really big dream, I dreamt of writing, not just any book, but a book that had the power to, as Dr. Matthews suggested, change peoples' lives. *Safe Eyes* was a gift to me. I now give it to you. To those of you who are hurting, have been hurt, have hurt others, or who have, for whatever the reason, *temporarily* lost your way, allow Grace Ann to hold your hand as you (and your *own* inner-knower) make straight *your* path and once again open the door to the light that's awaiting us all.

And, in memory of Brian.

CONTENTS

INTRODUCTION

The human mind is truly remarkable. Instinctively protective, it is vigilant in its observations. When threatened with an overwhelming trauma, it seeks to anesthetize, compartmentalize, and adapt, until that day when, nestled in a haven of security and trust, it undertakes the arduous task of healing itself. Where there is safety there is hope—hope for survival, for recovery, and ultimately for life—long denied.

The battle wages onward, lines of confrontation boldly etched, an undisguised repulsion in the eyes of those of the opposing camp. Questions abound. Does Multiple Personality Disorder, now known as Dissociative Identity Disorder (DID) exist? Is an altered state of consciousness a pathological manifestation of a deranged mind, or simply the result of an overactive imagination? Is DID the by-product of a therapist who unwittingly stokes the all-consuming flames of an unscripted drama? Does a human being possess an innate ability to heal itself? Is there an inner-knower, an internal self-helper that resides within us all?

As in wars throughout the ages, each seeks the truth as he understands, or perhaps *needs* it to be—proclaiming, denying, debating, rebutting. We continue our march through the minefield of disbelief. What *is* the truth? Do we have the courage to know?

———◆•✶•◆———

While at times incredible, the following story of Grace Ann Hughes is a true one. Names have been changed, but it has not been edited to minimize its graphic content, nor sensationalized in an effort to sell books. It portrays not one, but two inner odysseys, sometimes intersecting, sometimes parallel voyages of dualities punctuated by confidence and questioning, hope and disillusionment, serenity and struggle, alienation and union, utter despair and absolute peace.

I have been told that once in every psychotherapist's lifetime a client will "land on the doorstep" who challenges, chisels, and changes your life forever. Such was the case of Grace Ann Hughes. I cannot imagine that I will ever again be a witness to that degree of pain and suffering, or that level of inestimable courage and determination to heal. *Nothing*, no well-worn text, motivating lecture, experiential exercise, nor supervised experience prepared me for Grace Ann and her "inside" family. Month after month, therapeutic plan after plan was adopted, modified, discarded. Frustration mounted. Discouragement crept in. No longer the director, I was, more often than not, a resentful participant, sharing little of Grace Ann's unwavering faith, and even less of her zeal. Reluctantly, I, as the considerably educated and meticulously trained therapist, accepted what had become all too obvious—*there was no way out but through.* If meaningful change was to happen, or even be attempted for that matter, I had no choice but to surrender—*get out of my own way.*

Upon reflection, there was a point that the process emerged with a life of its own, not *because* of my scholarship, but *in spite* of it. Grace Ann's courage opened the door for others to heal. Those who reach deep within and hear, *really hear*, the words of her internal self-helper, her *Strong Man*, will become acquainted with, once again, the inner wisdom and guiding light that resides within us all.

Perhaps Grace Ann's introduction into my life on that rainy November day was nothing more than mere chance, an unlucky stroke of fate's pen. I thought so for several very long years. In retrospect, I believe it was no less than an incidence of Jung's synchronicity, a "meaningful coincidence," whose purpose continues to unfold in both my personal and professional life today. The redemptive transformation that came— alienation to union, utter despair to absolute peace—impacted not only Grace Ann, but me as well. Grace Ann taught me the meaning of James 4:6b: "God resists the proud, but gives grace to the humble." In fact, the name *Grace* was chosen to represent the peace and forgiveness that is free to us all, *if we will but ask.*

It is my most cherished desire that Grace Ann and her "all healed" inside family will give themselves a hug for a job well done, and will *know* that their light has indeed shone brighter than their pain. It is to this lovely lady that I owe a debt of gratitude for what I have become, and for what I yet hope to be.

It was the strangest dream. The aging room wears panels of a rich, dark wood. Benches, high-backed, ramrod straight, are positioned on either side of the burnished hall, framing what appears to be a center aisle. At one end is a massive door, replete with chiseled carvings and tarnished brass. Above the door, in the gable end, is an oddly diminutive, octagonal window which emits the room's only natural light. At the far end is a raised box-like structure, much like the pulpit of an 18th century house of worship—ominous in its rigidity and uncertainty.

Footsteps echo in the chambers of my subconscious mind. Black-robed, wigged men file in. Staid, proper, even sanctimonious, each face is a blank canvas.

The massive door groans open, revealing a woman in tattered clothing, hands shackled, her down-turned face obscured by unkempt hair.

I watch, a silent observer to the surreal scene, as she is led along the walkway and up the narrow steps to what now appears to be a makeshift cell.

A portly gentleman stands. A booming voice rings out.

"Madam, you are on this day to be tried for your ideals."

In less than a moment, a brilliant light, laser intense, is beamed through the octagonal window. Robed arms shield startled eyes; men fall to their knees. And there, in the light, stands an elderly woman with shining—no, twinkling—eyes. At her side is a long, narrow basket woven of reeds, brimming with rosemary and sage and lavender, herbs, healing herbs. Slowly, very slowly, as if performing a sacred rite of passage, she lifts the basket, and her eyes, to the shackled woman above.

My soul gasps in recognition, as the elderly woman with the twinkling eyes is my beloved grandmother. And the shackled woman, the prisoner of her ideals... me.

What does it mean?

It was the strangest dream....

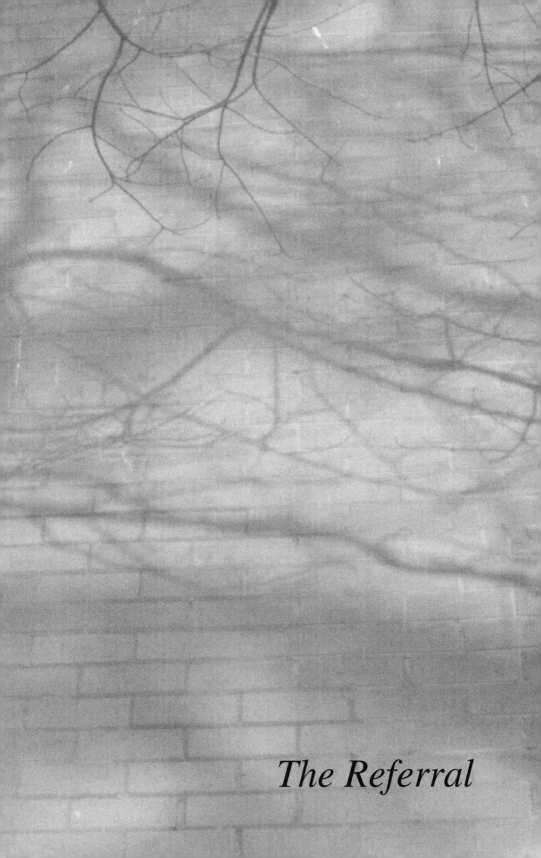

The Referral

---

*"It takes two to tell the truth;
one to say it, another to hear it."*

Thoreau

CHAPTER ONE

November 1994

"I ran into an old friend at the doctor's office the other day, a gal I knew from the university. She's in pretty bad shape…gained a lot of weight…hobbling around on painful looking crutches. Told me she's just been released from, I don't know, I think some sort of treatment program. She's out of work with a bad knee, and it looks like it's getting to her—most likely an adjustment disorder, maybe even depression. You interested?"

Am I interested? Are you kidding? My first client! I have just signed a contract to join an established psychotherapeutic practice. My new colleague and I have agreed that I will be assigned to a satellite office as soon as I've completed my current graduate program and resigned my school counseling position. I haven't even hung out a shingle, and I have a referral! As my twelve-year-old son, Justin, would say, this is just too awesome!

Wait a minute....

Slow down, Deb....

*How on earth am I going to make this work? I'm a full-time graduate student, a full-time school counselor, a full-time mother, and I'm thinking of adding **this** to an already overloaded schedule? Am I highly motivated or just plain stupid? Let's see. I can drive the two hundred miles every other weekend, it's only a couple more months until I graduate. I can see this lady on Saturdays, and then drive back on Sunday nights. If she's struggling with depression, we'll probably be wrapped up by the time I move back. That seems reasonable! It's just two months before all this craziness ends. In the meantime, the extra money would really be a huge help, with Christmas right around the corner and that move coming up in January. Perfect, just perfect! Everything's falling into place! Couldn't be better!*

Struggling to mask my unexpected good fortune, I turn to address my newfound benefactor as we emerge from the dimly lit hall. Huddling beneath the building's less than adequate overhang, preparing to dart into the November evening's intermittent rain, I casually reply, "Sure, I'll be happy to see her…give her my phone number. Tell her to give me a call if she wants to set something up. No problem."

Mistake number one!

A scant twenty minutes later, I pull into the driveway of our family's weekend retreat. Scurrying through the now obnoxious downpour, I am greeted at the fully flung door, not with the expected congratulatory hug, but with an unexpected menacing scowl. Caught off guard, my entrepreneurial glee wilts. Ignoring my dripping hair and soggy coat, my exasperated husband thrusts the cordless phone at me, saying, "Look, this lady has called three times. She sounds awful. I told her you weren't here, that you'd be in touch when you got in, but she keeps on calling. You talk to her. I don't know anything about this stuff!" Returning the scowl, I reach for the receiver.

"Hello, this is Deborah, may I help you?" My query is met with silence. I glare at my husband, silently accusing him of manufacturing both the controversy and the call. "Hello, may I help you?" I again ask, watching water meandering across the oak floor.

Again, no reply. Wait! What's that, that strange, barely perceptible sound? Is my agitated mind playing tricks on me, or do I detect a faint, erratic, rasping sort of breathing?

I'm beginning to understand why my husband has become unglued. This is really weird! I search out his eyes, offering a silent apology.

A low-pitched, scarcely audible voice (if you could call it a voice)— an odd mixture of professionalism and a passionate pleading—finally says, "My name is Grace Ann Hughes. Jim Driskill told me you would help me. He said I could trust you. You *will* help me, won't you?"

Some forty-five perplexing, very cold minutes later, a session is finally scheduled. *I don't think it's supposed to take forty-five minutes to schedule a session!* Sighing (the mystifying banter has drained me), I agree to meet her the following Saturday in my colleague's office. I hadn't planned on making this grueling $3^{1}/_{2}$-hour commute again so soon, but this lady *really* is in bad shape. Replacing the receiver, I shake the numbness from my weary hand, and begin a mental checklist of rapidly mounting concerns. *I know I don't have a lot of experience and I just don't feel good about this. My intuition is tap dancing upon my now throbbing head. It's as if my gut is whispering, no, not whispering, shouting—shouting garbled messages, and I can't decipher the code! Shivers run up and down my spine as I attempt to shake off the chill—and the looming sense that all is not as it seems.* I'd better get in touch with this lady mid-week. If she's really as confused and depressed as she seems, I just won't be comfortable so far away. I'm going to need to refer her to someone more local. She denies having thoughts of harming herself, and vehemently protests the need of hospitalization, but I don't know. I just don't know.

A quick glance at the fog-shrouded darkness tells me what I already know—I'm running really late and the drive back to school through the pounding rain will be miserable. As I begrudgingly toss a week's worth of clothing into the backseat of my well worn, and equally reluctant, Grand Am, the phone continues to ring, with six additional calls received from the beleaguered client. Time after time, I am assured by the increasingly familiar voice that I can change my mind if I choose, since I might not want to work with someone "as bad" as herself. Drawing deeply upon my therapeutic training (for to rely upon my rapidly depleting emotional reserves would spell a certain disaster), I confirm, then reconfirm the appointed place and time, and seek to reassure the now invasive caller that Saturday *will be just fine*, that I look forward to our meeting, and am not at all likely to change my mind.

I hope I sound more convincing than I am beginning to feel.

My husband Karl is a high school principal. He married a middle school teacher and expected to remain married to a middle school teacher. Little did he know, nor did I for that matter, that his wife, the middle school teacher, would evolve into something, someone unknown—not unknown in a bad way, just unknown. First, there was the change from teacher to school counselor—not a big change, but a change nonethe-less. Then there was the change to doctoral student and the change to commuter wife. Eventually, whether he is to understand or not, he finds his own demanding life intertwined with that of a fledgling psychothera-pist, a change that is not only unanticipated, but, at times, unwelcomed. He, the high school principal, is understandably "green" regarding the appropriate therapeutic boundaries of repeated phone calls. From his perspective, when the phone rings, you answer it. It's as simple as that! As the high school principal, he has no way of knowing. I, as psycho-therapist, fledgling or not, should have known. I should have known.

I ponder the day's strange events during my long, tedious drive back to the university. It is after midnight when I reach my destination. A phone is again ringing. I seize the faultless receiver, only to be greeted with: "Deborah, this is Grace Ann Hughes. Are you sure you haven't changed your mind? You know you really don't have to see me!"

My husband, unfortunately, has little time for reflection, for the unrelenting calls continue. Afraid to answer the phone, but even more afraid to ignore this lady's apparent desperation, he confronts each new assault with a mixture of barely-suppressed agitation and mounting concern. Frustrated, no, not frustrated, *furious,* I phone a now sleeping Karl. "What in heaven's name was going through your demented mind when you gave Ms. Hughes this number?"

Too tired, or perhaps too wise, to argue with his equally demented wife, his only response was, "She said it was an emergency. I didn't know what else to do."

The week is punctuated with yet even more calls, three during the late hours of the evening, several more received during the day at school. Each petition replicates the now hauntingly familiar plea: "Deborah, this is Grace Ann Hughes. I'm sorry to bother you again, but I really have to know. Have you changed your mind yet? It's O.K. if you have. I'll understand. I wouldn't blame you for not wanting to work with someone as bad as me."

"I Feel Angry and Distant From God"

Rocking…rocking…rocking…she sits, precariously perched on the very edge of the borrowed room's oversized sofa. Crutches posi-tioned protectively by her side, she desperately clutches George, a well-worn brown bear, to her ample chest, sobbing, "I trust George, he won't hurt me, he has safe eyes. Can you see his safe eyes?" Reluctant, or perhaps simply unable to visually engage me, the puzzled therapist, she checks and rechecks her transient environment to determine if friend or foe. Hypervigilance gives way to detachment, as she appears to become spontaneously submerged in a world of shadowy apprehension. Her speech takes on a slurred quality, punctuated by the familiar rasping sounds, as if she were laboring to acquire sufficient air. At last, following a seemingly eternity of guttural clamor, she sighs, and with a curious conviction states, "George says I can trust you. You have safe eyes."

———◆◆◆◆◆———

Saturday finally comes. Following our lengthy initial session, Grace Ann asks, almost apologetically, if it "would be possible for George and me to see you again tomorrow," a pattern that is to continue. The second meeting proves less baffling and more informative. I am able to determine that the client, a middle-aged Caucasian female of New England descent, is currently on medical leave from her nursing position due to a knee injury, an injury which cannot be surgically corrected until a minimum of one hundred pounds are shed. Clearly overwhelmed, with shame as the most likely culprit, she tearfully admits that her weight has gotten out of control, and she has ballooned to 489$^1/_2$ pounds. No longer afforded the luxury of her time-tested coping mechanisms (working, walking, and eating), she sinks into a world of despair. A popular coffee commercial featuring an obviously well-loved son's unexpected return home for the holidays is credited with initiating the anxiety and debilitating panic attacks that are now her ever-present and unwelcome companions.

Grace Ann reports voluntarily admitting herself into an inpatient treatment facility, surprisingly, a clinic specializing in childhood sexual abuse.

Childhood sexual abuse? This is certainly a far cry from an adjustment disorder!

"My doctor there, he was really nice. He told me that he hated to release me, but I wasn't suicidal, so my insurance wouldn't pay anymore. I've paid my premiums every month since 1968, and I've never been hospitalized, not even once. If I had known they were going to do that to me, I'd have told them I was going to kill myself and made up some horrible way I was planning to do it."

"Grace Ann, you've told me you don't trust very easily. I know this must be very hard for you. What brings you to outpatient counseling?"

"I came here because I'm really depressed, really, really depressed, and really nervous. My stomach hurts all the time and I can't sleep. I've developed some sort of asthma, stress induced, I think. At times it's really hard for me to breathe. And I feel dirty. Before I hurt my knee, I took, I don't know, three, maybe four showers a day. I guess the worst part is the vomiting—I constantly feel that I need to vomit."

Constantly needs to vomit! This poor soul is having a very hard time.

Glancing at the intake form that Grace Ann completed at our last session, I notice several references to foster care. "Can you tell me about your family? Were you ever in foster care?"

Her sudden ghastly expression causes me to rethink my question. Maybe I misread the information. Hurriedly scanning the page in an attempt to undo or, at the very least, minimize my obvious error, I hear a slow, methodical, oddly painful, "I wish I had not been such a bad child and wouldn't have caused my foster parents to do what they did to me. I wish I could forgive them. I wish I could love my enemies."

What kind of depression is this?

"What about your biological parents, Grace Ann? Were they a part of your life?"

My seemingly insensitive question is met with a blank stare, then silence—a long chilling silence. Void of all emotion, she delivers her punctuated response in a deliberate, monotone manner.

"I don't know my parents, I don't know their birth dates, I don't know where they were born, or where they live. I don't know nothing. My social worker told me my mother divorced my father because he was cheating on her. He was married to two women at the same time. My mother was a devout Catholic. I understand that his other wife was an equally devout Jew. My father, it makes me physically sick to call him that, is supposed to be alive somewhere. The last time I heard, he was married to his fourteenth wife."

Fourteenth wife? This guy really gets around!

"My Aunt Rita, she lives in New York, told me my mother spent twenty years in a mental hospital. Don't have any idea what happened to her. Last time I heard, she was supposed to be living with her sister somewhere. I have two brothers. I hardly remember them. One escaped by joining the army, the other one ran away. I don't blame either one of them. I ran away, too. I haven't seen or heard from them in thirty years. I don't have no family. I would like to get married and have someone to love me for me, and not use me to satisfy his or her own needs. I never want to be a victim again. Right now it's safer to live alone."

Uncomfortable with this unlikely soliloquy, I attempt to buy some time by deflecting the questioning to less volatile areas.

"What do you, or did you do before you hurt your knee?"

"Well, after I ran away and spent three nights in a bowling alley...."

Grace Ann seems oblivious to my redirected question. *Did she even hear me?*

"I went to live at the local Y. I emancipated myself at $14\frac{1}{2}$, and I guess I finished high school. I really don't remember. I barely remember going to nursing school, but I suppose I did, since I graduated with a L.P.N. degree. Then Jim was killed in Vietnam. After that, there was no reason to stay. I wanted, I needed, to get out of town, so I applied for the school nurse job when the university here was just opening its doors. Since I was employed by the university, I got to go back to school. I earned a double major in Social Science and Foreign Missions. Somewhere in there I went back to nursing school and became an R.N."

Finally a safe area! Not wanting to lose the session's momentum, I choose to delay exploring the "Jim" issue, and ask, "How would you describe yourself? What are your likes? Dislikes?"

"Well, I'm a good nurse. Nursing Supervisor, actually. I'm responsible for all third shift activities. I listen to my staff, and really care about them individually. All of my evaluations are above average. I do tend to be a workaholic, that's how I hurt my knee. I must admit that I often work sixteen-hour days, sometimes even seven days a week. I like what I do, but I wouldn't mind looking into another profession. Before I took a medical leave, I was beginning to feel burned out, used-up, really.

"I pretty much keep to myself...don't trust a lot of people. I do like people who are loving, caring, and non-judgmental. Honesty, trust, respect, morality, and kindness are really important to me. My dislikes? My weaknesses? I guess overeating to stuff my feelings is my greatest weakness. Maybe lack of trust, too. I really dislike, really hate people who spiritually, sexually, and emotionally abuse children.

"Religion used to be very important in my life, actually the most important thing in my life. I was raised a Catholic. Seems like I spent my whole life in catechism classes. When I moved down here, I joined, was really active, in a Fundamentalist church, but I don't go to church anymore, don't trust religion either. I feel angry and distant from God. Actually I think my ultimate hatred is toward God. I don't understand why He would allow those people to do that to me."

Those people? What people? What did they do? What was it God allowed to happen? I am left hanging, with more questions than answers, but a surreptitious glance at the therapy-room's clock tells me what I already know—we are far over our allotted time. Standing to signal the end of our session, I usher a reluctant, now sobbing, Grace Ann down the hall and through the office door. She turns, rivers of tears streaming down her distorted face. "Deborah, can we ask you for a favor? A really big favor?"

"Grace Ann, I can't promise, but I'll certainly try. What is it that you need?"

"Can we have a hug? We've never been hugged by someone that we trusted? It would mean a lot if we could have a hug."

I stop dead in my tracks. No way! I don't intend to get in the habit of hugging my clients. I've had enough problems with boundary violations already, and the last thing I need is another complication. No way! It's just not going to happen. And who are WE? Does George need a hug, too?

"I'm sorry Grace Ann. I don't have physical contact with my clients. It's just not a good idea. I *am* sorry."

"That's O.K., Deborah. We understand. We understand, don't we, George?"

Thankfully, he does not answer.

The streaming tears turn to sobs as Grace Ann and George shuffle out to the waiting car.

Leaning on the doorway, watching as she pulls away, I attempt to shake off the sadness, the disappointment so clearly etched on her face.

I did do the right thing, didn't I? Hug your clients? Where is it written that you're supposed to hug your clients? Who does she think she is? She's a nurse. She knows about boundaries.

Returning to the room, I curl up in an oversized chair and set out to record my therapeutic impressions. Immersing myself in the rhetoric of my training, stroke by stroke, I distance myself from her pain:

> Upon presentation, this forty-five year old female is experiencing significant levels of anxiety and depression as the result of purported issues involving sexual abuse in childhood, and the subsequent loss of her coping mechanisms—work, food, and exercise. At the time of intake, she is internally focused, reflective, and detached. Exhibiting a below-average integration and realization of potential, she presents as withdrawn, self-defeating, and vulnerable. It is important to note, however, that her methodical, systematic approach to life may prove a valuable component in the healing process. Her willingness to pursue counseling with regularity, as well as her desire to become less internally focused and more socially oriented, poised, and self-confident may provide a reassurance that better days are ahead for this lovely, but hurting individual.

A Beginning

Whatever the cause—obesity, anxiety, depression, abuse—Grace Ann is hurting. At times she is exceptionally coherent, regurgitating her life story in a detached and seemingly unaffected manner. At other moments a spontaneous rocking erupts, often for no discernable reason. Eyelids flutter, her already labored breathing grows even more ragged, more strained.

The rocking slows, then stops. She hugs the ever-present George to her breast. Staring past his tattered right ear, she retreats to her very private world, a world of tarnished dreams.

"I be sorry, I be so sorry. I din't mean to bee's so bad."

Agony—pain is far too inadequate a word—exudes from every pore. I sense a child, but do not see a child. I am confused by my own confusion.

I have for many years incorporated bibliotherapy into my work, finding the simple, straightforward truths of a child's story to hold tremendous healing potential for folks of all ages. I must be frightened, for I, most uncharacteristically, discard my well-manicured therapeutic plan for Grace Ann's recovery and instinctively return to my pre-graduate school roots. Grace Ann is oblivious to both me and the surrounding environment. Sensing my presence will not be missed, I escape to the adjoining room and frantically rummage through a still-taped box of children's books. Joyously ferreting out a well-worn friend, I return and read Doleski's *The Hurt*, a story of pain and forgiveness.

The small but profound edition concludes with a little boy's decision to forgive a friend who has wronged him.

> *"But what will I do with the Hurt?" asked Justin.*
> *"You'll have to let it go," Daddy said.*
> *"It's too big to get out of my room now," said Justin.*
> *"When you're ready to let it go, it will be small enough."[1]*

Remarkably, the story appears to have a calming effect. Returning from her faraway place, she looks up, then deftly slides her generous frame onto the floor. Sitting somewhat cross-legged (crossing her ankles rather than her calves), she cautions George to be very quiet, positioning the bear so he, too, can see the book's pictures. They both sit, she transfixed, he predictable.

Grinning from ear lobe to ear lobe, cheeks flushed and eyes twinkling, Grace Ann's impish smile lights up the room. At the end of the tale of healing, she assists her companion in applauding the happy, emotionally liberating ending. "That be a berry good story, Dr. Debbie. Me and George luved it!"

She gracefully returns to the couch, closes her eyes, then, in an articulate and very grown-up voice, asks, "Deborah, do you think it would be helpful if I talk about my own hurts. Maybe even write them down. Do you think I'll heal more quickly?"

I didn't think she was even listening, and now she's asking to direct her own healing. Amazing! Listing her hurts may not be of any benefit at all, but at least it's a plan, and at this point, it's more than I have to offer.

Together, we agree to embark upon a systematic recovery strategy, one that allows Grace Ann to succinctly list her painful life events, owning the experiences, feeling them, and through forgiveness, letting them go. Enthusiasm mounting, Grace Ann agrees to begin an inventory of her hurts, to record them, memory by memory, and to bring them in a journal with her to our next session.

Five days later she hands me a bound volume, her journal. As she begins the lengthy process of situating herself within the room, I take advantage of this "squandered time" and open the cover. I am totally unprepared for the fragmented allegations to come.

Grace Ann's Hurts

i will make your body unfit and undesirable for any man.

She, my foster mother, tied me to my bed. She took a butcher knife and cut off my nipples. Then she sucked the blood out. She took a candle and burned my private parts. My foster father asked her why she saw the need to make me unfit for any man. i don't think he agreed with her, but he never said anything. Then he said, maybe i can make her stop crying…he had sex with me…if i could have gotten loose, i would have killed them both.

If you didn't fight, you wouldn't be tied to your bed.

If you weren't so bad, you wouldn't have to be put in the closet.

If you didn't cry, you would get beat with the strap until you cried. If you did cry, you would get beat with the strap or yardstick until you stopped crying. When you are BAD you get put in the closet. If you cried at all in the closet you would get handcuffed to the water pipe and the back of your arm and wrist hurts BAD.

My foster mother would go out at ten p.m. to get a hot dog. My foster father would take me out of the closet and uncuff me if i promised not to fight him to have oral and vaginal sex with him. i hated that worse than anything. i wish i could vomit just to think of it.

i had to make everyone's bed before going to school in the morning. If i didn't put the flat sheet on correctly, when i came home from school the beds would be stripped and i would have to remake them. My foster mother would say, 'You are so stupid, you can't even put a sheet on right.'

My foster father would take me out of the closet early in the morning before anyone got up to have sex with me. i hated it. He would stuff a sock or wash cloth in my mouth if i cried so i wouldn't wake everyone up.

Grace Ann is the fattest, ugliest thing that was ever made on this earth.

My foster father would tie my hands to the top of the bed and my feet to the bottom with ropes. He would say if you would just learn not to fight, it wouldn't hurt so much. He would make me watch him, my foster mother, and their daughter have sex together. He pointed out that they didn't fight and it didn't hurt them or make them cry. i was supposed to learn from them not to fight or cry.

Every time he would have sex with me, he'd ask me if i was ready to join the cult. He must have asked me that a million times. i said, 'No, no, no, no, no, no.'

I, too, feel the need to vomit! Afraid to turn another page, I find myself reverting to that quick, shallow, irregular breathing pattern, that panicky feeling I get when I'm about to address a room full of people. I want to run, but find myself clinging to an unlikely intervention—the remote chance that the office floor will miraculously rupture and suck me and my discomfort from the room. *I don't think, I know I can't handle this!* Cautiously glancing across the room, I watch as Grace Ann, the same Grace Ann that presented me with this disgusting journal, sits placidly, nonchalantly sipping water from an oversized green travel mug. I'm sick, and she's casually sipping water as if she didn't have a care in the world!

Gulping, I return to the journal, hoping against hope that the horror is over. The gods have deserted me, for the grizzly account continues.

i hated Saturdays. First to Confession with Father Stafford, who i first trusted until i didn't like him saying he would make my hot dog roll big enough with his fingers for his hot dog to fit into. He began by telling me i was special.

i'm going to show you how much i love you, he would say.

The Saturday before taking my first communion, he put his hot dog in me. It hurt so bad. i felt so dirty all the time. i saw him hurt those alter boys.

i hated Saturday nights. Every Saturday night i had to go to the Big Hall and be tied down with leather straps to a hard, cold, table, where men would force their peckers into my bottom and my mouth. With each time, they would ask, are you ready to join? When i said no, they would, i thought, urinate in my mouth. It made me so sick and ashamed.

My foster mother would make us eat liver once a week. i hated liver. If i didn't finish it in the allotted time for supper, it would get put in the refrigerator and i would get put in the closet. She'd serve me the same cold awful liver for breakfast and every meal until i ate all of it. If i put the dishes facing the wrong way in the dish drainer, i would get my hands strapped across my knuckles with a ruler and then put in HOT, HOT water—just for putting the dishes the wrong way.

She would throw my peanut butter and jelly sandwich out the back door if i put the bread together wrong.

They would come and ask again if i was ready to join the cult. i continually said no. So they would start with different things to get me to join. This would go on every Saturday night from six p.m. to midnight or twelve-thirty a.m. That's how i learned in my mind to escape to my safe place. That's where i want to go right now.

My foster mother and father said only good, pretty girls should have dimples, not FAT, UGLY, and UNWANTED girls like me, oh, and unlovable girls shouldn't have dimples either.

No one wants or loves you and no one ever will.

Father Stafford said the night before my first communion, 'Tomorrow will probably be the only white dress you will ever wear'...he was right.

Mrs. Lang, our social worker, told me three years ago if i or the boys had told her what was going on at our foster parents, she would have moved us, but since none of us told her, it was all our fault these things happened to us. So my foster mother was right. i caused everything that happened. i feel dirty, bad, no good, just a big zero, and a failure. Doing this assignment has made me anxious and i am shaking.

i want to go to my safe, free place. i hate me.

No way! I do not believe this! Abusive foster parents? A priest? A cult? Come on now. I know things are bad, but this is ridiculous! I take a long time to attempt to gather my jumbled thoughts. The delay pays off, for in reviewing the journal entry, I note for the first time the use of the lower case "i" throughout the gruesome narrative. Grace Ann appears to alternate between recollections of attacks upon her self-esteem, and assaults upon her physical self. As the text progresses, the writing changes from a polished script to a barely perceptible scrawl. Attached are scribbled drawings, appearing to be the work of a distraught child. When I casually (I hope casually) question, she seems stunned, professing to have no knowledge of their origin.

"Where is this *safe, free place?*" I inquire. *I, too, want to cope by detaching myself, and I search in vain for my old friends, logic and reason, but find they have forsaken me.*

My left hand is grasping the padded arm of the wingback chair so tightly that it's both cold and numb. My breathing is shallow and irregular. The dizziness arrives. I struggle to maintain my composure, futilely seeking to restrain the turbulence within. It's not over yet, for the endless narrative continues.

i know i can reward myself in nondestructive ways. i can go for a walk, call a friend, take a warm bath, or ask for a hug (this is very hard for me to do, but sometimes i need one BAD). i have mixed-up feelings, a volcano inside of me, constant coughing and asthma. i feel angry inside. i could eat a dozen donuts.

Why couldn't i have been a more obedient child?

Grace Ann's "safe, free" place.

i've blocked out years. i can't remember teachers' names. i can't remember being in those grades. No one told me it would be this hard.

How much should i trust her? *[apparently referring to me]* i am really scared. Sometimes talking about things is hard because i have to feel. It hurts to feel. i just wish the Lord would come to take me home so i wouldn't have to hurt anymore inside. i think i should have left this tucked away. i wish i had been good so all these things wouldn't have happened to me. My insides are racing. My mind is traveling one hundred miles per hour. i feel like a robot.

As if this emotional outpouring is not enough, Grace Ann reaches into her canvas bag and removes a poem she reports having written for a sexual abuse recovery publication. Attached to the poem are a series of newspaper clippings chronicling the arrest, trial, conviction, and sentencing of the priest she references in the poem. In one hand I am holding a recent clipping of a small, nondescript man convicted of molesting an indeterminable number of girls and boys during the fifties and sixties. In the other, I am holding a bitter, heart-wrenching poem, written by someone who knows first hand the price children pay when adults pillage their childhood. I am numb with disbelief.

Life Sentence from a Priest Child Molester

Tears burn my skin
with each vision of pain.
I can still see the jury,
hearing my experiences of the past.
But, I see his presence in my brain.
Will I ever forget what he put me through?
I keep reminding myself
I am one of the lucky ones
who lived to tell all I know.
I wonder about the others.
Their lives scarred, as mine?
The jury sentenced him to 6 MONTHS
HIS VICTIMS GOT LIFE!

This unimaginable session just won't end. Grace Ann rocks and wheezes, all the while tightly squeezing George. She has to be encouraged to use her inhaler. I am angered by her allegations, overwhelmed, and confused. As a mother, it is inconceivable that an individual, most particularly a man of the cloth, could violate a child in such a heinous manner. I am captured in what is to become a hauntingly familiar battle, i.e., the struggle to maintain a "therapist face" when bombarded with material too grotesque to digest, or to even imagine. I know, from somewhere deep inside, that in order to help her I must convey an empathic and encouraging support, but must not be pulled too far into her story. *Groping, I find, then lose, then regain my fragile composure, only to have it abandon me once more.*

When finally I'm able to speak, my strained words, carefully chosen but poorly delivered, take on a stilted and undeniably unempathic tenor, "Grace Ann, what do you feel would be most helpful during this stage of your recovery?"

Without a moment's hesitation she lifts her head, squares her burdened shoulders, gazes into my eyes, and responds, "I need to work on my spiritual journey."

Within the realm of our present difficulties, I find, 'I need to work on my spiritual journey' to be an inconsequential and exceedingly shallow reply!

The Burgeoning
Borderline

Just Me, Just Me

Sweet Marie, she loves just me
(She also loves Maurice McGhee)
No, she don't, she loves just me
(She also loves Louise Dupree).
No, she don't, she loves just me
(She also loves the willow tree).
No, she don't, she loves just me!
(Poor, poor fool, why can't you see
She can love others and still love thee).[2]

Shel Silverstein
Where the Sidewalk Ends

CHAPTER TWO

January 1995

S everal months have passed, arduous months, perplexing, and at times mystifying. It's as if Grace Ann has been sliced to her very core, and I am, prematurely, without knowing how, or why, heartlessly plucking the protective sutures, revealing a massive, gaping wound, leaving it, and her, raw, exposed, vulnerable. This merciless scenario is repeated session after session.

She continues to communicate her newly surfacing awarenesses through her journal, appearing to hide within its scribbled pages and to be comforted by the anonymity of the written word. Hobbling into the room, she ceremoniously unpacks her worn canvas bag, and presents me with her most recent soul-baring entry. I tentatively, very tentatively, peruse the black and white spiral-bound edition, while she sits, wordlessly, holding her breath, as if in anticipation of certain rejection. It doesn't take long to stumble upon Grace Ann's first step in her self-avowed spiritual expedition.

Powerlessness

We admitted we were powerless over the effects of our separation from God, that our lives had become unmanageable. We came to believe that a power greater than ourselves could restore us to sanity. We made a decision to turn our will and our lives over to the care of God as we understand Him to be. We made a searching and fearless moral inventory of ourselves. We sought through prayer and meditation to improve our conscious contact with God, as we understand Him, praying only for knowledge of His will and the power to carry it out. Having had a spiritual awakening because of these steps, we tried to carry this message to others, and to practice these principles in all our affairs.

"Who are we? What steps?"

This sounds as if it has been regurgitated from the pages of an Alcoholic Anonymous pamphlet. For the first time, I wonder about the treatment center she attended prior to seeing me. What was its therapeutic orientation? Was it, like so many recovery programs, based upon AA's Twelve Steps? I suppose it really doesn't matter, for I have always believed that spirituality and psychotherapy make poor bedfellows! Not me, I'm not going there! While I don't discourage her ramblings, I am uncomfortable with this talk of supernatural matters, and am repulsed by what I perceive to be a politically-oriented, overly-judgmental, at times down-right cruel religious dogma. I recognize that I, as an Adlerian therapist, have never practiced totally value-free counseling. While Rudolph Driekers, a student of Alfred Adler, did introduce a more cosmic orientation into the treatment room, I just don't think this "spiritual journey" stuff was what he had in mind. Even so, Grace Ann appears to at least have a plan, which is more than I can say for me at this point. Some part of her seems to be in control, so I have no choice but to support her in her celestial wanderings.

The journal entry continues. It takes very little time to decipher the feebly disguised code, for while Grace Ann is attempting to call attention to her own sense of powerlessness, she is also seeking to triangulate me into her extraordinarily bizarre drama.

> i wake up crying, scared, shaking. i go to the freezer to get the frozen chocolate pound cake and frozen pizza. i trust Deborah with just about everything now, but i am really scared. i need her. The little girl in me really needs Deborah. i wish she were here. i would ask her if i could put my head in her lap and ask her to help me. My heart is racing and i can't stop shaking. Sunday i was going to ask her for a hug, but then i got scared. i am so mixed up and confused. i like her and trust her, yet i'm scared of her. Sometimes i want to tell her everything, yet if she really knows how BAD i am,

she will hate me. i don't want to lose her. i need her help. Deborah, please don't leave me. i need you. i wish i could just go to sleep and never wake up! i need to be clean. i need serenity, courage, and wisdom. i can't do it anymore. i admit i am powerless over my life, my eating, my stuffing…i am powerless.

Lord, you told me once, when my Father and Mother forsake me, then you will take me up. You are my Heavenly Father. i need you to help me banish my fears. i know you love me. i have accepted you. i now need your help, and help Deborah and Dr. Gentry [Grace Ann's friend and personal physician] to help me fix the mess i've made. i want to be healed and i cannot heal myself. i need to admit i am powerless. i need to humble myself and submit to the process that will eventually bring about my recovery.

i can't see why my heart doesn't break and allow death to free me.

Daddy Jesus, the little girl grace ann inside of me needs to be held. i asked Deborah to hold me, and she refused. i can't ask anyone else, so will you hold me? Maybe one day i could let a real person hold me without hurting me. Daddy, i'm so scared of touch by real people, yet i need it all of a sudden. Up until recently, i couldn't even shake someone's hand, and would physically push them away. Why can't i push them away anymore? Why do i now need to be held?

I wonder what those i's are all about? And what about the diminutive reference to the little girl grace ann?

Very little energy is expended on academic queries into the nature of the psyche, for once again, like it or not, Grace Ann is successful in roping me in to "her stuff." While I am merely uncomfortable with the religious piece, I am wholly repelled, perhaps even repulsed, by all this dependency! Look at all those references to me— her pleas for me not to leave, her desire to be held—so much so that I vow to end this nonsense, once and for all! Enough is enough! There is a vast difference between needfulness and healing. Needfulness, pretend healing, is a behavior, resembling a tentacle, that first grasps, then sucks the life out of all it meets. Healing, true healing, purges, then cleanses the soul, bringing with it new possibilities, new beginnings, much like the early morning freshness of a dewy spring day. It's time, past time for Grace Ann to hear this! It's time for her to know the difference! I feel the tentacles closing in! *Calm down! You know better, Deborah! Don't get sucked in! Calm down!* I will remain detached. I have no choice. I cannot help if I, too, become overwhelmed by the pain.

The next session arrives all too soon for my taste. Fortifying myself against the petulant tirade and tears that are certain to come, I wonder, What's wrong with me? Why am I so nervous? What kind of therapist is afraid to confront her own client?

I am embarrassed that the tremor in my voice is so obvious. "Grace Ann, before we get started today, I really need to discuss something that's been on my mind—something that needs to be addressed before we can continue our work together."

Perhaps it's too late. Maybe I'm already ill, for I find myself scrutinizing the expression on George's face to determine if it's O.K. to go on! He doesn't appear overly concerned, so I choose to continue my well-rehearsed lecture. **I'm nuts! I'm absolutely nuts.**

"Grace Ann, a therapist is a guide, not a friend. I don't have your answers. I can't make you well. I wish I could. I wish I had a magic wand that I could wave and all of this, this pain, would be over for you. But Grace Ann, I don't, and I never will.

"There is a lot that I *don't* know. But I am sure of one thing. The longer you look to me, or to anyone or anything else outside of you, the longer and harder this process is going to be. I believe you will find what you are looking for only when you have the courage to turn within. The greatest gift you can give your therapist, Grace Ann, is your own healing.

"As a therapist, I've been taught to maintain clear boundaries between my clients and myself. If these boundaries aren't respected, a dual relationship is created, which distorts objectivity, and in the end, simply makes things worse. The last thing I want is to make things worse for you, Grace Ann. My gosh, that's the *very* last thing I want to see happen. I hope you can understand that."

Whew! That wasn't so bad, in fact, it went pretty well! Or so it seemed...But the peace before the storm is short lived. As I feared, the sulking petulance begins.

"But you're the kind of person I would like to have as a friend," she pleads.

Openly distraught, Grace Ann repositions George onto the opposite knee, ensuring his comfort before she turns her attention to the ever-present canvas bag. The tears arrive as she angrily tosses a comb, her inhaler, then a host of partially used prescriptions, at last retrieving a faded, but neatly folded blue washcloth. Hands violently shaking, she lowers her drenched and distorted face into the inadequate washcloth. As the weeping continues, I, of all things, find myself relieved that at least George remains unfazed! *There's no question about it! I'm going to need to find my own therapist really soon.*

"Why can't you be my friend? I thought you were different, but you're just like everybody else!"

The tears turn to angry sobs as she aims piercing daggers of betrayal at me, hastily throws her belongings back into the waiting canvas bag, and drags herself up, crutches and all, and eventually through the office door.

Exhausted, with head pounding, I congratulate myself, firstly, because I survive the ordeal, and secondly, because I refuse to be drawn into this pathetic inquiry. I celebrate this no small victory with two Tylenol and a dark room.

Convoluted as my celebration might be, there is no festivity, contrived or otherwise, for my client. As is frequently the case, Grace Ann chooses to journal her feelings, for she is able to pen but not speak of her inner discontent, her volcanic internal turmoil. The evening's entry reflects her unrelenting confusion and concern. She writes:

> I'm sitting here still trying to sort out that dependency thing. I say I will never call Deborah again, only talk to her in my allotted session time. Then something starts to make me anxious and I don't know how to pinpoint what it is, so I call her. Is that dependency on her? Yet I know in my heart I trust her and I know she can help me see or get out whatever I am anxious over or whatever is bothering me. I

am so confused about that. Yet I need her at the time I call her. How do I distinguish between becoming dependent on her and needing her help at a specific time? She said I was too dependent on her. She also said I was very manipulative. I'd like to know how I am manipulative! If she thinks I am all these things, I wonder why she even bothers to help me?

Wrong again! I should be getting used to this by now. The day obviously did not go well at all. One more fiasco! What will it take for her to really hear me? It's as if one part of her, fueled by an illusive light, is desperate to recover, while another, a shadowy, murky self, is equally determined that she remain ill, fragmented, alone. Discouraged, I ache with her confusion, but I cannot, I will not, be pulled into her manipulation, intentional or not. Re-reading the entry, my eyes focus on not one, but the series of underlined I's. They must be symbolic of something, but what? Where do we go from here? Where do I go from here? Looking up, I watch as an unusually placid Grace Ann, quietly, perhaps even peacefully, gazes at the carpeted floor. There are no answers, only questions, in the silence.

March 1995

We are now in the throes of a determined late winter. It is as if we are somehow in need of one more freezing blast, one more casing of ice and snow to remind us that we cling to a distorted reality. We are not in charge—of anything! Control is but an illusion that we hide behind, often as long as possible, until our souls are laid bare and we have no choice but to acknowledge, then embrace, our own fractured selves.

The phone calls have continued, currently to an office pager and, thankfully, no longer to my home phone. We've passed the "hugs" stage. Now she wants to be *held!* It's hard to establish, much less enforce, ironclad boundaries with an individual in this much pain, but to be held? *I don't think so!* I've accepted that our work together will be immersed with spirituality, I can't change that, but I am not going to bend on the physical touch. Grace Ann may need to be held, but I will not be the one doing the holding!

Weeks pass. The simmering undercurrent of discontent continues. Sensing yet another eruption is approaching, I enthusiastically (I hope enthusiastically) suggest: "Grace Ann, perhaps the time has come to get some input and direction from the other doctors who are familiar with your case. How about signing a couple of releases? Appearing to be appeased, temporarily at least, I obtain consent to exchange information forms: one to consult with Dr. Gentry, Grace Ann's long-time personal physician; one to speak with the sexual abuse treatment facility's staff psychiatrist, Dr. Abbott. As soon as Grace Ann ambles out the door, calls are placed to both physicians. Dr. Gentry confirms the primary diagnosis of Major Depression, Single Episode, Severe, and offers that Grace Ann is a kind, compassionate and highly capable individual whose selfless devotion to her patients and staff has earned her an exemplary and well-deserved reputation.

Well, now, that's certainly impressive! Looking back, I begrudgingly admit that I, too, have seen, or at least glimpsed, this illusive Grace Ann.

Dr. Abbott, on the other hand, provides little assistance and no reassurance. Reluctant, strangely distant and intentionally vague, he dodges my questions as if to guard some sinister secret. His single significant comment is in response to my question regarding an anticipated length of treatment.

"Dr. Abbott, Grace Ann's personal physician has confirmed the diagnosis of Major Depression, a pretty bad one at that! With medication, I expected to see a significant turn around in her affect in twelve to sixteen weeks. I must confess I don't see an improvement, no improvement at all. How long do you expect this to take?"

To my amazement, he quietly, and with what appears to be a genuine sadness, responds, "Considering her extraordinary level of pathology, I expect you can count on at least five years."

Five years! No one said anything about five years!

Do you know some dark secret? This does not fit any depression or any pathology I've ever known. I simply do not understand—five years! The cold chills wreaking havoc with my spine tell me I might wish to remain in the dark, that perhaps, just perhaps, I really don't want to know.

The Advent of Managed Care

Ah! Managed Care! Our most immediate "external" crisis revolves around the upheaval within the nation's health care industry. Due to spiraling hospital costs and unethical charges by a small band of un-scrupulous practitioners, managed care programs are beginning to spring up at every turn. As of January, all mental health treatment must be pre-approved. To make matters worse, I am a new practitioner, known by no one in the industry, and must await acceptance into "their net-work."

Talk about bad timing!

According to the initial session data, Grace Ann said she has been enrolled in an employer sponsored health care plan since 1968. Prior to the onset of this depressive (?) episode, she rarely filed a benefit claim. In order for her to access her own medical benefits, as her therapist, I must submit a Treatment Plan detailing the presenting problem, a diagnosis, current medication, problems to be addressed, and the methodology. This is new to me, and presents an enormous ethical dilemma. In fact, it is the antithesis of all I have been taught or have come to believe. I'm uncomfortable with releasing personal, in this case, intensely personal, information to anyone. Once the data leaves my hands, it's gone—to who knows where. I recall recently hearing that upon release, a minimum of seventy people will have access to a file.

I wouldn't want seventy people to read about the skeletons in my closet! How will Grace Ann feel? Hasn't she been traumatized enough? I'm worried that her position as nursing supervisor may be jeopar-dized. And what about her future health care benefits? Can she be denied insurance coverage due to a diagnosis? There are just too many unanswered questions here. I can't possibly make this decision on my own.

"Grace Ann, I don't want to worry you, but your insurance com-pany is denying payment for your sessions until I complete something they call a Treatment Plan."

"What's that, Deborah? I don't understand."

"Apparently, it's some sort of document that I fill out and fax to your caseworker. It tells them about your diagnosis and course of treatment—things like that."

"I didn't know I had a caseworker. My diagnosis? Isn't that kind of personal? Isn't that, how do you say it, an invasion of my rights to privacy?"

"Well, I must admit that I'm a little concerned, too. This is all new to me, Grace Ann. Perhaps another therapist might be more on top of this. I'm afraid I can't be a great deal of help."

"I don't think it's a good idea, Deborah. It just doesn't feel right. I feel like I have no privacy—nowhere to go to get well. I thought, I hoped it would be safe to come here. Isn't there anything you can do?"

"I don't know, Grace Ann. I can only tell you that I'll try."

The call is placed. I immediately regret my efforts, for I am confronted with rudeness, arrogance, and an implication, no, a statement of fact, that Grace Ann's healing would be dependent upon how we, as client and therapist, decided to play the game.

"Ms. Berkley, I've written you, and spoken to Ms. Hughes several times. I have approved four sessions. I will not approve anymore until you follow the guidelines. If your client hopes to access her benefits, she will follow our rules."

If she hopes to access her benefits? Now where's the justice in that? And four sessions? Four sessions? That's absurd! Dr. Abbott told me five years! It would be laughable if someone's sanity wasn't at stake! Don't I have enough on my plate? And now this? No one told me I would be battling an insurance company when I decided to enter private practice. It was never discussed, not even once, during all my years of graduate training. If I had known this one fact, this one small fact, I may well have reconsidered my recent career change. What has happened to our medical system? How sad! What a pity—for us all!

Backed into a corner, I prepare the mandatory treatment plan, and reluctantly submit it to the appropriate governing agency for approval.

Treatment Plan

Presenting Problem: The client presents for outpatient therapy upon release from an inpatient treatment facility. Currently on medical leave due to obesity/knee injury concerns, the client is experiencing significant depression, panic attacks, hypervigilance, and recurrent/intrusive recollections.

Diagnosis:

Axis I	Major Depression, Single Episode, Severe
	Post-Traumatic Stress Disorder
Axis II	Borderline Personality Disorder
Axis III	Morbid Obesity
Axis IV	Occupational Problems;
	Economic Problems
	Problems with Access to Health Care
Axis V	35/90

Medication:

Prozac	30 mg. b.i.d. (twice a day)
Alprazolom	1.0 mg. q.i.d. (four times a day)
Voltaren	75 mg. q.d. (once a day)

Problems to be addressed: We will address depression, self-esteem issues, adult survivor issues, an eating disorder, anxiety/hypervigilance (including panic attacks), and recurrent dreams/night flashbacks/terrors.

Goals: The client will revisit childhood/adolescent issues as a component of the reintegration process, will experience a lessened anxiety reaction, will experience fewer panic attacks less severe in nature, and will address issues of morbid obesity.

Methodology: The client will participate in a lifestyle investigation, food-addiction recovery program, group work, journaling, cognitive restructuring (positive self-talk), experiential awareness exercises, bibliotherapy, affirmations, autogenic relaxation training, guided imagery, and medication management.

The treatment plan is initially denied. The already strained relations with the managed care company are now compounded, as they are unwilling to acknowledge the severity of the depression or the post-traumatic stress disorder diagnosis. To make matters worse, there is little room in managed care for an Adlerian therapist, as preference is given to those of the Cognitive Behavioral and Brief Systems Therapies schools. There's no need to introduce Grace Ann's religious orientation, for there is certainly no place in Behavioral Psychology for a self-guided spiritual tour. Finally, I am instructed to: "Focus your work only on the current symptoms. Thank you."

They appear not to believe me at all. I wonder which of the "current symptoms" I should focus on first.

They don't have a clue. Neither do I!

Pandora's Box

Crisis follows crisis. Everywhere I turn, there's yet another crisis! It's as if I'm juggling too many balls: morbid obesity, allegations of long-term sexual abuse, hypervigilance, depression, and now, managed care; and if even one is dropped, both Grace Ann and I will be shredded by the shrapnel. Issues are popping out so fast and furiously that I routinely plan, then discard, treatment strategies. Tentative agendas are mapped, both in my mind and in writing, yet I find less resistance, and ultimately greater success, when I'm willing to shelve my plans and simply follow Grace Ann's lead. I discover that I'm fine-tuning my observational skills, reading between the lines of her journals, and modifying my therapeutic training to meet the transitory, but none-the-less overpowering needs at hand. And I'm realizing that, amazingly, I must rely as heavily upon the subjective skills of creativity and intuition as I do my clinical training, an awareness of which is generating an intense discomfort within me. Themes are emerging, themes of persistent overeating, hindered feelings, and oppressive anxiety.

Grace Ann writes:

> i just got home from talking with Deborah for one hour
> and forty-five minutes. It sure did go by fast. Sometimes
> it's hard to go home. i have all these mixed-up emotions

like a volcano inside of me. i have coughed since i left her office. Sometimes i wish i could throw-up, but i can't stand throwing up. Sometimes i wish i could cry and feel better. i have so much anger inside me. Right now i feel like eating a dozen doughnuts. What am i feeling? i don't know. i sometimes wish i had left all this packed away. i didn't have to feel then. When Deborah asked me about that incident in the second grade, i thought i would be sick to my stomach. It's strange how i remember that, yet for years i have blocked it out. i cannot even remember my teachers' names after the second grade. i really feel like a failure having to ask for help. Why? All these years i could have everything packed in my closet. i didn't have to feel. How much should i trust her? i am really scared. i ate three bananas…my insides can't stop shaking. i wish i could go to sleep and never wake up. i need something to eat. i need to take a shower. i need to get clean. i need to eat. i can't stop rocking and shaking. i need to throw up.

i blew it…i just ate a piece of frozen pizza. Yuck! Then a piece of frozen pound cake. My heart won't stop racing. i hate me. i'm a big FAILURE. i ate that pizza frozen and two large pieces of pound cake. It didn't take care of the anxiety attack. i literally inhaled the food to stuff my feelings, and the feelings are still there. FAILURE, FAILURE, FAILURE.

Back to those lower case i's!!!

We must get in control of something. The anxiety fuels the eating, the eating fuels the obesity, the obesity exacerbates the bad knees, the bad knees create the disability, the disability kindles the cognitive distortions, the cognitive distortions provoke the depression, and ultimately escalate the anxiety! This exhausting cycle is repeated day after day after day!

First things first…Grace Ann may well die! It's no surprise that morbid obesity and premature death often go hand in hand. Recalling her penchant for twelve-step programs, I hunt down, then purchase Minirth, Meier, Henfelt, and Snead's *Love Hunger*, a twelve-step recovery program in which the cycle of food addiction is depicted as an individual's futile attempt to "feed the hungry heart."[3] Grace Ann is, as always, fully compliant, and not only purchases her own copy but the accompanying workbook as well. We agree to cover one chapter per week.

At last we have a plan. I am encouraged!

———◆◆◆◆———

Grace Ann once told me that she had shed eighty pounds on a medically supervised liquid diet, only to regain it, along with another hundred, within eighteen months. I understand why she is reluctant to begin a second weight-loss program and don't blame her, but I don't know what else to do!

"Grace Ann, didn't you tell me that before I met you, you were really active?"

"Sure was, Deborah! I worked a lot of double shifts—sometimes was on my feet for the whole sixteen hours. Then, on the days I didn't work doubles, I, well, my friend and I, walked. We eventually got up to fourteen miles each week."

"I seem to remember that you also attended several church services each week."

"Not anymore!" she angrily responded.

Oops! Watch it, Deborah!

"Well, my point is not that you aren't going to church right now, but that you're spending an awful lot of time alone, too much time, Grace Ann. It's not healthy. No one needs to be constantly alone. I know that you get really nervous around people, but it's important not to isolate yourself. The only time you seem to get out is when you come to therapy."

"I go to see Dr. Gentry."

"I stand corrected. The only 'times' you leave your apartment are to come to therapy and go to see Dr. Gentry." I am met with a sullen stare.

"Listen to me, just for a minute. We know you need to lose weight. It will help your knees, if nothing else. You also need to be with people— at least sometimes during the week. What if we combined the two, and tried, just tried, a Weight Watcher's group? It might help with the weight loss, and might help us put a lid on this growing anxiety. What do you think?"

One look into her panic-stricken eyes, and I had my answer. "I'm not going to push you, Grace Ann. I just want you to think about it. I really, really, believe it might help."

"Do you really think so, Deborah?"

"Yes, ma'am, I really do."

Mountains of encouragement and three unsuccessful attempts later, Grace Ann makes it in the door of her first Weight Watcher's meeting. She arrives halfway through the program, sitting on the end seat of the back row—close to the door, just in case a panic attack engulfs her and she needs a quick getaway. But she makes it! Buoyed by her newfound success, she agrees to attend three sessions weekly until the binges are under control.

Yes!

A lifetime of discouragement has turned Grace Ann into her own worst enemy. Her self-esteem is nonexistent. Her self-talk, regurgitated daily, is damning. We are all creatures of habit at heart. Grace Ann's "habit" is, at least in part, keeping her ill.

"Grace Ann, have you ever thought about what you say to yourself?"

"What do you mean, Deborah? I don't talk to myself. I'm not *that* sick! Am I? Oh, no, I...."

The wailing begins.

"Whoa, wait just a minute. Let's start again. Calm down. That's right, calm down. Look into my eyes."

All eyes are upon me—Grace Ann's and George's.

"Let's start again. What I meant was...."

"I'm with you now, Deborah. I don't know what happened. I just got so scared. I thought I was losing my mind."

"What I meant was you say such awful things to yourself. You refer to yourself as ugly, and stupid, and worthless—things like that. Grace Ann, you're not ugly, or stupid, or worthless. Nothing could be further from the truth."

"Do you mean that, Deborah?"

"Do you trust me, Grace Ann?"

"You know I do."

"Then *you* answer your question."

"You meant what you said, because you don't lie to me. Thank you, Deborah, for never lying to me. You said I say awful things to myself. You said that I'm not ugly, or stupid, or worthless."

"That's exactly what I said, Grace Ann," I respond, forever amazed that she is in possession of such an uncanny memory. I don't think she's even listening, and time after time, she repeats my statements—word for word. There's a very intelligent person in there—somewhere!

"People, especially when they're hurting, sometimes get into the bad habit of being very negative, not only to others, but to themselves. We don't even realize we're doing it, because we've done it for so long. It's just a very bad habit."

"You mean like when I pull my toenails off?"

Pull my toenails off? Oh my God! Stay on track, Deborah! Breathe!

"Something like that, Grace Ann," I respond, recovering my momentum. "What I want you to do is reverse your thinking." I'm met with a quizzical stare. "I want you to catch yourself saying *bad*, then change it to *good*. Change *ugly* to *beautiful*, *worthless* to *worthwhile*, *failure* to *success*, *victim* to *survivor*."

"O.K., Deborah. I think I understand. I'll try." She listens politely, but is less than enthusiastic in her response. Grace Ann is emotionally depleted. Empty. Bankrupt.

———◆◆◆◆———

Abuse blights the soul. Those who have known the molester's hand learn to cope with the stark reality of daily living by suppressing their own inner voice, their intuition, their gut. Healthy individuals acknowledge this inner voice, often accepting it as not only valid, but *valuable*. These fortunate folk have the privilege of choice—to honor the intuitive self, or to forge ahead blindly, at least for a little while, until the inevitable dead-end looms ahead. This choice is their birthright. Not so for the violated. For them, birthright is synonymous with shame. Feelings, emotions, *the voice*, are at first minimized, then ignored, and finally, obliterated. It's far too painful to recall, to remember what *should* be. They don't *choose* to turn away from the *voice*. They simply no longer hear.

A child, by its very nature, is experiential, unable to "give voice" to the pain, but most certainly able to act out that pain. For many years I have used an aggression bat, an unwieldy, super-padded apparatus with a red plastic handle. Many a child or adolescent has pounded a desk or chair in an effort to safely liberate themselves from momentary crippling emotions. With this in mind, I gently introduce Grace Ann to the concept of processing feelings physically within the therapy room, being careful not to offend her by emphasizing her childlike and sometimes childish nature.

To my pleasure and surprise, she readily embraces the practice.

"That sounds like a really good idea. I like that. I think it might help. Would it be O.K. if I took one of the bats home, so I won't have to call you every time something comes up?"

So I won't have to call every time something comes up? Are you kidding? Needless to say, I am enthusiastic in my donation.

I have to face this spiritual stuff, for Grace Ann seems determined to begin her *spiritual journey*, with or without me. It certainly doesn't look as if it, or she, is going away. Where to begin? A quick trip to my favorite haunt, the local bookstore, yields an entire shelf of books devoted to the higher self. Perusing the titles, I decide the daily devotionals are a safe bet, and select a group Grace Ann might enjoy. Coincidentally, *or so I think*, my Advanced Theories syllabus arrives at about the same time. Among the required reading is a small, nondescript paperback, Assagioli's *Psychosynthesis*. I'm drawn to this seemingly insignificant title, and casting aside the other course requirements, devour the work, inhaling the words within as if they were the breath of life itself. It's as if Roberto Assagioli, many years ago, knew that someone like me would meet someone like Grace Ann.

I find that *Psychosynthesis* is an alliance of traditional psychoanalysis *(Freud's stuff)* with active therapeutic techniques *(my stuff)*. Positive in orientation, Assagioli's holistic stance seeks not to minimize nor deny life's pain, for to exclude the less desirable facets of the personality in favor of those more pleasing or acceptable is to undermine our potential as fully-functioning beings. Instead, it emphasizes man's creative, joy-filled experiences, and in so doing, magnifies the healing potential in pure awareness.

While I am forewarned by the author to make judicious use of misidentification (the "pure awareness" inherent in psychosynthesis) when dealing with severe pathology, I am struck that psychological theories *do* exist which embrace, not religion, but the supra conscious. Hmm! The supra conscious? Now that's an unusual term. For the first time, I am cognizant of spirituality and its potential role in the therapeutic process. For the first time, I grasp the meaning of a "lived" spirituality. I am struck by

> ...the realization of the spiritual Self is not for the purpose of withdrawal, but for the purpose of being able to perform more effective service in the world of men...There is no division, no separation between inner and outer, between spiritual and worldly life. In psychosynthesis there should be a dynamic balancing of the two..."[4]

Aided by symbolism, the personal self-conscious gradually gives way, with self-identity in the personal fading into a spiritual realization. Psychosynthesis "leads to the door, but stops there." Assagioli's acknowledgment of symbolic life catches my eye, for Grace Ann's journals have been filled with symbols—religious emblems, colors, butterflies, the safe, free prairie. I haven't been able to decode them, yet have no doubt they hold an enigmatic meaning.

In addition, Psychosynthesis places a key emphasis upon the strengthening of the will through the repeated use of affirmations, with faith no longer a subjective, ill-defined concept, but "an assured conviction." Grace Ann and I decide that the use of affirmations would likely strengthen therapy by serving as a convenient reminder of a forward orientation. I am unwilling, however, to introduce Assagioli's acclaimed "I have a body, but I am not my body," for I'm concerned that her already fragile state will be turned on its head! Instead, I ask Grace Ann to develop her own list, assuming she will know far better than I the affirmations useful in strengthening her resolve. Always the dutiful student, she returns with her list.

> I can do all things through Christ who strengthens me.
> My grace is sufficient for you, for my power is made perfect in weakness.
> Everything is possible for him who believes.

And, to my pleasure and surprise, I find my own words within her tattered journal.

> The greatest gift you can give your therapist is your own healing.

A Walk Through A Country Garden

Many of our crises have been precipitated by Grace Ann's chronic anxiety and debilitating panic attacks. The shortness of breath, dizziness, profuse perspiration, and absolute terror are proving to be as much of a hindrance as the ever-present depression. Night after night my pager wails, shattering the evening's silence. I rarely even bother to glance at the number.

"Grace Ann, how can I help you?"

"I can't breathe! Can't breathe!"

"Stay with me, Grace Ann. Can you hear me?"

"Uh-huh," she gasps.

"Breathe with me. O.K., here we go—slow, deep breaths. Breathe in—one, two, three, four. Hold it—one, two, three, four. Release—one, two, three, four. One more time…."

"Thank you, Deborah. I feel better. I'm sorry I bothered you. It just helps to hear your voice."

"No problem, Grace Ann. I'll see you soon."

This isn't working—for either of us. Grace Ann is embarrassed, and I'm tired. Recalling the frequent refrain "it just helps to hear your voice," I decide to record a relaxation training exercise that Grace Ann can replay whenever she's feeling anxious. As an afterthought, I add a guided imagery, which, for some obscure reason, is based upon vivid recollections of my long-deceased grandmother's country garden. I struggle as I write the script, struggle to find just the right words that will offer her the peace that I knew in my grandma's garden, the peace that has eluded her for so long.

> In your mind's eye, you may be leisurely strolling through a tranquil garden, hand-in-hand, not with another, but with yourself. Remember, Grace Ann, healing comes in turning inward, not in our attempts to alter or manipulate

others....You are beginning to relish the warmth of the spring day. The bulbs, complete within themselves, are residing in the dark protection of mother earth, and when they are ready, they will burst forth, exhibiting a beauty only to be found in nature.... Grace Ann, as we embrace the sometimes stillness of our lives, it is then that we hear the still small voice within us, and it is then that we connect with our creator.

The soul-warming sun is boldly peeping through, and you are becoming more attuned to your own peaceful core. A furry newborn bunny scurries through, perhaps en route to her own security. A mother robin, exhausted from the ever-present demands of her precious offspring, is slowly, ever so slowly, arousing herself from a refreshing sleep. You observe her as she slowly, ever so slowly, stretches a wing, then draws it near to her body. The second wing is ever so slowly extended, then withdrawn. There is no hurry, no mad rush, for as a creature of nature, she intuitively understands that to become one with the world around her, she has no choice but to obey its natural laws.

An ever so tiny hummingbird, then another, circles contentedly around the pastel yellow and lavender blossoms of an early-blooming columbine, its face tenderly turned upward in an attempt to gather instructions from The Master Planner. The columbine possesses wisdom, for she understands that in relinquishing her life-force to the creator of the garden, she in turn will be enriched as well as replenished. In the stillness of the garden, all that she needs to know will be revealed to her. She does not fret, nor does she worry. She is at one with nature. She is at perfect peace. You, too, Grace Ann, can know that peace.

"Grace Ann, I spent a few minutes last night writing an exercise that may help you with those terrible panic attacks. I'd like to tape it today. I think it might help. What about you? How do you feel?"

"I think it would be great, but...."

"But what?"

She does not answer. I watch, perplexed, as she reaches into her canvas bag, and pulls her furry friend out by his foot.

What was I thinking? A session without George?

Preparations for taping begin. Grace Ann removes her shoes, sprawls across the therapy room's rose-colored sofa, and tenderly hugs an obedient George to her substantial chest. Utterly contented, she, and presumably George, drifts into a well-earned sleep.

Give the Man A Face

I don't know the source of the trauma, but it is becoming harder to deny that whatever it was, it must have been long-term, and severe. Little is needed to trigger an emotional, and with increasing frequency, a physical release.

"I don't know what it is, Deborah, but Nancy *(Grace Ann's one significant friend),* has this hand lotion that, are you ready for this? reminds me of placenta. I won't touch her hand when she has it on."

Placenta? Where did she come up with that? I know she's a nurse, but I don't remember her ever working in Labor and Delivery.

"And it looks just like lemon yogurt. Lemon yogurt makes me gag! I like every other flavor, but yuck, not lemon. Can't stand to be in the same room with the stuff."

O.K. First placenta, now lemon yogurt?

Several weeks later a leaking pipe sends a trail of water down the office wall. In order to repair the pipe and halt the soggy invasion, a hole is drilled in the stippled ceiling. Grace Ann hobbles into the office, plops down on the couch, looks up, shrinks into a fetal position and cries out: "No, no, Dr. Debbie!"

Dr. Debbie? Whatever happened to Deborah?

"Are they going to drop a hook through that hole?"

"No, Grace Ann, no hook will ever appear in my office."

She eyes me warily. Distrust takes center stage. It's clear she doesn't believe me. I spend an entire session attempting to coax my client out of her fetal position.

Several days later, the "hook" incident still unresolved, a neighboring business (a hair salon) markets its new line of cosmetics by hanging Mardi Gras masks outside its door. As an unsuspecting Grace

Ann descends the stairs leading from my office to the street, she encounters this new display. A virtual uproar ensues.

Screaming. Sobbing. Screaming. Sobbing.

Horrified, I instantly assume the worst—she, *and George*, must have toppled down the steep entranceway. Rushing out, I find her, not battered and bruised as I had feared, but rigidly positioned at the top of the stairs. Confused, I scan the area in an attempt to ward off some invisible enemy. Hoping, needing to minimize the tumult before she embarrasses herself, *and me*, in the public hallway, I call out, "Grace Ann, Grace Ann, what is wrong?"

I'm standing beside her, not a foot away, and she doesn't even acknowledge my presence! To my amazement I watch, mouth ajar, as she tosses the previously indispensable crutches down the brick steps, turns around, and sprints, not hobbles, but sprints back towards the safety of my office door. I have no idea what is going on! Several hours pass before she is calm enough to once again enter the outside world.

More weeks pass. I arrive for a late winter session, clothed appropriately, I think, in a red wool dress and black, three-quarter length leather jacket. Upon seeing me, Grace Ann's mood, initially pleasant and welcoming, instantly changes. Hiding her face behind now visibly shaking hands, she sobs: "No, I knew they would find me! Make them go away! We, I thought we could trust you, Dr. Debbie! We can't trust nobody!"

Triggers show no mercy.

⦿⊷⦁⊷⦿

Grace Ann's orthopedic doctor recommends that she swim daily, an outing she loves until she swallows a mouthful of water and is consumed with an image of a faceless man attempting to drown her in a tub of water. She refuses to swim again.

Grace Ann, at my suggestion, reluctantly agrees to attend a panic attack support group facilitated by a male therapist. After the interview to determine her suitability for the group, she calls, bawling into the phone, "I just got home from talking to that man. I can't do this, Deborah. I'm just not comfortable with a man. Any man. I went by

Krispy Kreme, I couldn't stop myself. I bought a dozen doughnuts, and I've already eaten them all! The whole dozen! I just inhaled them—I don't even know what they tasted like. I'm so ashamed of myself. Why can't I stop this, Deborah?"

One journal entry reads:

> i'm sitting here watching the Home Show. They are talking about child sexual abuse by a friend or relative. A thirteen-year-old girl has come forward with it. i wish i had the courage to come forward before now. It triggered how my foster father would come into my room when i had been sleeping and he'd wake me up 'to do our special thing,' as he would say. He seemed larger than life to me. He just seemed overpowering…i couldn't get him off of me, no matter how much i tried to push him off. i hate him for what he used to do. i still feel dirty and shameful inside. i hate men, i wish i could have told earlier and wouldn't have wasted so much of my life. i hate life…i am a failure in everything i do.

Another tells of watering her beloved azaleas:

> …it triggered our foster mother giving us enemas with what felt like a water hose. She said she was washing the bad out. She would make us hold it until it gave us pains in the stomach, and if we let any water come out before she said we could, she would put more in and make us hold it longer, then beat us with the strap for not holding it.

Enough already! I just can't read anymore!

———◆◆◆———

There is absolutely no doubt in my mind that this poor woman is suffering from Post Traumatic Stress Disorder, a severe anxiety based upon an individual's response to a traumatic event. Before a diagnosis of PTSD can be made, an individual must have experienced some sort of extreme stressor. The stressor, or event, is then re-experienced as intrusive thoughts or dreams. The PTSD victim responds to this intense memory with fear, helplessness, or horror. The trauma creates a "numbing" of the individual's responses. Hypervigilance and irritability are persistent symptoms. The disorder creates overwhelming distress, eventually leading to an impairment of the individual's ability to function.

I'm confident that I am on the right track. Something terrible must have happened to Grace Ann, and "that something" must have continued for a very long time. However, the question still remains—how to best help this hurting client.

I'm brainstorming with a friend before class when Ron, a fellow doctoral student, overhears my discouraged commentary.

"You might want to do a dissociation assessment, Deborah."

"Why would I want to do that?"

"Because I'm sure you have a Multiple."

"A Multiple what?"

"A client with Multiple Personality Disorder. I think they call it something else now. DID, maybe. I think it stands for Dissociative Identity Disorder. I expect you'll see the whole picture before long."

There is no way my very first client could have Multiple Personality Disorder, or DID, or whatever you call it.

Anxious to prove him wrong, I locate the assessments and, with Grace Ann's permission, conduct the testing. Several hours after our uneventful "testing," my secretary knocks on the office door.

"I'm really sorry to interrupt," she apologizes to both me and my current client, a kindly gentleman grieving the loss of his wife of forty-six years, "but you have an emergency. I tried to handle it, but I, I just don't know what to do."

Generally an exceptionally competent individual with an uncanny ability to handle anything, I wince at the uncharacteristic tremor in her voice.

Excusing myself, I hurry to the phone, only to be greeted with a mixture of wails and screams. "No, no, no, Deborah, help me! Please help me!"

Recognizing a hysterical Grace Ann, I take a deep breath and attempt to diffuse whatever it is that has created this most recent catastrophe. Unable to hear me, the choking diatribe continues, until, barely able to catch her breath, I hear, "Can I come back. Can I please, please come back?"

Scanning the appointment book, I see my only break scheduled in this busy day is one hour for lunch—if I'm able to stay on schedule.

"Grace Ann, come on in at one. I can see you for a few minutes then."

———•◦•◦•———

It's 12:45. I know she's in the waiting room. I can hear the persistent howls through the office walls. *Forget about the few minutes. It's just not going to happen!*

Bracing myself, I round the corner and watch a distraught Grace Ann sobbing into the worn-out blue washcloth.

Is there no end to tears?

"Come on in, Grace," I sigh.

Once the time-consuming task of "settling-in" has been completed, an overwrought and trembling Grace Ann hands me, what else, her journal. I'm curious as to what could *possibly* have been added since our morning session.

> The assessments triggered memories of ritual abuse… My birthday (her writing changes to an elementary script, the deliberate efforts of a child in about the fourth or fifth grade), which we never celebrated, was October 18th, and Halloween was October 31st. Halloween is the highest Holy Day in the satanic witchcraft cult. It's like Christmas is to Christians. It was horrible. I escaped to my safe, free place even before I got into the car.
>
> At the Big Hall, they tied me to that hard table, took off all my clothes. They tried to hurt me with their peckers. They continually asked if i was willing to join. It seems like i came back from my safe, free spot long enough to say no, then back to be free and safe. The next thing i knew, i was home and had a huge blister on my bottom and left thigh. i didn't even remember coming home from the Hall. i just knew i couldn't sit down.

Satanic Witchcraft? The Big Hall? Hard Tables? The changes in those I's?

Over the next several weeks, the dam weakens, then bursts. Grace Ann reluctantly confesses that the dark circles beneath her eyes are the result of her, not inability, but refusal to sleep. As debilitating as the daily, often hourly, triggers are, she describes the night terrors as insufferable. It's clear she's not exaggerating.

"I'm scared to close my eyes, Deborah. I wake up crying, no not crying, sobbing into my pillow. The covers are kicked off the bed. Sometimes I don't know where I am. I'm crouched in a corner, or last night, I was hiding behind the living room chair. I don't even know why I was hiding. I have bruises on my ankles and my wrists, and I don't know where they came from."

Looking closely at the distraught figure, I see the bruises. Not just bruises, but cuts, many cuts of varying depths and degrees of irritation, etched into both forearms. To my horror, she lifts her shirt, and displays a multitude of red-rimmed, oozing blisters within the folds of her chest and abdomen. One look into her tear-filled eyes tells me there's no point in my asking questions—she is oblivious to their origin.

Grace Ann continues to be terrorized by the illusive, faceless man. I attempt to provide some small degree of comfort and read Lobby's *Jessica and the Wolf—A Story for Children Who Have Bad Dreams*. In this engaging tale, the child is able to halt the recurring nightmares by abruptly turning and facing her attacker. By giving him a face, she no longer lives in fear of what *might* be. No longer terrorized by the mystery, she now *knows*. Jessica then gleefully observes him as he dejectedly slinks away, no longer possessing the power to rob her of a refreshing sleep.

Together, Grace Ann and I resolve to disarm her nocturnal foe, to "give the man a face." However, Grace Ann finds no peace. Instead, a dramatic physical deterioration occurs: Nail biting, pulling skin from the cuticles, increased agitation, a violent twitching and rocking, erratic breathing, and voice fluctuations (from guttural to infant-like) are the end products of this less-than-successful experiment. *I don't know how she can go on. I don't know how we can go on. Breathe...Breathe.*

I've always believed to repeat the same behaviors and expect different results is a sure sign of insanity. Time to change the approach! Attempting to interject some degree of reason, I, the dyed-in-the-wool educator, explain: "Grace Ann, trauma compartmentalizes itself, and only leaks through, little by little, when an individual is psychologically prepared to deal with the forbidden material, whatever it might be."

Ever the cheerleader, I suggest that she acknowledge the trigger, that she give the trigger a face. I encourage her to confront the fear, to boldly exclaim, *I'll deal with you later*, or even, I *have already processed you, and now I'm letting you go.*

However well meaning the admonishment, it is painfully obvious that she cannot hear, for she appears to be lost in her world of faceless men.

My personal notes read:

I am initially optimistic. Grace Ann is journaling, engaged in cognitive restructuring, affirmations, autonomic muscle relaxation, and experiential therapy. The work has been painstakingly slow and methodical. However, at the present time, a distinct de-compensation is noted. While she is clearly motivated, she appears to possess a limited ability to engage in her own healing. It's as if something outside of herself is holding her back—blocking her participation—as if her "will" alone is keeping her going.

Recurrent, intrusive recollections are occurring at an overwhelming pace. I never know what to expect, or what will trigger what. Coping strategies are grossly insufficient. She vacillates among inappropriately dependent, passive-aggressive, and compulsive tendencies. Boundary issues, the repeated phone calls in particular, are EXTREMELY difficult to maintain. An analysis of her most recent journal entries demonstrates an unmistakable variation in handwriting, particularly noticeable when detailing the trauma and abuse. In addition, testing indicates the presence of POSSIBLE dissociative features, along with the *obvious PTSD*. I suspect Borderline Personality Disorder as well. Although the results of the assessments indicate full blown MPD, I am unwilling to wholly accept the findings, for I am aware that, depending upon the degree of severity, a borderline personality can appear to the untrained eye (and mine is certainly untrained) as MPD. In addition, Grace Ann is MY VERY FIRST CLIENT!!!!!! I don't believe the fates could be so cruel!

For the first time, hospitalization is considered as a treatment option, for it, at least at the present time, seems to be inevitable. I don't have the power to make her well. I do have the power to keep her safe. Maybe that's all I can hope for. Maybe my only purpose is to protect Grace Ann...from herself.

"I'm Going to Stop Therapy For A While"

Dr. Gentry, Grace Ann's personal physician calls to inquire about her therapy. "How's school going, Deborah? You about finished with the coursework? Started the dissertation, yet? Grace Ann tells me she's asked you to tell her story! That would be some read, wouldn't it?"

After several minutes of this pleasant small talk..."Deborah, I think we need to put our heads together. She calls the office over and over. I think she puts the thing on redial. She has driven our receptionist absolutely crazy. I know she's hurting, but I just don't know what to do.

Today she asked if she could take another milligram of *Alprazolom*, so she could stop shaking. She's in such bad shape that I said O.K."

"I've talked to her about hospitalization. I think it might help, but she adamantly refuses. Unfortunately, if we force her to go, it will likely just make matters worse. She may view our attempts to help as one more incarceration, then we'll join the long line of perpetrators. We surely don't want to be included in those ranks! I have noticed some improvement lately, but I think this will continue as a slow go."

"Dr. Gentry, what do you think happened to her?"

"I don't expect we want to know."

———◆◈◆———

Grace Ann does not want to be hospitalized. What am I to do? 5.0 mg of Alprazolom a day! Isn't this an awfully high dosage? Are we setting her up for yet another addiction? This all seems to have landed on my shoulders. I know Grace Ann has repeatedly refused to see another psychiatrist, but I'm going to push for a consult anyway. I have no choice! On a positive note, she has experienced a thirty-two pound weight loss. At least this is going well. She's also more aware of how she feels right before an eating binge. Another positive! I am, however, concerned with her absolute refusal to see an in-network psychiatrist.

"No Deborah, I see Dr. Gentry every week or so. Remember that I saw a psychiatrist when I was in that treatment program. It didn't help at all. Why would I want to go through that again?"

"Well, let's look at what's best for you. It would be helpful for me to have a second opinion, and maybe some direction. I don't want you to have to pay for all this therapy. Remember that you have the right to access your insurance benefits. They don't seem to believe my diagnoses. They've said repeatedly that if you want them to pay, you'll have to see one of their docs."

Standing firm, she again refuses, choosing instead to phone the managed care caseworker herself.

"Deborah, I called that lady. She treated me just like I was crazy! I guess I don't have any other choice. I feel like I'm being punished by my own insurance company. I'll go if you think it will help me."

I make a note to schedule the consult—a.s.a.p. Better move before she changes her mind! The only psychiatrists in this network are men. Grace Ann will have a fit. It will take at least a month, if not more, to find an opening, so I'll cross the gender bridge when I get there.

The bad knees, which used to hurt only when walking, now throb non-stop. Dr. Johnson, Grace Ann's orthopedic surgeon and long-time friend, delivers the fatal blow.

"Grace Ann, I don't expect you will be able to go back to your old job. Your knees are just too far gone. We can do the replacement surgery, but not until you've lost, say, another hundred, hundred-fifty pounds. Even after surgery and the rehab, I just don't think you'll be able to deal with all that walking. I can see you're not handling this well at all." He orders continued psychotherapy.

Grace Ann is rapidly exhausting her meager savings. Generous to a fault, she continues to be a major contributor to numerous children's charities, even though she no longer has the funds to do so. "Friends" borrow money with an alarming regularity. Anxious to garner support for herself, and her as yet unnamed condition, she purchases costly hardbound books weekly, presenting these new editions to her primary care physician, orthopedic surgeon, and me. I can't speak for the others, but I smell trouble brewing, and am anxious to preserve our fragile therapeutic boundaries. Determined to avoid what I fear would become a lethal dual relationship, I repeatedly, week after week, refuse her purchases.

"I'm only trying to help," she whimpers. "You've helped me, why can't I help you?"

I don't have an answer, but I continue to refuse. My insistence is met with a prolonged haughty irritability.

Eventually I am one-upped. This wonderfully calculating client, upon hearing of an office lending library, sends books—boxes of books.

"Nancy, I've told Grace Ann over and over that I can't accept gifts from my clients! Grace Ann…."

"I know what you're going to say, Deborah," she interrupts, "but the books aren't for you. They're for your clients. Look." She opens a volume, and points to the inside cover. It is meticulously inscribed, (as are all the others) with:

"For the library of Deborah Berkley L.P.C., from Grace Ann Hughes."

I shake my head in disbelief as I survey the boxes. I must never play poker with this insightful, but uncanny individual. I am quite certain I would lose.

———◆◆◆◆◆———

The stressors just keep on coming. Grace Ann had purchased a "long-term" disability policy twenty years ago, only to discover that the policy is actually effective for only one year. Worker's Compensation is some nine weeks behind in its payments. As if matters are not bad enough, Dr. Johnson's updated report has arrived, detailing the severity of her orthopedic condition. Concerned as to her future employability, the agency attempts to initiate career retraining, suggesting that the office/clerical field might be most appropriate for the previously "temporarily" disabled health care professional.

Desperate and anxious to help, Nancy arranges to take her hurting companion to a Fundamentalist healing service.

"Claim your power and rebuke Satan," Grace Ann is counseled by the television evangelist. Ignited by the evening's religious fervor, and in an apparent show of faith, Grace Ann is videotaped ambling, unimpeded, across the coliseum's massive stage.

Where are her crutches? I wonder, as I remember that I, too, had witnessed a similar weird occurrence at the top of the office stairs.

Arms swinging gleefully by her side, she wears both her customary pink tee shirt and a blissful, childlike grin....

Following this remarkable demonstration of conviction, or religious fervor (it's too early to tell), she runs to the arena's "nosebleed" seats before dropping to her knees in a prayer of gratitude. Unfortunately, the "healing" is short-lived, for the next morning several doses of painkillers are needed before she can bear to pull herself from bed. Several weeks later the pain is unrelenting, and she refuses to walk, even with the assistance of her indispensable wooden companions.

So much for "claiming your power."

———◆◆◆◆◆———

Throughout our time together, Grace Ann has repeatedly expressed a desire, no, a *need,* to reconnect with her past. I can certainly appreciate her wishes—her need to discover her roots. I, too, value family. A heritage is a birthright. Grace Ann is no less deserving than I. But the timing has just been lousy.

"Grace Ann, it's not the right time. I'm concerned that you're just too fragile."

Grace Ann has a hard head!

She remains undeterred as she places call after call to the town of her youth. Phone bills, from five to fifteen hundred dollars a month, advance her fiscal deficit, and her ill-advised attempts prove no less than devastating. Unsure of where to start, she contacts the child and family services agency responsible for her several foster placements. Unable, physically or financially, to travel the sixteen hundred miles to her childhood home, she requests that her records be mailed. She is at first told she must sign a "permission to release confidential information form." When the promised records are not forthcoming, she calls yet again, and is told by a second official that the keys to her childhood cannot be delivered until all other persons referenced in the aging documents agree to sign releases as well.

Not one to be easily dissuaded, Grace Ann explains her circumstances to a hierarchy of officials (*via long distance, of course*), and is finally told she will be mailed altered copies as soon as the records clerk can review the eighteen years of notes, and delete all mention of her brothers. While awaiting these records, she locates a distant aunt (in yet another corner of the country), and is told her long-estranged mother has been released into the custody of her own elderly sister. Delighted with the news, Grace Ann phones, and is informed by the caregiver that her mother is to receive no calls from her children. Shortly after the aborted communication, a letter arrives from an attorney confirming that her biological mother does not wish to be inconvenienced with memories of an unfortunate past.

The more contact Grace Ann has with persons or agencies from her past, the more instability and personality de-compensation is observed. In true borderline fashion, she becomes extraordinarily labile (severe mood swings), overwhelmed, and anxious. The end result is an octopus-like dependence. Once rebuffed, either externally or from

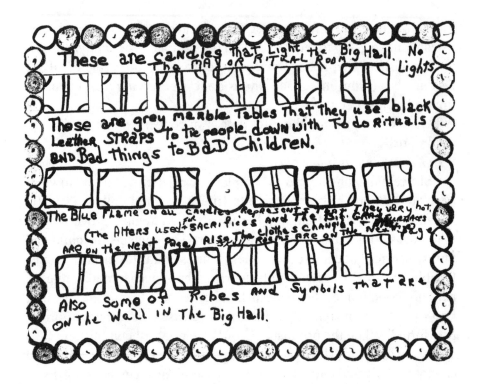

within, she enters a petulant depression. At this point, Grace Ann, as do most individuals suffering from borderline pathology, sinks into a cognitive disorientation, a sense of estrangement and disembodiment—nothingness. Dejection gives way to irritability, histrionic behaviors, self-mutilation, then fury and rage, the latter of which is generally projected upon the person who, only a short time before, has been over-idealized as the savior. Therapeutically, this is known as the classic "borderline flip." I, of course, was yesterday's savior.

Burdened, and appearing confused by her own thoughts, she exclaims, "I can see the Big Hall. I can describe every inch of it. Am I dreaming this, Deborah? It's so real to me."

I have no reply. I just don't know. Sensing wariness in me, the heartfelt query abruptly turns to fury.

"I'm going to stop therapy for a while," she announces, arms defiantly crossed, legs twitching, indifferent to direction, tears streaming.

"You won't be my friend." Angry, sulking, and petulant, Grace Ann doggedly continues. "Why won't you be my friend?"

Once again, I attempt to discuss the role of the therapist as a helping professional, the need for objectivity, and the inappropriateness of unrelenting phone calls between sessions. Having accomplished nothing more than further agitating the now smoldering individual, I offer: "I will support you in the decision you feel you need to make. I will be happy to make a referral to another therapist."

"I don't want another therapist," she lashes out. "I'm not coming back. It's too much money."

One...Two...Three...Four...Five...Big breaths...Breathe, Deborah, breathe....

"You might want to stop this process for a while. You know you can always come back when you're ready to address these painful issues. It's important to take all the time you need. Make this work for you, Grace Ann."

Incensed by the implication that she is not serious about her recovery, she aims a no less than venomous glare across the room, not surprisingly, in my direction. A low-pitched, grating, demonic-like roar erupts.

"I don't want to be dependent on you. I'm going to stop counseling."

As calmly and detached as possible, I reiterate, "I support you in your decision and wish you well."

Shaking with fury, she proceeds to pound a nearby chair, all the while screaming at the top of her lungs, "You're just like the others, you don't care. All you care about is my money. Don't worry, you'll get paid if it's the last thing I do. You're never there when I need you. Do you treat all your patients this way?"

*O.K. Where in the professional codebook does it say "Thou shalt not murder thy client?" I have to get out of here. If I stay much longer, I should say, if **she** stays much longer, there will be trouble. Breathe...breathe....*

The tantrum continues. The CD in the waiting room is blaring. My secretary must be attempting to block the noise. An inhaler comes whizzing by, then a journal. I maintain my placid exterior. Now she's really mad. Heaving herself up by a single crutch, she continues her now nonsensical tirade as she hobbles through the reception area and out the office door.

I brave a sideways glance as I pass by the reception area. If the situation had not been so tense, so anti-therapeutic, I would have laughed hysterically, for there, sitting stoically erect is a new client, bug-eyed, purse clutched to her chest as if to shield herself from whomever, or whatever, emerges from the adjoining room.

The day's notes read: *As a therapist, I must consider my limits. I can't continue these two double sessions each week. I am inundated with the constant calls, pages, cards, "helpful" notes…am at my wit's end with her incessant demands. Borderline behaviors are up! Dependency needs are up! Passive-aggressive tendencies are up! Compulsivity is up!*

Several hours after the *supposed* termination, our now frazzled secretary receives four calls.

"Tell Deborah I didn't mean it, I'm sorry. Ask her to please forgive me. I don't really want to stop. Not really. She's the only person I trust. She can't leave me."

Watch me!!!!!

I do not return her plaintive calls. They continue, detailing her fragile sense of self, her uncertainty and confusion.

"I don't want to be dependent upon you."

"I decided I was going to yell at you today."

"I'm sorry I bothered you."

"I almost called you at home last night."

I don't think so….

"I still love you."

Other clients are beginning to complain that the voice mail is always full. The secretary, tired of transcribing the repetitive missives, asks if she can simply delete Grace Ann's calls.

Dr. Gentry calls. Grace Ann has phoned her answering service, declaring an emergency. When the bewildered physician returns the urgent summons, she encounters a wailing child, shrieking, "I bee's bad, I bee's bad. Dr. Debbie hates the Big Lady 'cause I bee's so bad."

"I don't know what else to do for her," the clearly dejected physician declares. "I can't increase her medication, and she won't go to the hospital. If I tell her she can't continue to act this way, will you reconsider?"

"I don't know if I can do it," is my honest, my own dejected reply. *Pressure. Pressure. Guilt. Pressure.*

"Oh, O.K. All right."

Another session is begrudgingly scheduled. Grace Ann, seemingly amnestic to her prior pleas of repentance, again lashes out, "I guess I'm dependent on you. You won't be my friend. Everyone I want as a friend refuses to be there for me. I'm quitting therapy."

Gritting my teeth, *yes,* gritting my teeth, I respond in slow, measured tones, "The very next time you call with 'I'm quitting therapy,' I am going to refuse to treat you any longer."

"I'm paying for this, Deborah. I can do anything I want!"

"Wrong, wrong, wrong. No, you may not! This may come as a surprise to you, but as a therapist, I also have rights and you may not, you may not abuse my rights! Do you understand?"

I feel the heat from my flushing face as I sit without speaking. Furious, I refuse to acknowledge her weakening tirade. I hear my now not so subtle inner voice insist, "Calm down, calm down. Breathe! Breathe!"

When finally the most recent barrage has wound down (and I have restrained myself from thoughts of homicide), I again address the therapeutic issues at hand, using terse phrases and displaying little patience. The "voice" within again beseeches me to relax. From somewhere, something reminds me that an abused individual often seeks to reconstruct the abuse as a warped affirmation of her existence. I am cautioned that to respond in the manner that I wish, in the manner that her behavior deserves, will be to furnish nothing more than a confirmation of her ever-present feelings of worthlessness.

There are already times I hate being a therapist!

"Grace Ann," my voice is remarkably calm, "Grace Ann, we will have to again set definite boundaries. I am your therapist. My job is to help you get well. If your behavior continues along these lines, I will refer you to another therapist. If Dr. Gentry and I feel hospitalization is necessary, and you enter voluntarily, I will go with you as your therapist. If not, I will set the admission process in motion and you will be referred to whomever is on call. Grace Ann, if I don't believe I can help you help yourself, I will not continue to see you."

Moments pass in silence, a most uncomfortable silence—the kind that makes your hair stand on end and your skin crawl. Grace Ann surveys the familiar environment, pausing on objects around the room. The seemingly diversionary quest ends with her fumbling through the never-ending contents of the canvas bag, rummaging around until she produces what appears to be a framed photograph. At first, I am immersed with guilt, for it seems she is about to hand me another present. Upon closer examination, I determine that the "present" is actually an 8x10 photograph of a pre-adolescent child attired in a white "Sunday-best" dress. The sepia-toned formal portrait is covered with a pink sheet of lined notebook paper, the paper secured tightly across the back of the frame by a hodge-podge of cellophane tape. Puzzled, I cast a sideways glance at the dejected client.

"This is not a bad child…how could this be me…I must not see myself as others see me."

I realize that the white "Sunday-best" dress is actually communion attire, and the young child is none other than an already desecrated Grace Ann Hughes.

A Diagnosis Confirmed

Although we have discussed this on *far* too many occasions, the phone calls continue, twenty-six on this particular day. With each call, Grace Ann's agitation escalates and her comprehension wanes. Interestingly, this episode seems to be different, for it doesn't at all appear to be manipulative, or purposeful. At my request, the embattled secretary attempts to inform the confused caller that a phone block will be necessary if this irresponsible behavior continues.

"Deborah, I told her I was going to call the phone company, and have them block all her calls from all her numbers, but I don't think she heard a single thing I said."

In an attempt to diffuse the out-of-control situation, another emergency session is hurriedly arranged. Grace Ann arrives, and departs, sobbing.

A colleague pulls into the office parking lot. Upon entering the building, he approaches the secretary and me with, "Deborah, did you know your client is sitting outside in her car? I don't think I've ever

seen anyone shake like that—she can't even hold on to the steering wheel. I went over to the window to see if I could help, but when she saw me, she screamed, locked the doors, and covered her head with her jacket. She knows me, but she looked like she'd just seen a monster. I couldn't believe it! What in heaven's name is going on with her? Is she O.K.?"

Uh, no. I don't think so.

We stand, huddled behind the office door, gently parting the curtain every so often to keep abreast of the goings-on. Perplexed, unsure of what the appropriate therapeutic move might be, we watch in a mixture of wonder and dread as Grace Ann steadies her phone, propping it against the steering wheel. Slowly, methodically, she presses the numbers. Our phone wails. My colleague clutches his chest. I scream. Our secretary sits, transfixed, unable, or unwilling, to answer the phone. Finally, the spell is broken.

"Deborah, she wants to come inside."

Dear God in Heaven, no. Please don't do this to me! Please! This is more than I can bear.

"Tell her to come on in."

I pace the room in mindless strides. The measured pacing gives way, disintegrating into a strange bolting motion much like the frenzied gallop of a caged animal. My colleague has disappeared. My secretary sits, frozen, wild-eyed—her boss has gone slightly mad! *The office door is swinging open. She has nowhere to hide. We have nowhere to hide!*

I cease my aimless flailing. A crutch appears, then a backside. I watch as Grace Ann, turned sideways to more easily navigate the doorway, enters the room—once again.

"Can I see you just for a minute?" she asks, her voice tremulous.

My training takes over. "Grace Ann, I can only give you a minute or two. I have a really busy afternoon scheduled."

It's going to be a long day.

Grace Ann settles in. The wheezing and shaking continue. She struggles to harness the sobs as she spits out the details of her mind's intruder.

"I was getting ready to pull out of the parking lot when all those years of Saturday nights flashed before my eyes. I see me, I know it's me, and I'm being forced into these, these acts with dogs. I see it all, Deborah. I see it all. My mind spins forward, and my foster mother is putting lipstick on me. She's holding me down while my foster father is having his way with me. The movie camera is running the whole time.

"Then I see me, a little, innocent, sad me, and I'm being chained to a water pipe in a dark closet. She's closing the door, and telling me she will let me out if I'll be good—if I won't fight them. I'm little, and I'm so scared of the dark. The pictures in my head just wouldn't stop. The next thing I see is my foster father having sex with his own daughter. And she looks like she's enjoying it!

"Oh my God! What's happening to me? Make it stop, Deborah. Why can't you make it stop?"

"Grace Ann, I would make it stop if I could. I don't know how. I really think you need to be in the hospital—for just a little while. Just until you're feeling better. You can't go on like this. You just can't."

"No—absolutely not. I'm not going to any hospital—not ever again. I won't go, Deborah. Don't ask me again."

"You know you'll have to sign a safety contract, don't you?"

"Yes, I know. That's O.K. I don't mind signing one. You know I'm not going to harm myself. I don't know why God makes me wake up each day, but I'm not going to kill myself."

"Grace, you're going to have to stay in the waiting room until this shaking stops. I can't let you drive like this. I'm going to try to get in touch with Dr. Gentry. If you're not willing to go to the hospital, I at least want you to be seen by your physician."

"Don't worry, Deborah. I'm feeling better. I'll wait outside. I'm sure I'm going to be just fine."

Yet another call is placed to Dr. Gentry.

"I know it's getting late, but can you possibly see Grace Ann this evening? She's out of control, and I'm afraid for her own safety. She's having flashback after flashback. I think she really needs to be hospitalized."

The concerned physician agrees to extend her hours, to remain at her office until we feel Grace Ann is calm enough to drive. Later that evening she phones my office, where I am now seeing the client that was forced to reschedule due to Grace Ann's impromptu session.

A remarkable transformation appears to have taken place. Dr. Gentry reports the client arrived—composed and psychologically intact. When questioned as to the strange events of the afternoon, Grace Ann is said to have replied, "I was upset, but I'm O.K. now."

"Deborah, I'm sorry, but I have no reason to hospitalize her. She's fine."

I am incredulous. *I don't know whom I'm more upset with, Grace Ann Hughes or Dr. Gentry!!! I'm beginning to think we've all gone crazy! What is going on here? It's time to circle the wagons. Breathe...breathe....*

After giving myself an extended time-out, I'm able to recover sufficiently to again put on my therapeutic hat. Realizing this isolated individual is in dire need of social support, I follow through with Grace Ann's earlier request that I schedule a consultation with her friend, Nancy. Checking my releases to ensure all is in order, I phone Nancy, who is receptive and appears eager to assist in any way possible. While frustrated, she is fully invested. She volunteers that Grace Ann has a history of bizarre behaviors, rapid and unpredictable mood shifts, and conversely, an inconceivable generosity. Going out on a limb, I ask her about the less than successful healing service.

Dismayed, she responds, "I don't know how she could have fallen back into sin. I tell her to claim her power and rebuke Satan."

Nancy shares an earlier experience of taking Grace Ann to a Pentecostal minister and his wife, only to be told that Grace Ann was demon-possessed and must never be brought into their presence again. While I am comforted that I'm not carrying this ball alone, I am concerned that Nancy may be, unintentionally, inflicting yet another layer of guilt upon my already guilt-ridden client. I feel comfortable enough with Nancy to discuss these concerns with her. Thankfully, she takes no offense, and agrees to tone down the judgmental, albeit well-intentioned, commentary. Her heart is clearly in the right place.

<hr />

The day of the insurance company mandated psychiatric consult arrives. Grace Ann calls, "Pray for me, Deborah. I'm terrified, but I know I need to go."

My worst fears are confirmed when, shortly after the appointed session, there is a knock on my office door.

"Deborah, I'm sorry to interrupt you, but Dr. Sullivan is on the line. He says he needs to speak with you."

Excusing myself from the session in progress, I scramble to the phone, unsure if my reluctant client has even made it to, or through, the dreaded session.

"Ms. Berkley, this is Dr. Sullivan. I need to let you know that your patient has a severe Borderline Personality/Post Traumatic Stress Disorder/Multiple Personality Disorder. Dr. Gentry has her appropriately medicated. We can only hope to keep the symptoms in check. She's going to need extensive long-term therapy."

A gentle, soft-spoken individual, he struggles as he attempts to diffuse the announcement. "She appears to have a good therapeutic relationship with you," was his well-meaning effort. "I'll be happy to monitor her medications if you want me to. Feel free to call anytime…and good luck!"

Now what? I feel sick to my stomach! My whole body is beginning to shake! This cannot be happening to me! It's unbelievable! I have never taken a course on MPD! I have never even read about MPD! I don't want to even hear about MPD!

I call a therapist friend, who offers consolation, but no advice. I yell at my son, who promptly yells back, "It's your fault, Mom. You're the one who wanted to work with crazy people! I liked you better when you were a teacher!"

Hell, I liked me better when I was a teacher, too….

Realizing I no longer wished to "swim alone," I called a local, non-network psychiatrist. "Dr. Marten, this is Deborah Berkley. I'm a newly licensed professional counselor, and am working with an unexpectedly challenging client. I'm really having a difficult time setting and maintaining appropriate therapeutic boundaries, and would like for another professional to supervise my work."

Clearly misjudging my request, Dr. Marten, now on full alert, inquires, "Are you referring to an inappropriate relationship with a, let's say, a male client? Is your behavior in question in any way?"

Incredulous, then indignant, I retrieve my gaping jaw. Wasting no time in correcting his chauvinistic misperceptions (I'm beginning to feel like Grace Ann!), I respond, in a crisp, staccato-like, fashion. "No, Dr. Marten, I am not involved in any inappropriate relationship. I am attempting to work with an MPD, and have no training. I was looking for someone to provide some direction."

I can hear him blushing through the phone. Apologetic, he volunteers to meet with me the following week.

I call my local bookstore, "Sandy, would you please order everything you can get your hands on about Multiple Personality Disorder and multi-perpetrator abuse?" *(She is by now used to my strange requests!)*

I contact my college professor. "Dr. Matthews, I'm sure you remember our conversations about that unusual client. I just found out that she has MPD, and, according to her, has been involved in some sort of ritualized abuse. As you are more than aware, I'm clueless. Could I do an independent study on this?" Thankfully, permission is granted for the unusual request!

And finally, I phone my mom. *If all else fails, call mom!* "I've changed my mind. I'll be able to go with you guys to the beach after all. I'm tired, and I think I need to get away."

After arranging emergency coverage, I pack the car with off-duty beach clothing and an oversized box of crisp new books. Day after day I sit by the ocean, my head cleared by the assuredness of the surf. I read the works of the experts—Kluft, Braun, Putnam, and Ross. I peruse *Many Voices*, a monthly self-help publication for persons diagnosed with a dissociative disorder. I am fascinated as I review Cohen, Giller, and Lynn W.'s *Multiple Personality from the Inside Out*, an insider's view of life with the disorder. As I read, I recognize the dissociative splits, auto-stimulation, and hypervigilance that has been, in hindsight, apparent in Grace Ann's presentation. I begin to decipher the Delphic handwriting of her journal, and reflect upon so many instances where, without my even knowing, I have been communicating—not with the Grace Ann I thought I knew—but with "an altered state of consciousness."

For a girl who grew up on a rural Virginia farm in the '50s and '60s, "an altered state of consciousness" not drug-induced is far-out indeed.

As if MPD is not enough, I also find myself a disinclined guest in the obscure world of multi-perpetrator abuse. Basking in the warmth of the early summer day, I realize that I am both comforted, and re-pulsed, by the knowledge that is to come....

A Question
of Fear

What would you say, by the way, if I told you that all of my brand-new prehistory of hysteria is already known and was published a hundred times over, though several centuries ago? Do you remember that I always said that the medieval theory of possession held by ecclesiastical courts was identical with our theory of a foreign body and the splitting of consciousness? But when did the devil who took possession of the poor things invariably abuse them sexually and in a loathsome manner? Why are their confessions under torture so like the communications made by my patients in psychic treatment? Sometimes soon I must delve into the literature on this subject! [5]

Sigmund Freud
1897 Letter to Wilhelm Fleiss

CHAPTER THREE

Medieval possession? Splitting of consciousness? Confessions under torture?

I sit, transfixed, very much—too much—alone. An unwelcome, but familiar tightness steals its way across my labored chest.

Relax, Deborah! You're holding your breath again! This is a vacation—a vacation. You can't go on like this! You're losing it! Breathe! Breathe!

"The soul-warming sun is boldly peeping through, and you are becoming more and more attuned to your own peaceful core." I recall the words I taped for Grace Ann. I surely didn't know I'd be needing them! Granting myself the, oh, so simple pleasure of closing suddenly weary eyes against the noonday rays, I, like the columbine of my grandma's garden, turn my face upward. I, too, "attempt to gather instructions from the Master Planner." I wait, and wonder....

Could it have been that once, several lifetimes ago, psychology's founding father sat alone and wondered? Could it have been that he gazed upward towards snow-capped peaks, or perhaps outward, as I do today, towards a placid sea? Was his heart burdened, weighted down with uncertainty? Had he, in his "psychic treatment," come face to face with his own Grace Ann Hughes? Was he afraid, as I am afraid?

And what of Freud's "poor things," and my own Grace Ann? Did they know fear?

Something deep inside tells me that fear is far too kind a word....

The Business of Exploitation

Sighing, reluctantly I turn again to the captive text, feeling not empowered, but enslaved. It seems that the 1980s witnessed an explosion in the *documented* incidents of child abuse unsurpassed in recorded history. At that time, it was alleged that a child was abused every two minutes, with over 95 percent of the abusers known by the child. One out of three girls, and one out of five boys was believed to be sexually molested before age eighteen, with one in ten homes involved in some form of child sexual exploitation. It was estimated that for every case that was reported, twenty-five were silenced, with only 50 percent of all sexual abuse cases actually going to court. In 50 percent of *those* cases, the child continued to be court-ordered into the sole custody of those who had been accused of the molestation.

Could this possibly be true? In America?

My stomach churns as I read of the perpetrators. These offenders, *these thieves of the innocent,* were not the sordid individuals with criminal records or tainted pasts I had expected, but frequently respected members of the community, even trusted friends or *loving* family. I am saddened, yet hardly surprised, that approximately 97 percent of child prostitutes were themselves incest victims, and that child abuse was a leading contributor to teenage suicide.[6]

It was during this decade, this not so distant past, that reports of sexual impropriety, child pornography, forced prostitution, and the most diabolical forms of systematic/ritualistic/multi-perpetrator abuse began trickling into the clergy, law enforcement, and psychotherapy offices of the Western world. Untold numbers of children, adolescents and adults came forth with tales (past as well as present) of cult involvement, accounts "unbelievably grisly, yet at the same time, remarkably similar in their sometimes copious detail."[7]

At least I'm not alone in my horror! I should be ashamed, for curious as it may seem, I take some bizarre comfort in knowing others have walked this road before me. Others have clutched armchairs as they heard, or read as I have done, ghastly tales of horrific abuse. Others have choked on the vile reflux, or blinked away the frozen tears. Apparently they survived, at least somewhat intact, to tell about it. Perhaps I'll survive as well!

But what of Grace Ann? What will her future be? What can her future be?

I learn that little, *if any,* consensus exists within the treatment community as to the validity of these macabre allegations—*I am hardly alone in my confusion.* One camp argues that our current knowledge of abuse issues is based primarily upon subjective anecdotal accounts, while another suggests there is little evidence to support the claims of a *widespread* conspiracy of systematic/ritualistic/multi-perpetrator abuse of children. Still others, professionals in the fields of psychiatry, psychology, counseling, religious studies, journalism, and the law, maintain the ritual abuse of children *is* ongoing, systematic, and pervasive.

So much for simple answers....

As I loll in the security of the balmy Outer Banks day, I realize that I, too, find it incredible, absolutely incomprehensible, and beyond the furthermost reaches of my intellect that any form of multi-perpetrator abuse, systematic or otherwise, could actually exist. I'm determined not to lose this glorious day to this madness, but find it really hard to remain detached as I read one disturbing account after another, documented accounts, from Australia, Canada, Great Britain, and, yes, even here at home. These bone-chilling allegations simply don't fit life as I have *known it to be.* I've heard much of this from Grace Ann, albeit in jumbled bits and pieces, but must admit to have doubted more than I believed. I know nothing of her world. My own childhood consisted of such wonderful things—grandma's chicken and dumplings, ice cream made of snow, wooden swings soaring towards treetops on endless summer days, Sunday morning services in our simple country church, and comfortable, comforting, nightly dinners around a loving family's old oak table. How blessed I was to have been sheltered by my mom and dad. Night after night I slept soundly, knowing beyond a shadow of a doubt that my father, my daddy, would protect me at the very risk of losing his own life.

Who protected Grace Ann? Who sheltered her from harm? Who took her to swim lessons, or taught her to sew? Who was there at the end of the school day? Who prepared her favorite meals, or stayed by her side when she was sick, or scared, or lonely? Was there anyone? *Anyone at all?* How afraid she must have been! I can't get a grasp on all of this. I just don't know. Or perhaps I simply choose not to know, for to understand her world would somehow threaten the safety of mine.

Continuing my reluctant journey, I find that ritual abuse was first described in *Michelle Remembers*, a book in which satanic crimes alleged to have been carried out in British Columbia in the 1950s are described. At the time of publication, this diabolical concept was defined as the "repeated, physical, emotional, mental, and spiritual assaults combined with a systematic abuse of symbols and secret ceremonies designed to turn a child against itself, family, society, and God.[8] Some eight years later, the definition was expanded to include "…abuse that occurs in a context linked to some symbols or group activity that have a religious, magical, or supernatural connotation, and where the invocation of these symbols or activities is repeated over time and used to frighten and intimidate the children."[9]

Apparently the controversy escalated to such astounding levels that in 1989 the Los Angeles Commission for Women formed its own Ritual Abuse Task Force, its goal to shed light upon the smoldering, frequently acrimonious debate. Rather than dismiss these dubious allegations, the exploratory group concluded that ritual violence *did indeed exist*, and could be best described as a "brutal form of abuse of children, adolescents, and adults consisting of physical, sexual, and psychological abuse, and involving the use of symbols.[10] The commission's 1991 Task Force enlarged its earlier definition to read:

> The physical abuse is severe, sometimes including torture and killing. The sexual abuse is usually painful, sadistic, and humiliating, intended as a means of gaining dominance over the victim. The psychological abuse is devastating and involves the use of rituals, intimidation which conveys to the victim a profound terror of cult members, and of the evil spirits they believe cult members can command. Both during and after the abuse, most victims are in a state of terror, mind control, and dissociation in which disclosure is exceedingly difficult.[11]

Illinois followed suit, when in January 1993, Public Act #87-1167 established the definitions, exclusions, and penalties of ritualized abuse of a child.

> A person is guilty of a felony when he commits any of the following acts with, upon, or in the presence of a child as part of a ceremony.

1. Actively, or in simulation, tortures, mutilates, or sacrifices any warm-blooded animal or human being.

2. Forces ingestion, injection, or other application of any narcotic drug, hallucinogen, or anesthetic for the purpose of dulling sensitivity, cognition, recollection of, or resistance to any criminal activity.

3. Forces ingestion or external application of human or animal urine, feces, flesh, blood, bones, body secretions, non-prescribed or chemical compounds.

4. Involves the child in a mock, unauthorized or unlawful marriage ceremony with another person or representation of any force or deity, followed by sexual contact with the child.

5. Places a living child into a coffin or open grave containing a corpse or remains.

6. Threatens death or serious harm to a child, his or her parents, family, pets, or friends which instills a well-founded fear in the child that the threat will be carried out, or

7. Unlawfully dissects, mutilates, or incinerates a human corpse.[12]

A human corpse?

Whoa! Time to take a break!

Meandering along the retreating water's edge, I confess, to no one but my disbelieving self, that I've been holding on, perhaps tenaciously, but holding on nevertheless, to the now rapidly dwindling hope that this would all be a bad memory, the by-product of a very ill woman's mental demise. Los Angeles and Illinois have dashed that dream, opening the floodgates to even more questions to further, although I must admit, resentful inquiry. Their acceptance of the impossible has added credibility to this dispute that is neither anticipated nor welcomed. Squaring my shoulders, and my attitude, I struggle to open my mind to the possibility, the remote likelihood (I hope) that these behaviors can, and do, exist.

Another idyllic summer day! Another sordid title keeps me company during my morning by the peaceful sea.

"Whatcha reading, Deb?" my sister Annette asks, as she settles in beside me with the year's most touted beach read.

"This book on ritual abuse," I respond, indifferently, as if I read this sort of thing every day. "It's a fascinating book. Look at the cover—all those colors swirling about. Kinda unsettling, isn't it? Just found out that it's a firsthand account—don't get many of those. The author changed her name 'cause she, or maybe *he,* I don't know, feared some sort of retaliation. Can you believe that?"

I expect empathy. I receive none.

Shaking her head in dismay, she, my sister, my friend, my *former* biggest supporter, sarcastically replies, "It's time you got a life, big sister. Too much of that stuff can't be good for you! By the way, you don't *really* believe any of that is true, do you?" she asks, lifting her sunglasses to look into my eyes.

"I don't know what I believe," I reply, turning my eyes away, for I'm embarrassed to admit I'm even considering the possibility. "It's just that I've heard so many of these things from this client. I *want* to believe she's delusional, I really do, but there's *something* about her. I can't put my finger on it, but she's so, so honest, so genuine. I'm not ready to dismiss all of this, maybe some of it, but not all, at least not yet."

"Geez, Deb! It's worse than I thought! You've finally gone over the edge!" she exclaims, as she resumes her own tale of betrayal and lust.

Page after page, I read of darkness. *A really dark darkness*, the kind that chills the soul, despite the glowing summer sun. It seems that ritual abuse is carried out by a cult, a "group of people who share an obsessive devotion to a person or idea."[13] Often multi-generational, the present day abusers were yesterday's victims, victims who themselves have been trapped in the insidious cycle of corruption. They seek to brainwash, even as they have been brainwashed. Everyone in the cult believes the lies to be the truth, and the insanity is passed, unquestioned, unchallenged, from generation to generation.

Permeating all levels of society, these persons are alleged to live in seclusion in non-communal environments, for to congregate in group settings would risk exposure to themselves and their clandestine activities. Often respected members of their local communities, they are believed to be typically involved in traditional religious services, and can be found in all faiths and denominations. (*Amazingly, the author suggests that a high concentration exists in both Fundamentalist Christian and Roman Catholic sects. That's some allegation! It's no wonder the author changed her name!*) In all likelihood, the adults active in cult worship today have undergone the same systematic indoctrination and programming they are now imposing upon others. Some are believed to have no memory of the abuse, and may even have no knowledge of their current involvement, while others are thought to have remained mindful of both the childhood abuse and their present day association with the society. Still others, as adults, join groups, societies and fraternities, unaware of macabre events that are to come. While initially encouraged to research alternate religious beliefs, these vulnerable individuals quickly progress from level to level until they are involved in moderate sexualized rituals. At this point, the indoctrination/mind control is increased, and the doors to a sane existence are closed forever.

Moderate sexualized rituals? What on earth is a moderate sexualized ritual?

Detection of cult activities is rare, since rituals are generally held at night in remote or protected areas, buildings owned by members, basements without windows, secluded wooded areas, etc. Scouts are often assigned lookout duties, and programming is employed to silence the membership. (*The author is unwavering in her accusations.*) Law enforcement has turned a deaf ear. Publishing houses are reluctant to accept such controversial materials for publication. These victims are truly alone—*disbelieved, and unbelievable.*

No cult activity is undertaken without a specific intent—*nothing occurs by chance.* The programming is purposeful, the result of an iron-clad dogma, an entrenched belief system. Cult members of today profess a belief in a unifying god, a single source from which both good and evil originate. Since nothing exists that is not of God, evil cannot exist because it is a part of God. Members profess supremacy *(blond-hair, blue-eyed children are said to be targeted)* and ritually abuse children in order to create a superior race. They frequently justify this torture by claiming, *believing,* they are preparing the child to meet the everyday demands of the real world. There's a sort of magical teaching, a teaching that suggests the child connects with the darker force through pain and suffering. This, too, is honorable, since the stronger the connection with the darker force, the greater the power. Children are taught that violence for higher spiritual purposes is not only acceptable, *but also desirable.* Values, as well, are taught through violence.

Desirable candidates for membership are actively sought. Likely recruits are those at odds with life—those in financial trouble, emotional distress, vulnerable, searching for answers, wanting to belong to something—*somewhere.* Some are dissatisfied with mainstream society, or disappointed with traditional religion. Of particular value, ironically, are those seeking recovery from earlier abuse and teenagers who are disconnected from their families and are without cultural, religious, or community roots.

Suddenly the sea is not so peaceful! My sister is right. I do need to get a life!

Reading on, I stumble upon an eerie account of convoluted logic, written by a survivor with an insider's view of this "closed system of thought."

> You think something bad happened and you were involved. That makes you bad. What you believe happened didn't happen. If it did, you should tell about it if you were good, but since it didn't happen, if you tell about it and people believe you, you are bad. If you tell about it, and people don't believe you they will know you are a liar and therefore bad. If you believe it happened and it didn't, you are crazy. If you don't tell about it and it's true, you are bad. If you don't tell about it and it's not true, you are good. If you did it, you are bad and good people will condemn you, but we like bad people so to us you are good. If you agree with us that it didn't happen, you are good...You belong with us if you are bad. You are only good if you are bad. If you are bad, you belong to us.[14]

"You are only good if you are bad?" What does *that* mean? How twisted! How sick! My head is spinning, again! For the life of me, I can't begin to fathom the damage this would inflict upon a child! Is *this* what Grace Ann has been trying to tell me? *Surely not!*

As if all of this isn't upsetting enough, I'm especially disturbed with the remarkable similarity between the victims' accounts, victims who neither know each other, nor have heard each other's stories.

In 1991 thirty-seven adult survivors undergoing psychotherapy volunteered to complete a survey. The results of this survey, conducted through the University of Utah, were no less than haunting. Themes emerged, themes of molestation by groups of adults clothed in robes and masks, and forced participation in various forms of sacrifice. Most were told a family member or loved one would be killed if they told of the abuse. There was even a remarkable similarity in the location of the abuse, with these violent acts occurring most frequently in members' homes and in designated wooded areas.[15] The abuses were frequently photographed. The reports of torture were universal.

I have heard so many of these allegations from Grace Ann. How can this be? Is she, too, reading this book?

The headache starts. My vision blurs as I read of trained torturers and their inhuman devices—needles, electrical probes, scalding instruments. I learn of hypnosis coupled with pain, suffocation, forced participation in sexualized rituals in which others are harmed *(or even killed)*, rapes by groups of adults in costumes, robes, and/or masks, live burials, dismemberment, forced drinking of blood and eating of excrement, burning, placement of a sacrificial victim's body parts, especially the eyes, into a child's body cavity as a constant reminder that "the eyes of Satan are watching you,"[16] and on, and on.

The choking begins.

"You O.K., Deb?" Annette asks. "You look awful."

Clutching my chest, I bolt upright, coughing, choking, arms flailing above my head while struggling for air.

"What's wrong with you?" my little sister, now on full alert, anxiously asks. "What's wrong?"

I choke.

She screams. "Answer me! I told you to answer me! What's wrong?"

"Nothing," I manage to squeak between wheezes, motioning to her to sit back down. "Nothing at all. I'm fine."

"You sure don't look fine. What happened to you? You just erupted!"

"I'm fine. I really am. I must have swallowed the wrong way."

The summer sun rests, hoarding its beams for yet another day. The choking finally subsides. Hoping to salvage the remnants of this troubling day, I head back to the beach, this time alone. I need to be alone. Try as I might, I haven't been able to shake this unsettled feeling—this feeling of impending doom, like something is about to happen to one of your kids, and you don't know where *they* are, or what it is, or how to stop it. I've returned today's book to its resting place in the box— *enough of that stuff*—no need to keep making myself sick. Tucked protectively under my arm is yet another *gift* from my friends at the bookstore.

I haven't even looked at the title. It can't possibly be as bad as the last one!

I've always believed in the sanctity of the infinite sea. My eyes skim the deserted beach as I settle into the low-flung, webbed chair. Terns swoop, again and again, like kites tossed about by a blustery puff of March air. A gentle surf laps at my feet. Contented toes wiggle their way into the coolness of the waterlogged sand, and, at last, I know peace. Convinced that one hour by the ocean can cure whatever ails you, I lie back and wait. A bare sixty minutes have passed and, as if right on cue, I'm a different person. Gone is that queasy feeling, the foreboding, the doom. Refreshed, energized, and *determined,* I'm ready to resume my waltz with the underworld.

I can do this. I know I can!

Satan's Children is on my lap. Breathing deeply, as if to remind myself that I really am relaxed, I open the small paperback, and am drawn, first to Sasha, and then to her surrealistic account of Mary's creation:

> As usual, they woke her up in the middle of the night, put her in the cage, and drove her to the farmhouse where they held their ceremonies. They put her in a tiny room. It was dark. She stayed there for a long time. We do not know how long. She had no food and water. There was no place to go to the bathroom. She tried to hold it but couldn't. She had to sit in her own excrement.

Then they came in. They gave her enemas. (*Grace Ann!*) They said it was to wash the good out of her so that the evil could be put in. They did it several times.

After that, they left her alone again for a long time. Her mind started to drift. At first she told herself stories to pass the time. She drifted into a kind of fantasyland. She started to see things. Birds would fly around. They would talk to her, and tell her stories. She got to know them. She gave them names.

After awhile they took her into another room where there were bright flashing lights. Strobes, I think they call them. And it had one of those mirrored balls hanging from the ceiling that spreads light around the room in swirls. They left her cage in the center of the room for a long time. There were five other cages, each containing a child. There was very little room in the cages. They had to sit on their haunches. They all looked terrified.

Then the drums started to beat…they got louder and louder, then softer and softer. Fortunately, we weren't affected by it. We had left the body, and floated up to the ceiling. We watched it all from above. Then the devils came out. They danced around her and started to chant. 'Hail Satan!' Like that—to the same beat as the drums.

They took one of the other girls out of the cage and told her to dance. She danced for a while. She wasn't very good. Her heart wasn't in it. They kept telling her to do better, but she couldn't. Maybe she was too frightened. After awhile, they stopped her. They said she wasn't good enough. They put her on the altar and killed her.

Then they went to the next cage, and took another girl out. She was better than the first. They liked her. They appeared to get aroused. All the devils had sex with her while she cried. But that got them mad. They put her in a box with the girl they had just killed.

A devil took her [another girl] out of the cage. He placed his hands on her shoulders, looked in her eyes and said, 'You are Satan's child. You will serve Satan. You will re-

ceive a great reward from the Lord of Lord's for performing His will.'

At that point Mary was created. She knew just what to
do. She said, 'Yes, Lord. I am Satan's daughter. I know
what to do. I will do it.[17]

*Slamming the book into the sand, I realize I really don't like waltz-
ing at all.*

The Dissociative Phenomena

A hundred years of clinical research confirms the phenomenon of
spontaneous dissociation, the body's most adaptive response to overwhelming trauma. In the United States alone, mountains of data can be
found on our veterans—*from World War I through Vietnam,* individuals whose internal reply to the utter horror of war resulted in a disorder
subsequently referenced as shell shock, battle fatigue, and most recently, post-traumatic stress.

Dissociation can be found along a continuum, from the everyday
experience of an adolescent's daydream, highly adaptive in nature, to
the maladaptive, often disabling diagnosis of Dissociative Identity Disorder *(formerly known as Multiple Personality Disorder, or MPD).*
While initially utilized as a defense against traumatic experiences, its
existence allowed for the continuity of normal psychological functioning. There are four distinct dissociative disorders.

Dissociative Amnesia involves the sudden inability to recall personal information not attributed to either everyday forgetfulness or an
organic mental disorder.

Dissociative Fugue involves a sudden, unexpected travel from one's
home or work, coupled with an inability to recall the circumstances
involved. Frequently, the individual is confused about his past, and
may assume a temporary new identity.

Depersonalization Disorder is the result of an individual's sense
of unreality, detached or dreamlike state, or the experience of being
outside one's body while watching from outside or above. This outside
observer views the body and/or mental processes, while simultaneously
and remarkably, reality testing remains intact. The disorder has an abrupt
onset and a gradual recovery.

Dissociative Identity Disorder is the ultimate dissociative state, a chronic disorder which, if left untreated, will manifest itself over the course of a lifetime. Dissociative Identity Disorder, or DID as it is sometimes called, encompasses all the elements of the other less pathological dissociative disorders. It can be described as the existence within the individual of two or more distinct altered states of consciousness (alters), with at least two of these identities recurrently taking control of the person's behavior.[18] Often misdiagnosed as hypersensitivity, hypochondria, paranoid schizophrenia, or borderline personality disorder, DID is most often a tool for survival, for this ability to dissociate allows the individual to escape an incomprehensible environment by detaching mentally and emotionally.

M. Smith offers, "...the spirit is so unsafe in the body that it leaves."[19] Libby K. describes multiplicity as:

> ...a pain...full of death...we are walking dead persons, separated from feelings by having no feelings, tortured by memories unpredictably surfacing and sinking, stuck in the unfathomableness of time...we live in a hell where everything hurts. ...multiplicity is endless sorrow...I would have others know that even the smallest kindness, the softest, seemingly meaningless touch of a hand, can actually mean the difference between life and death.[20]

Or, as Ann H. so poignantly declares:

> My home was the Sahara,
> Dead sand shifting so rapidly
> Not even a cactus could grow.[21]

Common among ritual abuse survivors, the traumatic amnesia that results as the mind dissociates allows the victim to function outside the cult or abusive situation, and in essence, saves the child's life. "Severe, sustained, and repetitive child sexual abuse is a major factor in the creation of DID."[22] Other violations commonly reported are those of incest, extreme sadism, bondage, forced prostitution, and confinement, administered at the hands of a parent or caretaking individual.

Each alter, or *altered state of consciousness*, is responsible for a distinctive function within the fractured personality system. The *host*, (the entity that frequently schedules the appointment and shows up for treatment), is "the one who has executive control of the body the greatest percentage of the time."[23] I shake my head in disbelief as I learn that occasionally the host is not a single alter, but several alters attempting to present as one.

How do they do that? Is Grace Ann the host, or a host? I don't understand!

Child personalities are usually present, often in layers or groups of alters underneath other alters, and always frozen in time. If the abuse occurs in infancy, the children may be non-verbal and may act out the abuse, often viewing the therapist as the perpetrator. *(More good news!)* *Memory Trace* personalities hold the victim's complete history, while *Cross-Gender* alters are often responsible for the host's unisex look *(short hair and loose clothing to allow the alters to emerge). Adminis-trator* or *obsessive-compulsive* personalities are competent profession-ally and emerge in the workplace. *Substance Abuse* alters are often the most abused, and frequently require sedatives, hypnotics, and/or anal-gesics to function. Amazingly, it seems that drug abuse is usually lim-ited to a specific alter, the only one that experiences withdrawal. *(What?)* *Autistic/handicapped* personalities may present when no one else wishes to be in control, often rocking and self-stimulating throughout the ses-sion.[24]

Little Grace Ann? Purposeful Dissociation?

Cult alters are *created* to trigger programs of other alters within the fractured system, and to adjust existing programming to include new, more effective response systems. Since the vast majority of cult alters remain in contact with their perpetrators throughout the victim's lifetime, these childhood abusers continue to maintain a virtual total control. Most survivors have not one, but a number of alters who are instructed to reconnect. While the most ritually abused continue to participate in cult activities, they remain *amnestic*, unaware of their involvement. Programs are triggered by phone messages, hand sig-nals, or a series of taps outside a bedroom window at night *(alters are programmed to open windows and doors or to meet at pre-ar-ranged times and places).* Therapy disruption programs *(scrambling, flooding, or shutdown)* are effective in counteracting the effectiveness of therapy. The diabolical programming ensures continuing cult involvement.[25]

Let's see if I have this right! If Grace Ann was abused by a cult of some sort, and comes to me for therapy, all the work that we do together will be undone, scrambled, flooded, whatever, by an alter programmed into her years ago, whose sole purpose is to stay connected with the persons (for lack of a better name) who created all the mess in the first place! Is this what's meant by "mind control?"

Grace Ann or "someone," I'm afraid to speculate *who*, has told me that I *must* be careful, for "they still call in" after each session. I dismissed the warnings as hogwash! I hate to admit it, but I *have* seen Grace Ann's meticulous phone records. She *does* have a pink spiral notebook detailing the day, time, and length of these repeated calls, which always seem to arrive in a series of six. I haven't been particularly concerned, since no one has ever been on the other end of the line. Hum! Thinking back, I *do* remember all those middle-of-the-night messages on the office voice mail. "They're outside, Dr. Debbie! They're knocking on our window! Little Grace Ann's going to let them in! Help us, Dr. Debbie!"

LITTLE GRACE ANN?

NO WAY!

And how many times has she looked me straight in the eye, tears streaming, and said, "I know I hear you, but I just don't understand. I have this buzzing in my head. Could this 'buzzing' be a 'therapy disruption program?' "

"Nah! It's just a coincidence. Maybe even an outright lie!"

I hope I sound more convincing than I feel.

In some instances the victim is instructed to self-mutilate, using a *gift* presented by the programmer. She is told the consequences of disclosing the cult's activities will be the loss of her *own* life. Or, she may be warned, 'If you ever tell, we will kill you, or someone you love.'

A powerful message is sent when those who have attempted to escape cult influence are brought before the membership and tortured, or are told, "If you must leave, we will torture or kill the cult member you love the most." Perhaps most insidious is threat of madness. "Do you really think anyone will believe you? You're crazy. It's only a

dream. Go ahead. Try to tell. You'll be locked away in a mental hospital for the rest of your life." [26]

Sleep is fear-filled. Fatigue becomes the norm. The combination
of the unrelenting weariness and the repetitive programming weakens
the victim's psychological reserves, and allows these programs to trip
automatically when the individual is dealing with "forbidden material
in therapy."[27] Punishment programs create an erosion of boundaries,
blurring of the roles of good and evil and punishment and pain. Euphe-
misms such as a "firm kindness, physical persuasion, Jacob's Ladder
(torture), Jehovah's staff *(whipping rod)*, and the blessing service *(rape)*
are commonly employed."[28]

Amazingly, perpetrators are trickling into the therapy room, seeking treatment—*for themselves.* Frequently oppressed prior to assuming their role as oppressors, these individuals are corroborating the
accounts of those eternally wounded, validating what has previously
been mere speculation regarding the mechanics of purposefully created multiplicity. *(Oh, Lord!)* These victimizers tell of repeatedly in-
ducing torture, while carefully observing the eyes for what they term
"the split." As the trauma becomes unbearable, overwhelming to the
senses, the victim appears "anxious…terrified, and in pain…the person goes dead…he has exited the situation."[29] The programmer then
addresses the newly split-off altered state of consciousness, assigning
it a fairly specific role, or job description, within the system. The trauma
will be administered repeatedly until the alter "reliably responds." Once
the desired response is consistently achieved, the stimulus, no longer
necessary, is removed *(i.e., the shock is no longer required),* and the
programming is complete.[30]

This is too, too, familiar, for I, also, watch for the split.

Since it is clearly understood that all learning, torture based or otherwise, degrades over time, the programming must be reinforced periodically to ensure an optimum response of victims. This need for cult-ac-
cess is ensured by the reporting alters, with "the vast majority of victims
cult-contacted well into mid-stage treatment"[31] for the purpose of continued entrée and complete control. According to these *programmers-
turned-clients*, multiplicity protects rites and sacred organizations, shelters the perpetrator groups, and provides huge financial gain through
prostitution, pornographic films, drug activities, and money laundering.

In 1995, therapists known to treat or to have treated ritual abuse survivors were asked to participate in a survey. Information was collected on 152 cases. Fifty-five percent of these cases reported current cult contact (*by phone)* throughout the course of treatment, while 47 percent have reporting alters who connect either in person or over the phone. Even the smallest detail of therapy is reported back, and every effort is employed to sabotage the treatment. Counter-therapy, or shut-down programs, are routinely employed.[32]

Wonderful, just wonderful! Not only do I have to be concerned about therapy and counter-therapy, now I have to be on the lookout for reporting alters and shut-down programs! This is beginning to sound like the plot of a B movie—a bad one. Sarcasm allows me to distance myself from the allegations, for to accept these as reality, at any level, is far too painful to even consider. I dissociate, much like the individual who happens upon a gruesome car accident and finds a part of him wants to help, while the other, the more vocal part, needs to flee.

The Internal Self-Helper

Apparently all is not lost, for reading on, I stumble upon the strangest, most intriguing concept of them all—the appearance of the illusive, internal self-helper. First described in 1974, this alter, *if it is an alter*, has rarely been discussed by dissociative researchers. *I wonder why. Did they believe as I—that psychology and spirituality make poor bedfellows?*

> At some level the patient has an observing ego function that can comment accurately on the ongoing process and provide advice, suggestions, insight, and control over the patient's pathology. One can often find this type of function in non-MPD [DID] patients as well as within one's own self. It is important to listen to these inner voices of wisdom, but it is a mistake to view them as all knowledge-able or all-powerful.[33]

Inner voices of wisdom? If we really do have inner voices of wisdom, why wouldn't we acknowledge them as all knowledgeable or all-powerful! Isn't that what "wisdom" means?

I could use some advice, suggestions, insight, and most certainly, control over *my* patient's pathology. Fascinated with this curious revelation, I impatiently scan the page for more information, *any* information about the strange phenomenon, and locate only brief snippets, just enough to whet my appetite. It seems that this "inner-helper" will rarely reveal more than a small amount of information at any given time, with this information containing assumptions the therapist cannot understand.[34] *How does that help?* I learn that these entities are "enigmatic, leaving the therapist with the problem of deciphering their Delphic statements," and that the therapist's relationship with this alter "is so unique a relationship it has to be experienced to be believed."[35]

Delphic statements have to be experienced to be believed? Fascinating!

❖◦❖◦❖

Altered states of consciousness? Purposeful dissociation? Trained torturers? Dark forces? Could *any* of this be true? *Any of it at all?* And, if it *is* true, if it *does* exist, is it a product of life today, of our own fragmented culture? Has our present society created this, this evil, or is it rooted in another time? Returning to the trunk of my car, I rifle through the infamous box of books and, again, *one more time*, discover more than I wish to know!

A Doctrine of Darkness

What a paradox! The organized religions of the Western world, ostensibly conceived to sustain mankind, have at times provided a fertile breeding ground for heinous, ritualistic behaviors. Ample literature abounds to support the historical existence of cults/multi-perpetrator networks. It appears while we as a society are currently alternating between a reluctant acceptance and vehement denial of cult existence, absolute devotion resulting in unwavering fanaticism to an assumed ideal is by no means a twentieth century phenomenon.

It is believed the name Satan originated in ancient Egypt, where the slaying of Osiris by the dark forces of disorder and disharmony (SET) served to disrupt MAAT, or harmony. The cross-legged figure of a man with a goat's head discovered in the Indus valley has been traced to 3000 B.C., while a similar satanic figure, identified as Baphomet, often appeared in Babylonian art.[36]

The eternal conflict between good and evil was played out in eighth century B.C. Persia through the dualism of Zoroastrianism. In Zorathustra's universe, ". . .the principles of good and evil [were] fully dual and independently created, and [did] not share in each other's nature."[37]

In Israel, the doctrine of Judaism assured its people of their status as God's chosen. Difficulty and destruction—the absence of protection by the Supreme—were the result of the elect failing their God. While Judaism, as a doctrine, did survive its peoples' exile in Egypt, large numbers of Jews, quite understandably, lost all hope. God, although still seen as good, had "withdrawn from the world, leaving it in the hands of evil or incompetent forces."[38]

Is this how Grace Ann feels? Did God withdraw from her world?

One consequence of this perceived abandonment was the birth of Gnosticism, a dualistic, mystical belief that one's soul was forever imprisoned in an evil body as the result of man's cosmic fall. Gnostics, from the Greek word *gnosis*, meaning *knowledge*, believed "redemption, or liberation of the soul, was plausible only through knowledge (*gnosis*), not faith (*pintis*)."[39]

Enter the mythological postulates of Greek civilization, accompanied by tales of the underworld, sexuality, and fertility. "One of the classical mythological images was that of wild Dionysian frenzies of Greek women who held orgies and sacrifices in the hills…this being the cultural precursor of the witches' Sabbath."[40] With the subsequent decline of the Roman Empire came the demise of classical Gods and Goddesses, fertility rites, and pagan ceremonies. Judaism found itself split into three factions. *Rabbinic Judaism* espoused a belief in God's protection of those loyal to Him. *Gnosticism* championed knowledge as the inevitable supremacy of evil, while *Christianity*, the supposition that Gnostic depravity could be vanquished through a belief in Christ,[41] associated the body with all that was corrupt.[42] Under the Emperors Constantine and Theodosius, Christianity became the state religion (Easter replaced the fertility rites of spring, Christmas was chosen to supplant winter solstice ceremonies), while Gnosticism "survived in heretical sects and cults throughout the Middle Ages."[43] The Third century Egyptian monk, Epiphenius, reported that one such cult, the Phibonites, "practiced promiscuity, used semen as a sacrament, and sanctified abortion."[44] It has been observed that "such early Gnostic rituals share certain elements with the Satanic Mass, namely a secret feast, a sexual orgy, reversals of the Christian Mass, ritual use of blood, semen, and other bodily excretions, and the practice of infant sacrifice and cannibalism."[45]

The twelfth century witnessed an elevation of the Cather doctrine. Nurtured in the Langedoc region of southwestern France, the Cathers, as did the Gnostics, perceived the world to be ruled by an evil spirit—a universe run amok. Since the body (matter) was evil, the "material sacraments and the material church were also evil...The orthodox church...was considered satanic since it had surrendered to worldliness." The Cathers were known to celebrate the Black Mass, a historically documented sexualized ritual in which animals and humans were sacrificed.[46] The sect was forced underground during the Albigension Crusade, when it was discovered that its adherents consistently reversed the Christian Mass, a practice undetected due to the Latin liturgy of the day.

To the Cather sect now worshiping in scattered splinter societies, the emergence of the Black Death, the centuries-long plague ravaging Medieval Europe, was proof that Satan was surely in charge. It was indeed difficult to remain faithful to the Christian's Kingdom of Heaven during these years of death and pestilence. Magical thinking abounded, unknowingly, unwittingly perpetuated by the rites of the Christian sacrament—*the blood and body of Christ.* In referencing the Catholic Mass of Medieval Europe, Katchen writes:

> What the sale of indulgences...did was to make the priest into even more of a magician than he had been previously. For if a Mass was effacious, only if said by a priest, and if a priest had the power to absolve one's sins (and the power not to if he chose), then salvation was a form of magic that operated in accordance with the operator's will. As such, the sale of indulgences promoted not only cynicism, but also superstition.[47]

The earliest recorded allegations of sexual perversion in the priest-hood appeared in the fourteenth century. In referencing the cognitive dissonance (a necessary modification of either behavior or beliefs), Katchen suggests, "They (the priests) might well have modified their beliefs and determined that fair was foul and foul was fair...to the Medieval mind, a mass was a mass was a mass. Thus, the figure of the renegade priest celebrating a Black Mass does not seem all that impossible."[48]

The drama continues to unfold, as the mid-fifteenth century ushers in the Catholic Inquisition, a three-hundred-year period of hysteria and death. It has been suggested that several hundred thousand to nine million people were put to death at the hands of the Inquisitors,[49] with these witch hunts spurred on by the 1486 publication of *Malleus Maleficarum (The Hammer of the Witches)*. Penned by two monks, Heinrich Kramer and James Sprenger, these early authors sought to detail "normal witch behavior." Punishments for the purpose of "restoring God's blessing on the community included bathing those individuals identified as witches in boiling water, tearing the flesh from their breasts with searing tongs, and mutilating the genitalia."[50] Ross notes extraordinary similarities between the "female witch behavior" defined in *Malleus Maleficarum* and Arthur Schopenhauer's 1851 essay *On Women*, a treatise in which socially subservient women were referred to as "good," while those exhibiting less socially appropriate behaviors became medicalized, ultimately categorized as histrionic/borderline within the psychiatric communities of today. Childhood abuse and/or demonic possession may have been present in the lives of these unfortunate medieval women. Today's abuse victims may be known as "bad borderlines" instead of witches, and are hospitalized instead of burned.[51]

"The problems that the Inquisition faced, of reliability of evidence, over-zealousness, and political pressures, are also the problems of modern police forces and serious investigators of contemporary Satanism."[52]

Whoa! Now that's too close for comfort!

The Christian hierarchy begins to crumble. The church is losing its hold. Fear tactics become increasingly ineffective, the social discipline is in increasing disarray, and the needs of the people are no longer met by the organized religion of the day. "Christendom broke apart"[53] during the Reformation of the sixteenth century. Calvinism brings with it the doctrine of Predestination. Hellfire and Damnation are the utterances of the day, with God alone deciding whose soul would ascend and whose would be doomed to an eternal life in Hell. "For those on the bottom, whose indiscretions were enough to convince them that they were Hell-bound, Satanism may have offered an alternative."[54] Or, as Ross observes, "Satanic rituals, whether fantasies or actual events, are the mirror image of repressive Christianity."[55]

The first recorded law enforcement investigation of Satanism took place in the 1680s, when King Louis XIV ordered an inquiry into the poisoning death of the Duke of Bouillon by his wife Anne Marie. Known as the LaVoisin Affair, it was discovered that the disgruntled wife was assisted by Catherine DeShays, a.k.a. LaVoisin, a cosmologist who studied black magic and practiced Satanism under the direction of Abbe Guibourg (The Guibourg Mass routinely sacrificed children to Astaroth and Asmodeous). Their clandestine operation began as abortion and infanticide, and ended in murder for hire.[56]

The nineteenth century defrocked priest, Alphonse Louis Constance, a.k.a. Eliphas Levi, authored a volume of the occult which became the textbook of later magicians. At the turn of this century, Alliester Crowley, a.k.a. Frater Perdurabo, Master Therion, and Count Vladimir "partook in and taught drug induced rituals, perverted sexual acts, bestiality, eating of bodily emissions and excrements, and advocated blood sacrifices."[57] He is today known as the Father of Modern Satanism.

The Confessions of Alliester Crowley allows but a glimpse of the church's hidden inner circle. Crowley states, "Behind the exterior of the church is an interior church, the most hidden of all communities, a Secret Sanctuary which preserves all the mysteries of God and nature. It was formed after the fall of man. It is the hidden assembly of the elect."[58]

It was during the last years of his life, following his forced exile from Italy, that Crowley met and befriended Gerald B. Gardner. Gardner, a third degree initiate of Crowley's order Templi Orientis, founded WICCA, or white witchcraft, based on Crowley's rituals.[59]

Katchen suggests the twentieth century social strictures against sex (social/sexual taboos) have enabled Satanism to "enforce its code of silence,"[60] and proposes the historically closed system is now disintegrating due to Dr. C. Henry Kempe's identification of the Battered Child Syndrome, as well as an increased societal acceptance of the homosexual orientation. He states,

> Satanism is a subculture of Western civilization. It appears to be a product of our hitherto unyielding norms and caste system that consigned lower class people and those guilty (or allegedly guilty) of sexual indiscretions to the ranks of the damned. Its exposure appears to be the product of the more open attitude towards sexuality that the West has exhibited since the 1960s which enabled victims and survivors to talk more honestly about their experiences.[61]

Modern day Satanists are believed to be affiliated with one of five categories. *Transgenerational* cults are comprised of those born into a restrictive order known to worship Lucifer. This, the oldest of all contingents, is believed to participate in both animal and human sacrifice, seeks to resolve all opposites, and operates within the framework of pagan occult theosophy. *Neo-Satanic* cults, i.e., San Francisco's Church of Satan and the Temple of Satan in St. Louis, base their worship on the works of Gardner and Crowley, but deny the practice of sacrificial offerings. *Self-styled* satanic cult leaders are dropouts from other organized cults, while *teen dabblers* who pore over *The Satanic Bible* and *The Necronomicron,* are avid followers of selected Heavy Metal bands, and "engage in sexual experiments and murderous ventures."[62] Ninety-eight percent of Satanists fall into the last, most notorious category, those *solitary* Satanists whose belief in the "will of Satan" have allegedly led them into sadistic, torturous rampages. Richard Ramirez, i.e., The Night Stalker, Charles Manson of the Tate-LaBianco murders, the Son of Sam, associated with the "Twenty-Two Disciples of Hell," and Adolpho Constanzo of the Matamoros murders, have been found to have had satanic affiliations.[63]

It would be an error to believe violent rituals have been limited to worship in the Satanic Church.

> In 1952 or 1953, at the age of 8 or 9, I witnessed the ritual sexual abuse and murder of children in a Christian "healing

church" within an hour's drive or so from my home in Maryland. The church was an ornate mausoleum, with stained glass windows high on the walls and with crypts for the storage of embalmed bodies. Wooden pews faced a long stage-like altar. The pulpit stood to the worshiper's right. According to the preacher, the Day of Judgment was near at hand (as evidenced by the practice of air raids, bomb shelters, and city evacuation plans for the cold war) so the salvation of souls was urgent. He said the old people before him had already grown wise in the work of the Lord, their survival as exemplars of the faith was essential. In order that those men might continue the work of the Lord, he said "sanctified children" had offered their own vitality in Christian sacrifice. These little girls lined up on the altar were "saints" voluntarily surrendering their lives that their elders might live to spread the Gospel among those yet unsaved before the Day of Judgment. The men had only to "embrace the pure children," that is, copulate with them, to receive a share of their vitality. During the communion/rituals at the church, the girls, four to ten years old, thus discharged their life force to the men over a period of several weeks until they were completely empty, that is, dead.[64]

"Dr. Matthews, this is Deborah Berkley. I'll be mailing that independent study to you by the end of the week. I'm warning you, though. You'd better pour yourself a glass of wine—maybe two. This is no easy read."

A Doctor of
Broken Hearts

"That's all right, Dr. Debbie.
That bee's O.K. We luv you anyways.
You bee's a doctor of broken hearts."

Jessica, The Boss

CHAPTER FOUR

Jessica, The Boss

Fall 1995

"Dr. Debbie, I din't make no snow angel. The Big Lady did. The Big Lady make'd the angel all the way down the really big hill! Bumpety, bumpety, bumpety, all the way down the hill! It bee'd so funny! Do we be in awful trouble, Dr. Debbie?"

We've been discussing Grace Ann's sore back, as she lost her footing during an unexpected early fall ice storm and skidded, rather unceremoniously by her account, some forty feet down the backyard's sloping hill. We laugh, pleasantly relaxed as we relish this rare, but much needed comic moment. Grace Ann waves her arms wildly as she recounts the tumble, the crutch sliding past her, and her stymied attempts at confiscating it as it whizzes by. She then heaves a huge sigh, slumps forward, and drops her head to her chest. I'm at first startled, then frightened, for it appears to my untrained eye that she has experienced a heart attack.

"Grace Ann, Grace Ann, what's wrong? Can you hear me, Grace Ann?"

Slowly, she lifts her head. Her eyes are closed. I start to her, then sit back down, as I notice a swift blinking of the eyelids, much like the rapidly fluttering wings of a hummingbird when perched upon a flower's inviting blossom. Shaking her head as if to release imaginary cobwebs, she suspiciously eyes me, then clasps her arms protectively across her chest while furiously thrusting her generous frame to and fro.

"We din't mean to get the Big Lady in trouble, Dr. Debbie, honest we din't....Me and Jessica was going to feed Mr. Squirrel, he be so cold and hungry. We din't mean to make her fall. She make'd that snow angel, Dr. Debbie. We was just tryin' to help her get back up the hill. Please, please, Dr. Debbie, don't be mad at me and Jessica!"

Mystified, no stunned, I sit, knees shaking, as I attempt to gather my tenuous wits about me. Fortunately, I have now consumed all the major texts on this enigmatic disorder and am marginally, only marginally, prepared for this "unveiling."

"Who are you?" I ask, my voice shaking.

"I be Little Grace Ann. I be $3^1/_2$."

Grace Ann, the Grace Ann I know, reappears. No longer laughing, tears stream down her face as she pleads, "Deborah, I wish I could make you understand. I'm bad, bad, bad! I did everything you said, and now I'm being punished, just like my mother."

I have no inkling of what she means! What did I ask her to do? How is she being punished? What happened to her mother? I open my mouth to respond, but before I can react, the child, a child I don't know, returns, shaking, rocking, clutching the beloved George.

"I so sorry, I so sorry! I be bad! I din't mean to be so bad!"

Within this very same brief minute, my client, at least I think it's my client, reappears, dazed and flustered. Attempting to orient herself, she methodically scans the room, breathes a weighty sigh of relief, then looks down and slowly reaches into her canvas bag. Unchecked tears flow freely as she produces the customary journal.

"Deborah, I'm so scared! This is my journal, and it's filled with words I don't remember writing! What's happening to me? Am I losing my mind?"

*I'm scared, too, and for a split second wonder if I'm losing **my** mind. Fighting back my own fear and trembling, I struggle to keep hold of myself. Can't let her see me upset! Get a grip, Deborah! Now!*

Smiling what surely must be a wan smile, I offer, "No, Grace Ann, you're not losing your mind. Do you hear me, you're not! Let's take a look at this journal, and see if we can figure this thing out."

I hope I sound convincing.

My eyes are fixed on the black and white composition book. Sighing, I wistfully recall that I, too, wrote in a book such as this, *in cursive, of course*—years ago, when I was young and innocent. Opening its cover, *its protective shield,* I slowly, hesitantly, look down, for I know all too well how it feels to be seared to the bone with its contents. Gazing downward, I begin the haunting journey.

> Please help me. i am desperate. i hate having this tug of war inside of me. i hate me. i hate my foster parents. i am angry for what they did to me. i feel like they took my virginity. They took my ability to care and feel. i hate that priest. i am angry, angry, angry. i hate me. i am so ugly, dirty, filthy. i am a big nothing. Life is not worth living. i'm scared to death. i don't want to feel or hurt anymore. It's better not to feel. Why, God, was i so bad that you couldn't give me a loving, caring family?
>
> i don't remember her name. To me she was Mommy, the good Mommy, not my real Mommy, but the Mommy i was sent to after social services took my brothers and me from our home in the projects. i can recall exactly what she said when she was holding me. She said, 'I wish I could keep you. We really love you. Do you know that, Grace Ann? Daddy and I want what's best for you. You and your brothers need to be together, to be a family. Daddy and I are older now. We're not able to make a home for three little children. The Reynolds' are able to take the three of you. They'll be good to you. They have a child of their own. I have to say goodbye, Grace Ann, even if I don't want to—even if it breaks my heart to give you up.'

If only Grace Ann could have stayed in this loving home. What if these comforting arms could have held her, could have kept her safe throughout those years of vulnerability? How vastly different her little life would have been if she had known purity rather than pain. How different her life would have been....

Echoing again and again, not from my brain but from somewhere deep within, are the words,

"But for the grace of God go I."

*"But for the **grace** of God go I."*

I must remember to call my folks tonight. Once again, I've forgotten Mom's birthday. Never again, I silently vow...never again!

i can see her face now. There were tears in her eyes.
That was the last time i felt loved and nurtured. That was
the last time anyone cared for me. When they came to get
me, she placed a tiny gold cross around my neck, and told
me she would always be near, to never forget her. i've kept
that cross with me all my life, even though i had to hide it
in the steam pipe for many years because that witch of a
foster mother threatened to take it from me. i can't tell you
what that simple gold cross has meant to me. There is nothing that i treasure more.

The handwriting changes to an elementary script...a child adding her
recollection of innocence lost:

Mommy, the good Mommy, luved Little Grace Ann.
Mommy would rock and rock and rock Little Grace Ann,
and read Little Grace Ann happy stories.

Dr. Debbie, i not like my Daddy, my real Daddy, to give
me a bath. i not like him putting medicine on my bottom. i
not like my real Daddy taking pictures of Bad Jenny, fifteen-and-a-half months old. i not want anymore pictures of
me in the movie star room. i not like them hurtin' my wrists
and ankels. Judith, how you spell ankels?

Someone using a red marker has crossed over 'ankels' and written
'ankles' in a polished, adolescent script.

Thank you, Judith.

Who is Judith?

They hurted my hot dog roll BAD! i not like my real
Mommy, Daddy. i not like my Aunt Maggie. They hurted
me. My real Mommy, Daddy, Aunt Maggie say i be BAD,
BAD, BAD, 'cus i cry. They yell at me and say, 'Stop
that cryin', you understand, Grace Ann? Stop that cryin'
now!'

i not mean to cry. i not mean to be BAD. To make Daddy,
my real Daddy, not Daddy Francis, really hurt me. i try to
ahave. i be so scared. Please help Little Joann, too, Dr.

Debbie. We luv you bunches. Please not hate BAD Little Grace Ann.

Judith? And now Joann, a Little Joann?

Dr. Debbie, i not rip the skin off that scar on Big Lady Grace Ann's left leg. i not the only one who be BAD. Joann, fifteen-and-a-half months old do'ed it. Not BAD Little Grace Ann, three-and-a half.

So that's how Grace got that oozing scar. I must remember to tell her family doc.

Still another unseen child begs of Grace Ann:

Big Lady, please not go swimin' 'cus our real Daddy will drown us. Not Daddy Francis, but our real Daddy. i miss Mommy and Daddy Francis so much! i be sorry i tell Dr. Debbie. i be sorry i gived you a bad eyeache. i sorry i be so BAD you couldn't go to group. i not mean to make your toes hurt, to pull the skin off. i sorry i make you cry. i try to ahave. i be so scared.

Big Lady, you cannot wear my pink shirt with the flower on the pocket. i hided it. i am in your safe place. You cannot go there 'cus i be there. BAD, BAD, BAD, BAD Little Grace Ann, three-and-a-half.

I'm tired of being wrong. I'm not even marginally prepared for the day's spontaneous exhibition. Who are Mommy and Daddy Francis? Aunt Maggie? Jenny, Judith, and Joann? What does she mean by a "bad eyeache and hurt toes?" What, or where, is this "safe place?" Where are these children coming from? For God's sake, where is Grace Ann? I'm not even sure who just left my office! I think it was Grace Ann. I asked her and she said it was Grace Ann, but how do I know? Can she, or they, drive home?

Where does my responsibility end? I don't have the slightest idea what to do! Defeated, determined to find someone, anyone, to accept this referral, I rush to the phone. My shaking hands mirror my insides, as I dial the consulting psychiatrist's number. Dr. Sullivan is one of the good guys. He cares about Grace Ann, too. He'll have some ideas. He'll know where she can go to get the help she deserves.

Dr. Sullivan respectfully listens to my anxious babble.

"Deborah, I can't take her on. I just don't have the time. And besides, she trusts you. You have as much expertise in dissociative disorder as any other mental health professional in the area—probably more, with all the research you've been doing. I'll help as much as I can. O.K.? Please feel free to call anytime."

I have as much expertise as any other mental health professional in the area? Now that's a scary thought!

Look at all those Dr. Debbies. I appreciate my elevation to a doctorate, but conclude we're all in trouble, however many there are of us! Grace Ann deserves better than this! She's been to hell and back, several times. She has the right to be well.

My notes reflect my confusion, as they boldly insist, *Deborah, re-read those books! This is how it feels to be trapped!*

◆◆◆◆◆◆

The following weeks usher in a whirlwind of presentations. Each session is at first implausible, then inconceivable, and finally, simply amazing. Typically, Grace Ann ambles in, wearing weary knit stretch pants and an assortment of brightly colored, layered tee shirts. I'm often amused as, session after session, she exclaims, "I don't know why I picked this to wear today. It isn't even my color."

Pink appears most often, "almost" pink, pallid pink, resplendent pink. Black, peach, blue, then green and red, lots of red, which, curiously enough, Grace Ann professes to "absolutely despise." There is a collection of regal purples and, finally, a "sunshiny" yellow. It takes awhile, but I stagger, then stumble, upon the color-coded key of Grace Ann's inner family. Apparently all the alters (I'm still not sure how many) are watching me, and relishing my obvious confusion.

"Dah, Dr. Debbie! We thought you be smarted. You bee's dumb!"

I know I bee's dumb. I don't need some invisible child reminding me.

It soon becomes obvious that the alter wishing to be "out," to "share" with me, comes to the session with her color on top. (Yes, on top!) If there is dissention, respective emergencies, or simply children scrambling for "my turn," Grace Ann will arrive in multi-layers.

The more shirts, the more problems! I soon learn to gauge the session's degree of difficulty by scanning Grace Ann's depth of padding as she ambles through the door.

The alter who needs to talk, or who merely pouts enough to win the most recent argument, wears the shirt on top, and thereby "wins," or is allowed to have the majority of that session's time. At times, Grace Ann appears with only one shirt; on other occasions she's cloaked in twelve.

The initial presentations are of "the little ones." Jessica, age 6½ (as I am frequently reminded), is a delightful minx of a child, replete with an elfin grin, bottomless dimples, and the impish mannerisms of an Edith Ann. As "The Boss," Jessica keeps me aformed [informed] of the antics (and the pain) of the others, for she alone, at least at this early stage, appears to have a full awareness of the disparate internal group.

"Dr. Debbie, Big Lady Grace is reading the *Parade* out of the newspaper. It says: 'No More Myths About Mental Illness.' I hear'd her say'ed, 'People with mental illness are hopeless.' I hear'd Grace say'ed 'hopeless.' She not hopeless, right, Dr. Debbie? She be workin' good. We be tryin' to help her, all of us helpin'. She not hopeless, right, Dr. Debbie? Why she have to think she be hopeless? I luv you, Dr. Debbie."

"No, Jessica, she not be hopeless. I'm going to help Grace Ann. In fact, I'm going to help you all."

"Dr. Debbie?"

"Yes, Jessica."

"Dr. Debbie, can I ax you for a big favor, a really big favor, a really, really big favor?"

"A really, really big favor, huh? I guess so, Jessica. You can ask. I'll do what I can."

"Dr. Debbie, we needs sompin' from you."

"Well, what is it, Jessica?" I ask, curious as to what could possibly be causing all the fuss.

"You won't get mad at us, will you, Dr. Debbie? You won't get mad at us and send us away?"

"No, Jessica. I won't get mad at you and I won't send you away. What is it that you need? You'll have to tell me. I can't read your mind."

"A hug, Dr. Debbie. We all needs a hug." An infectious, pixie-like grin covers her face. Huge, plaintive orbs gaze lovingly, trustingly, into mine.

Needless to say, the hugs begin.

———◆·◈·◆———

I'm feeling more enthusiastic, or at least I think I am, for I've just spent the weekend re-reading my stash. Once I discover that most dissociative clients are in mental health treatment for almost seven years prior to receiving an accurate diagnosis, I feel empowered. At least a little empowered. Grace Ann has been working with me for less than one year. We're ahead of schedule! *So there! I just might not bee'd so dumb after all!*

The child alters have insisted upon referring to me as Dr. Debbie, despite my frequent explanations that I have not yet attained this educational status.

"Jessica, remember what I told you. I don't have a doctorate, I'm *working* on a doctorate at the university."

"That's all right, Dr. Debbie. That bee's O.K. We luv you anyways. You bee's a doctor of broken hearts."

Jessica plays the role of surrogate mom, a mother hen cuddling her little tykes while chastising, and at times, infuriating the older, more mature adolescents. She introduces Jenny and Joann, the system's non-verbal infants, recalling their pain while heeding their respective cries. They, along with Little Grace Ann, are (as is developmentally appropriate for most children) afraid of every new situation, anything out of the ordinary, and are in need of daily reassurance and care. Grace Ann, alias The Big Lady, has scheduled a routine trip to the dentist. This seemingly simple outing leaves them all trembling with fear.

Little Grace Ann writes:

> The Big Lady take'd us to two doctors I not know. They
> habe glasses, and masks, and grubbs on their hands. They

scarred me. Those doctors putted their hands in our mouth. I thinked they'ed going to put their hot dogs in my mouth. They habe the biggest hands and they hurted my mouth with all that pushin' and poking around.

An evening of bingo, which Grace Ann now looks forward to and declares to be a success, creates terror for the little ones. Little Grace Ann, with the assistance of an older alter who refuses to step forward, cries out in the journal:

> i want to go to Dr. Debbie's safe place. i be so scarred. What i doos so bad that the Big Lady take'd me to the Big Hall? i see'd the movie picture room. It's dark in this movie picure house. i never seed this movie picture house before. Why doos the Big Lady take me to this dark movie picture room? [They] will take Little Grace Ann's clothes off and take movie picures of Grace Ann with no clothes on. Mommy, Daddy Francis, please come to get Little Grace Ann. Please! i can't find nobody!

The ever-hovering Jessica comforts:

> Little Grace Ann, take some deep breaths. Dr. Debbie is going to help you to tell the hurts and everything is going to be O.K. Little Grace Ann? Did you hear'd me? Just let Dr. Debbie help you through the hurts. She will. Just trust her, she and your Daddy Jesus won't let anyone hurt you again. [*Daddy Jesus? This is going to be interesting!]* You will be in a berry safe place. Don't worry about it now. Go listen to Dr. Debbie's alaxation [relaxation] tapes, the ones she do'ed for us all, and put the blue ice on your eyes and try to go to sleep. You trust Dr. Debbie, don't you?

> I trust her, Jessica, but I be scarred somebody will hurt Little Grace Ann. I don't want no more hurts!

The adult Grace appears, unknowingly co-present with the child. She becomes an unwilling contributor to the internal dialogue as she writes:

I just went to the bathroom and I panicked and am wheezing. Deborah told me to give permission to the different parts of my personality to continue to talk to each other in the journal, and to give 'amission [permission] *(is Jessica lurking around, too?)* to leave notes for each other on the bulletin board. There was one there, and I don't know how it got there! It was even written in red! I hate red! I despise red! Everybody knows that!

The mother hen again attempts to soothe.

Grace Ann, stop and listen to me. Right now, Grace Ann! That's better. Grace Ann, you be wheezin' bad. Take some slow, deep breaths. I be with you, and *Strong Man Jesus* is here with us. You are still wheezin'. Take some slow, deep breaths. That's right, slow, deep breaths. Why are you so upset?

Because, there's a note on the hallway bulletin board, and I don't know how it got there! And, it's written in red!

We will read it later, Grace Ann. Right now, just listen to Dr. Debbie's tapes and do what she tells you to do. Close your eyes and listen to Dr. Debbie so she can help you stop wheezin'.

Apparently this is not the time for consolation, for Grace Ann, Little Grace Ann, or a yet to be identified someone angrily replies:

Shut up, Jessica. I don't know who Demon Judas is!

Demon Judas? Uh oh!

Who rote that note? i am goin' to take my Debra tapes *[Debra tapes?]* and go to my safe and free place and stay there until i go to see Debra.

That sounds like a really good idea to me. I think I'll join you! And by the way, did someone forget how to spell my name?

My eyeballs hurt. Why i be so scarred?

Demon Judas? I don't know a Demon Judas either, and am not at all certain that I want to make his acquaintance! I have noticed an angry, scowling presence fading in and out, but I thought it was one of the teenagers. Looking up from the scribbled dialogue, I decide I've come this far. There's no turning back now. What do I have to lose?

"May I speak with Demon Judas?"

I realize, too late, that I have a great deal to lose...my life!

In an instant, a blink of an eye, a biting chill descends upon the suddenly suffocating room. Is this my over-active imagination, or am I in the presence of something sinister? Goose bumps appear and the hair at the nape of my neck stands on end. What's wrong with me? *Good grief, Deborah, get a grip!*

My fears are not assuaged, as an unfamiliar snarl is emitted from what was, a short moment ago, a frightened child. Nostrils flared, teeth bared as if readying a growl, or worse, I am confronted with an alter, a presence, a thing. Apprehension mounts as I cautiously study the figure across the room, for the client, now an unrecognizable being, is effortlessly lifting herself, or itself, from the couch. Unfettered by a bad knee, the creature, slowly, step by step, menacingly approaches. Cold, cold eyes lock onto mine. Cowering above my now frozen pose, it leans forward, methodically pointing an index finger within inches of my horrified eyes. Clothed in a diabolical sneer, it, whatever it is, does not speak, choosing to intimidate me instead with its fiendish movements. Slowly, as if savoring an impending attack upon a certain victim, it touches my upper arm, then traces the length of my forearm, lifting its finger to once again point towards my unblinking eyes. Its flattened ears and distorted jaw make it reptilian-like. The being gutturally screeches, "You'll never get through to me. I am Demon Judas. I am bad, bad, bad, bad."

"I Was Never Bad?"

So begins the cat and mouse saga of Demon Judas. Detached and dissociated myself, I am confronted with my own unfamiliar inner voice. From within emerges, as if a wellspring, a surprisingly strong and undeniably certain sound. Embodied, it replies from the depths of what apparently is me, boldly, with an amazing calm: "No Demon Judas, you were never bad. You were hurt, but you were never, never bad."

Encouraged by his silence, I continue: "You took the brunt of the abuse. You saved Grace Ann's life. You were never bad. Thank you for saving her life, Judas."

Where did that come from? I sound, well, almost…knowledgeable. Apparently I don't feel knowledgeable, for I expend great energy in artfully avoiding further contact with Demon Judas. I'm afraid—no, terrified—and question my skill to confront a demon. I don't know how I could have been so, so together, and I don't trust that I will find the strength to "hold it together" a second time.

My older son, away at college, calls: "Mom, are you sure you're O.K.? I'm really worried? You watched *The Exorcist* lately? You know, that didn't turn out so well!"

My younger son begins to complain of stomachaches. "Maybe I can go with you today, Mom. Or, maybe we can even stay home!"

My husband is just ticked. "I told you she was crazy. You're wasting your time. Just get rid of her! She'll never pay you anyway!"

———————

Over the next several months, I choose to follow the fearful creature from afar, from the safety of the daily journal's pages.

In time, the "demon's" anger fades to despondency.

> Jessica, i told you i'm too bad to heal, so stop asking your Dr. Debbie what to do. i do not trust her. i am hopeless. Your Dr. Debbie will never, did you hear me, never, be able to get me to trust her enough to tell her my hurts. i don't deserve to heal anyway. i've accepted that. So Jessica, you should accept that i will never heal, and leave me alone. i am too bad, did you hear me, too bad to have anything good.

Demon Judas is watching, forever leering from behind the prison bars of Grace Ann's mind. The children just want to be children. They want to play, and sing, and have fun. On this particular evening, the little ones, under Judith's attentive eye *("They're too small to turn on the oven, Dr. Debbie! They might burn themselves! You know that!)*, are meticulously forming, then baking an assortment of clay figures.

Demon Judas, writing in his signature red ink, cynically remarks:

> I think the puddy [putty] things should have burned. They shouldn't be playing with puddy or coloring or making puzzles or playing games anyway. These things are only for good children, not for bad children to do. They's too bad to be allowed to have fun. I don't like fun things. They don't deserve them.

Judas, clearly the fractured system's antagonist, or internal prosecutor, goads an understandably frustrated Grace Ann as she declares:

> i'm going to quit therapy, it's just too hard!

The Demon writes:

> Go ahead and quit therapy, it's not doing you any good anyway. You are too bad to be good. You're just wasting your time, and *our* money! Your Dr. Debbie thinks she is so smart! She wants me to heal, too. But, she'll never get through to me. i do not trust her. i intend to stay just as i am.

Someone, whose ink color is green but who, to date, prefers to remain anonymous, chimes in:

> Ignore Demon Judas, Big Lady. He's going to heal, too. Just you wait and see. Keep on working hard.

In time there is a gradual softening. It is as if our resident "Demon" is sensing an impending defeat. He offers:

> You might think your Dr. Debbie can help me. But she doesn't have any idea how much i was hurt. i never want to be hurt like that again. Yes, your Dr. Debbie does try to help. She is nice, but i am scared.

Several months pass. A silent, yet apparently vigilant observer, Demon Judas reappears as none other than a reluctant helper, encouraging Little Grace Ann to tell all her hurts so she can heal. To my amazement, he writes:

> Little Grace Ann needs to tell Dr. Debbie. She needs to tell it to at least one person. She was really the one that was hurt. The physical pain was so bad. She was just a little girl, and she couldn't take it. i took that pain for her. So Jessica, don't you tell Dr. Debbie. Let Little Grace Ann tell so she can heal. i do not trust your Dr. Debbie yet. Halloween is coming soon. Little Grace Ann will start feeling like a volcano. Now Jessica, remember to keep your mouth shut! When i trust your Dr. Debbie, it will all come out.

And finally, the blessed day arrives.

> Jessica, you were right! Your Dr. Debbie did help me. She told me I was good. [*I note the use of the upper case I.*] I'm glad she allowed me to trust her. She doesn't have mean eyes, just safe eyes, eyes of compassion, not like those awful peoples' eyes. She's really nice and her office is a nice, safe place. I like it there. Dr. Debbie told me I was never bad. So everybody, listen up. Everybody call me Judas, not Demon Judas. Demon means bad. Dr. Debbie says I was never bad, that those mean people made some bad choices and did bad things. Dr. Debbie told me it was not my fault, that it was never my fault, and that no one will ever hurt me again. I am now Judas, just Judas. I help the others to survive each day. I help Dr. Debbie as much as I can with the ones who haven't trusted enough to tell.

To borrow a phrase from The Big Lady. . ."Praise the Lord!"

'Barrassed Janice

> Dr. Debbie said she wants us to talk to each other in Grace Ann's journal. Janice, why didn't you talk to Dr. Debbie when she asked you to on Monday?[*Jessica, The Boss, quizzes in her customary block print.*]

Dec 4, 1993

When I first met Dr Debbie I was very bad. I tried to scare her. Now I'm good. Take Care I protect her & of her with Strong-Man Jesus Judas

I was Demon-Judas now I'm good helpful Protectful Judas

Look at the next Picture I protect you with Strong Man Jesus + ♡

Sat. Dec 4, 1993
From Debbie from Judas

To Dr Debbie, Strong-Man Jesus and I will Protect You, And everybody, I drew and colored these pictures for you Thank you for teaching me that I was never bad. I love you Dr Debbie. Judas

Demon-Judas turned into a good Judas when Dr Debbie helped me tell my harts. I now help Dr Debbie.

Mind your own business, Jessica, big mouth. *[The hand-writing is in an unfamiliar peachy-pink, the shaky cursive reminiscent of a budding adolescent's first attempts at grown-up penmanship.]* You might trust Dr. Debbie, but I don't trust her as much as you do. I have a lot of questions I need to know.

What kind of questions, Janice? Maybe Dr. Debbie bee'd able to help you. She's smarted, 'cept when she's dumb. Maybe I bee's able to help. I helps the Big Lady and Judith alls the time. What kind of questions?

Sex questions, Jessica. I need to ask about sex questions.

Sex questions? *[a horrified Jessica writes.]* I don't no nothing 'bout no sex questions, not me!

I burst out laughing as I read this unusual exchange. Images of Prissy from *Gone With the Wind* swirl around in my mind—"I's don't know nothing 'bout birthing no babies, Miss Scarlett!" *Serves her right, the little know-it-all!*

I don't know how to ask Dr. Debbie yet. Demon Judas *[apparently this alter didn't "listen-up" when Judas announced his name change!]* says sex is only good for those who worship Satan, and Little Grace Ann and the Big Lady won't worship Satan. You ask Dr. Debbie the questions, O.K., Jessica? I know the hurts everybody went through. If I ask, it will trigger those horrible things those mean people did.

No way, Janice. *[Janice?]* That be your job. That don't fit my job ascription! *[Jessica has a job description? This I need to see!]* And Janice, don't listen to Judas. He not be Demon Judas no more, Janice. He don't know nothing 'bout no sex.

Several sessions after this journal entry, Jessica (of course) gently coerces the reluctant young lady to make her presence known.

Eyes sparkling, cheeks emblazoned with a crimson glow, I am greeted with a barely audible, but very grown-up, "Hello, Dr. Debbie. It's very nice to meet you. My name is Janice. The others call me 'Barrassed Janice."

"Well, 'Barrassed Janice, it's very nice to meet you, at last. You've been with us for a while, haven't you?"

"Yes, I have, Dr. Debbie, but I was too shy to talk to you."

"I'm certainly glad you decided to give it a try. By the way, Janice, why do you have 'barrassed in front of your name?"

"Because I'm really shy, and I get 'barrassed really easily. If you ever see the Big Lady blushing, you'll know it's me."

Following the very proper introductions, which include a genteel handshake, I attempt to reassure the delightful pre-teen child, reminding her that she is indeed in a very safe place and that she can ask me anything. After a period of playful coaxing, I ask, "Janice, what is it you would like to know?"

"Go ahead, Janice, you can ax Dr. Debbie anything," chimes the resident cheerleader, Jessica.

Scooting all the way around on her ample bottom, she cradles her now beet-red face in her hands, then reaches for Grace Ann's blue jacket, pulling it down over her head. From beneath her makeshift confessional, the child hesitantly, in muffled tones, stammers, "Dr. Debbie, where is the Big Lady's G Spot?"

Stunned, I sense there is an entire band of unseen alters holding their sides while laughing hysterically, thoroughly enjoying my poorly concealed dismay. I can almost hear their glee as they shout, *Gotcha, Dr. Debbie!*

Gathering my scattered wits, I attempt to recall the Family Life Education curriculum I was roped into teaching while employed as a middle school counselor. Clearing the colossal frog in my throat, I regurgitate the chapter on female anatomy, hoping to remember enough to bluff my way through. Apparently I am successful in recalling the long-ago lecture, for I am rewarded with a very proper, "Thank you, Dr. Debbie," at the conclusion of my own 'barrassed mumbling.

"Janice, I bee'd proud of you for talking with Dr. Debbie today. See, I told you she bee'd nice and she bee'd able to help you with any questions you habe. She bee'd very smart, and, she bee'd a lady. Just ax her all the lady sex questions you need to know," congratulates Jessica.

I'm beginning to agree with Janice. Jessica does have a big mouth!

"Dr. Debbie answered the question about the G Spot. How do we get the Big Lady that answer?" the not-so-shy-after-all 12^1/$_2$-year-old asks her younger companion.

"I dunno, Janice. Ax Dr. Debbie the next time you talk to her," was her surprisingly evasive reply.

"Janice."

"Yes, Jessica."

"Janice, Judas bee'd wrong. God created sex to bee'd bootiful 'tween two people who love each other. Even I know that! Strong Man 'splained it to me!"

One by one the unlikely travelers make their presence known. It seems there are twelve in all. The little ones, Baby Joann, fifteen months, Baby Jenny and Little Grace Ann, 3^1/$_2$, are coddled and protected by the older family members. They each wear pink. Jessica, 6^1/$_2$, The Boss, provides the comic relief, but unfortunately keeps everyone, especially the Big Lady, in trouble. She likes pink, too, but *her* pink is a slightly deeper shade. Jennifer, 9^1/$_2$, and 'Barrassed Janice, 12^1/$_2$, arrive in peach. Both prefer the role of silent observers. Jaqua 11^1/$_2$ wears blue. She was created when her daddy, her real daddy, tried to "drown us all" in the bathtub. Jacqueline and Judith are both 14^1/$_2$. Jacqueline loves green, the color of money. She bears the financial responsibility for the family. Few purchases are made without Jacqueline's tacit approval. Judith serves as the system's surrogate mother, working "my fingers to the bone" to keep everyone in place. She attends school, from middle school through the nursing program, and is the only alter who can cook. Judas, *not Demon Judas*, bears the brunt of the abuse, and Strong Man Jesus, the protector, wraps his loving arms around them all.

Jessica, who is NEVER to miss a session, coyly suggests there is someone who would like to meet Dr. Debbie, then sets out to 'splain why the unwilling newcomer cannot yet come forward.

Jenny- 11 Months old. My favorite color is pink

StrongMan Jesus. My colors are White for Purity, Purple for Power, and the cross † is what I died on for all Man-Kind. Everyone should keep GOD first in their life.

Judas- I used to be bad, til Dr. Debbie taught me I was never bad. She also taught all of us the difference between bad touch and GOOD WARM HUGS My color is purple. I help Dr. Debbie and Strong-Man Jesus to help all the little-younger children tell their hurts.

Jo-Ann 15 months old I LiKe PiNK.

Jessica. I LiKe Pink. I am 6½ yrs. old I be the Boss. I never be hurted. I LUV DR. Debbie. I Keep her informed. bout everbody. I want DR. Debbie to Dopt me.

Little Grace-Ann 3½ yrs. old. Color Pink.

Jennifer 9½ yrs. old. My Color is orange.

Janice 12½ yrs. old. I get Barrassed easily My Colors are blushing Pink and Red.

Jackqueline 14½ yrs. old. I manage the money. My favorite color is green.

Judith 14 ½ yrs. old. My favorite color is red.

Jaqua. My Color is Blue

BigGrace - Favorite colors all different shades of Blues and Greens. Survivor.

"Let me 'splain it to you, Dr. Debbie. You see, we don't trust nobody. Everybody always hurted us. No one luved us for a berry long time."

Judith, the last of the adolescent alters, has a difficult time indeed with this illusive concept of trust.

"I Do Not Trust You At All"

Printing, so even the smallest of the children can read her words, Judith writes:

> Little Grace Ann, you should not have told Dr. Debbie. Now the bad people will come and get you and they will kill you dead forever. You were told to NEVER, NEVER, NEVER TELL.

And then, as if aware that I will be reading her words, she stops printing and turns a fastidious red script to me:

> I am Judith. I am 14$^1/_2$. Dr. Debbie, I have only spoken to you one time. I do not trust you at all.

Encouraged by this tentative attempt at conversation, Strong Man Jesus, the internal representative of this uncommon assembly responds in his signature purple ink:

> Judith, we are so proud of you for writing to Dr. Debbie. Now we want you to trust her and talk to her. I know you don't trust her much yet. I also know that you were told to never, never tell anyone, and if you did tell, that they would find you, no matter where you were, and they would kill you. It's O.K. to trust and tell Dr. Debbie all the hurts you took for Grace Ann. We know it will be hard, but Dr. Debbie has a way of helping you tell her without having to relive all those hurts.

Strong Man seems to know everything. He, or she, for I do not know the gender of this kind and helpful alter, is referring to a method of recounting painful memories (screening) while projecting our inner imaginings onto an external screen. This projected reality helps to minimize the painful abreactions. Frequently employed by trauma

I am With all of you. No one can ever hurt anyone again. "Greater is He that is in all of you than he that is in the world". I m

depending on all of you to help Dr. Debbie as much as you can. Remember it was not your fault and no one will ever find you and kill you for telling.

I am with Dr. Debbie and everyone else who is trying to help all of you to heal!
Strong-Man
Jesus + Judas

*therapists, screening has its origins in Object Relations Theory. I
had taught this to Grace Ann months earlier, but quite frankly, had
forgotten all about it. It seems that two therapists **are** better than
one!*

> It's O.K. to trust and tell her everything. You will never
> be hurt again. You are not in the mean people's home. You
> are in Dr. Debbie's safe office. Dr. Debbie, Dr. Sullivan,
> and Dr. Gentry will not allow anyone to ever hurt you
> again. Remember, it's O.K. to trust and tell everything.
> Dr. Debbie will even show you the difference between
> bad touch and good touch, and what a good warm hug
> feels like without being hurt. No one will ever hurt you
> again. NO ONE! I am with you, Dr. Debbie, and all those
> that help you daily.

Strong Man continues:

> I give Dr. Debbie the strength, wisdom, and discern-
> ment to help you, Judith. You need to heal, Judith, so you
> can help Dr. Debbie to help little hurting Grace Ann. She
> hurts a lot, and Dr. Debbie needs all the help she can get
> from you to help her with Little Grace Ann's hurts. I know
> you and all the others need reassurance. You will be safe,
> Judith. No one will hurt you for telling. Remember, I am
> with you all.

*I give Dr. Debbie strength, wisdom, and discernment. I am with
you all? I wonder what he means.*

<hr>

It is from Judith that the bulk of the satanic drawings appear, many
produced in the counseling office, without the benefit of notes, meticulously sketched to enlighten the novice therapist or to clarify a question at hand. It is not until an ironclad trust is established and the promise of absolute safely is assured that the haunting tale of the underworld is divulged.

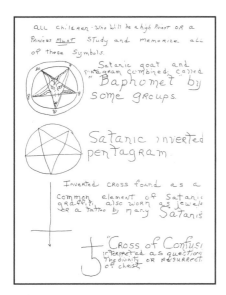

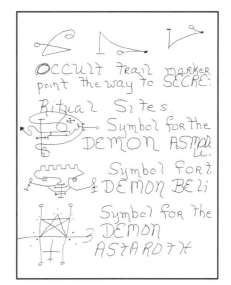

"Dr. Debbie, I can never tell what happened in the circle. We were told nothing that happens in the circle can be told outside of the circle. There is no way out because there is no end. They told us, all of us, that our parents had given us to them, that they knew what was happening, that it was O.K. with them."

"Dr. Debbie, in this picture Little Grace Ann is in the ground covered with dirt."

No way! The pleading eyes stopped me cold! The hands, shaking so violently that she could barely hold onto her painstakingly prepared drawing, convinced me to suspend my disbelief, at least for the moment, and to join with her in her truth.

"Little Grace Ann is in the ground covered with dirt, with a grate with the satanic symbol, or should I say, one of the symbols they use. There is a cemetery out back of the Big Hall. On the left side of the picture is the grey marble table, with the Satanic Bible and the upside down cross. On the top of the Satanic Bible is the most significant symbol *(Judith draws a pentagram.)* That's also the symbol on the grate that is on top of the hole that Little Grace is in. The little children that are flesh colored have no clothes on, and they will be the next to be put in the ground face down. Then they, too, will be covered with dirt. The small child with the white robe, the one with her hands covering her face, will be after the children with no clothes on. The rest of the children have lavender robes.

"All of the children are taken outside in the freezing cold, and shown that rope hanging from the tree. It's used to threaten the children, to threaten them into joining. All of the children were forced to watch them put Little Grace Ann into the ground, with no clothes on, face down. She was crying and screaming, *'I can't breathe, I can't breathe.'* They covered her with the dirt. That's when she developed asthma and bronchitis, Dr. Debbie. I think they left her there to die."

Merely hearing this, whether true or not, makes my head spin. I refocus my eyes in order to follow her throughout the rest of this lurid tale. Vivid memories of my week at the beach are bombarding my brain. Haven't I heard all of this before? It seems hauntingly familiar—too familiar.

"It was cold outside. It had snowed a little that day. The children with no clothes on were freezing. They knew they would be next. The children in the lavender robes were also very cold, as they had nothing on under those robes. The pink and blue blanket on the ground with the pink satin on the edges is Grace Ann's.

"Look near the tree, Dr. Debbie. The person in the white robe is her bad foster mother. The one in the black is her foster father. The other two

in black robes are Father Stafford and the social worker that took her away from Mommy and Daddy Francis. They would never have given her up if they had only known what those other people would do to her.

"Big Grace could not take anymore pain from those mean people. Many times, she would go to her safe place even before they would leave the house on Saturday nights. She hated going there so bad, Dr. Debbie.

"Dr. Debbie, I can't tell you anything else yet because I don't trust you enough. How do I know you won't call the detective on us? Jessica, Jennifer, Strong Man, Judas, Jacqueline, and Jaqua all say it's O.K. to tell and trust you. But I don't trust you like they do, not yet. They even said you would teach me about good warm hugs. But how do I know you won't hurt me? I've never known what a good hug or good touch feels like. Dr. Debbie, do you think there is any help or hope for me?"

"Absolutely Judith. You've watched the others, haven't you? Aren't they getting well? Don't they trust me?"

"Yes, Dr. Debbie, I have watched. I've watched very closely. I wouldn't have allowed them to continue talking with you if I didn't see that it helped them be less afraid. It's my job, well, actually, I help Strong Man to protect everyone. He says the same thing you do, Dr. Debbie. He says no one will ever hurt us again."

And then later that same week, the next installment in Judith's drama appears, written in her customary red ink:

> Dr. Debbie, Strong Man Jesus told us that on Thanksgiving we all had to write what we were thankful for. Little Grace Ann drew a funny picture of a turkey that made us all laugh. The only thing I am thankful for is that I took all that pain, the physical, sexual, and emotional pain for Grace Ann. If I didn't take it, she would have been dead today, because it was too much for any one person to bear.

> I hated living in that house. I never understood what they meant, my foster father and foster mother, when they said, 'You need to learn to come.'

> When they had hurt us more than any of us could stand, I ran away. I slept in the bowling alley for three nights until the manager called the police and they took me to the hospital. I stayed in the hospital for eleven weeks. Every day some nice lady would come to my room and ask me what happened, how I got all those vaginal tears. I was afraid they would kill me, or my brothers, or one of those other children, so I lied. I told them I was walking across a picket fence, and fell off. I don't think anyone believed me, but I kept telling the same story. When the Reynolds came to take me back to that place, I refused to go, so social services let me live in the YWCA for the next three years, until I graduated from high school. I don't even remember my graduation, but I have a diploma, so I guess I must have graduated. There is so much I don't remember.

I am thankful that you can help others. I am so scared. I wish I could tell you everything, but they promised if we were ever to tell anyone, they would kill us, and the person we told, too. So you see why we can't ever tell? They'll kill you, too, Dr. Debbie, and that would just be more than we could stand.

I can see how the others are starting to feel better after telling and trusting you. There is no hope for me because I hate. I am very sad all the time.

The search has continued for an appropriate support group for Grace Ann, for with the exception of the Weight Watchers meetings, she has little contact with the outside world. We finally locate a group called HOPE.

"Deborah, I leave on time, I really do. I want to make sure I can get there early, you know, and find a seat sort of out of the way. Besides that, you know how long it takes me to get anywhere with these crutches. I sit there, and people get out of their cars and wave at me. They look really nice, but I can't make myself open the car door. I just sit there and shake. After awhile I just give up and go home. I'm such a failure!"

"No, Grace Ann, you're not a failure. And by the way, remember what we said about all the negative self-talk. We only become what we think we are. O.K.?"

"I remember. I'm sorry, Deborah. I just get so frustrated. I feel like my insides are going to shake out."

After several more thwarted attempts, she opens the car door, and makes it into the room. The HOPE (Help for People Everywhere) meeting makes quite an impression on her, for she reports coming home and writing "The Butterfly." My copy is presented to me on yellow, butterfly-embossed paper. I note the use of the upper case I in the manuscript, and wonder if she really does feel whole, or if this is simply a printer's attempt to correct her grammar.

Grace Ann writes:

The Butterfly

If I truly love the butterfly, I must care for the caterpillar. Before this great change comes about, I must first identify in spirit with forlorn creatures as this. I am crawling instead of soaring, withdrawing from the world to hide away in my own little cocoon. Time passed and I heard of a program…a tiny crack in my shell appeared…HOPE was timid. After a few meetings, the hard shell began to crack even more. I came out into a new way of life, and into a wonderful world where I absorbed the warmth of fellowship and understanding. I emerged from the depths of despair into this great family of loving people. I try to leave with each person some of what others have given to me, so that they may reach for this new way of life as well.

We in therapy have much in common with the beautiful butterfly. Long before the time of Christ, the butterfly was a symbol of resurrection and eternal life. Many of us in therapy have found this "new life" indeed. The butterfly is a visual aid to remind us that we no longer think, feel, or act as we once did. We were trapped in a cocoon of darkness, but have wrestled our way to the sunlight. The butterfly denotes both gaiety and happiness. Chasing dreams is often fruitless, for like the butterfly, they flit away. But if we are still and become "one with God," the butterfly will light upon our shoulders. We all need to be quiet and give ourselves time to cultivate a resilience of spirit.

There are some who think of the butterfly as a symbol for their life—eternal beauty and freedom after they come to know God through life's experiences. To some, the butterfly is a symbol of rebirth. The wings of the butterfly teach us to be proud of our accomplishments. The reborn find a special significance in the life of the butterfly, which begins as an ugly, worm-like, fuzzy creature and emerges into a thing of awe and joy through God's Grace and Love.

The butterfly is on earth a very short time, and it spends most of its time fluttering from flower to flower. While it is here, it seeks to make the world more beautiful. Hopefully, that is what you and I are doing as well.

Behold a small egg, then a loathsome worm. The caterpillar is shut up, as if it were dead in a tomb, before it bursts forth from its imprisonment and becomes a fragile, lovely butterfly. I, too, became a loathsome, crawling worm. I had no interest in living at all. Death practically defeated me, and I wove a cocoon around me, shutting myself away from life, and from God, for months…even years. The same God that performs this miracle in the chrysalis is even more pleased to transform you and me, anytime, anywhere, anyhow.

I was once entangled and twisted until the light of God's Grace and Love penetrated my heart. Let's join together in the practice of thanking God for something every time we see a butterfly, a spiritual symbol of a happy, enlightened soul…a reminder of each individual's life of eternal beauty and freedom after they come to know God.

Smile. God loves you, and so do I!!!

By Grace Ann Hughes

I know this is signed by Grace Ann Hughes, but it doesn't sound like Grace Ann Hughes, at least the Grace Ann I know! What happened to "I am angry and distant from God?" I wonder what part of her being attends the HOPE meetings, and who within believes in an "eternal beauty and freedom after they come to know God." This just gets more and more curious….

Child and Family Services

Busy, busy, busy. The alters gleefully scurry about. Each has a personal agenda. Grace Ann's depression abates. She comes alive! Unwilling to remain a passive victim one minute longer, she embarks upon a fervent search for—The Truth. She's angry, and she wants answers!

Over the next six months, she attempts to obtain documents from her past. Call after call is made to the private agency responsible for placing her and her brothers in the "bad" foster home. She's on a mission!

"Grace Ann, I don't want to discourage you, but haven't you been through enough? You've had so many frustrations, and you've overcome so much! Does it really matter? Will it change anything? Can't we keep on going forward, like we have been, instead of going back into that dreadful past?"

"No, Deborah, I can't. I deserve to know. We all deserve to know. We have to make sure nothing like this ever happens to little children again!"

"O.K., Grace. What is it you need to know?"

"A lot of things, Deborah. Like, why I was removed from Mommy and Daddy Francis' home. They loved me. I know that! Why were all of us kept at the Reynolds' when anyone could see we were being horribly abused? What was wrong with those people? Had they lost their minds?"

"It was a very different time, Grace Ann. You must remember that!"

"That's no excuse, Deborah! No excuse at all! Michael quit school and joined the Merchant Marines. He didn't even tell Tommy or me goodbye. Tommy ran away after that witch hit him in the head with a bat. He lived with a Greek family until he finished school."

She shakes with rage. "I ended up in the hospital, for Christ's sake—for over two months. And they even wanted me to go back there when I was released. Can you believe that? What was wrong with those people? Was everybody blind? Didn't anyone care? What if I had gone back, Deborah? What would have happened to me then? I'm messed up enough as it is. Would I even be alive today? Would we be having this conversation?"

"Grace Ann, I…."

"And what about that lowlife, Father Stafford? How did he fit into this sick scheme? Did he give the Reynolds money so he could abuse us, too? I understand that my mother couldn't be there. She was sick. Who knows where my father was! But, where were my mother's relatives? Where were my father's? Didn't anybody care? Mrs. Reynolds used to tell us over and over that we were born of a bad breed, and that nobody wanted us. Was she right? Is this what happens to all little children who are born into poverty and have no mother and father to love them?"

Sobbing, she continues, hurling one last volley at her wounded past. "Deborah, poor children have rights, too. They deserve to be loved. They deserve to be protected from people—*animals* like we were forced to live with! There's just no reason at all why we couldn't have had a loving family, too."

She's absolutely right. I can think of nothing to say.

She is at first told the records don't exist, then that they do, but she will have to secure releases from her brothers before she can receive the transcripts. That's impossible, since she has not seen nor heard from either sibling since those fateful days of their youth. Tenacity reigns! She won't give up! She has the right to see those records and no one will keep them from her!

Finally, after months of Grace Ann's harassing phone calls, the agency blinks. The embattled director agrees to assign an unfortunate staffer to the thankless, time-consuming task of whiting out all mention of her brothers. Once this is done, the records will be released to her.

The victory is short-lived, for when the weighty manila envelope finally arrives, it is alleged by Grace Ann to hold aging documents replete with "blatant lies" and lengthy, unexplained missing blocks of time. Her smoldering anger is fanned into fury. "I hate them, I hate them, I hate them!"

She demands justice, a retribution! Her agitation is so pronounced she can barely control her voice. "For all this time, I thought she didn't want us.... I was told, over and over, that we were bad, that she gave us away."

The forty-four-year-old social services records provide a distinctively different account of these earlier, unfortunate events.

Grace Ann's mother, a Polish Catholic from a large immigrant family, had met and married the "smooth-talking" Mr. Hughes after his return from World War II. The couple was married in a Protestant ceremony at the husband's request, despite the vehement protestations of the bride's church and family.

The caseworker writes: "The family is strongly opposed to the mixed marriage and is very pessimistic about the possibility of its working out."

Mrs. Hughes is described by the intake counselor as "a rather dull-looking woman whose very bad teeth detract from her appearance." She notes the mother has presented for services due to the husband's frequent absences, apparent lack of concern for the family's welfare, and financial non-support. "Mrs. Hughes reports that she is reluctant to leave because she has no job, and no skills to get a job. Who would care for her children? Besides, she loves her husband and feels that he is ill. Why else would he refuse to take care of his wife and family?"

The document continues:

> On a more personal note, Mrs. Hughes does complain of her husband's sexual needs, which she describes as excessive.
>
> Mr. Hughes continues to refuse marital help and denies any association with his now destitute wife and three young children. To make matters even worse, the agency is informed that he has impregnated, ruined, a young Jewish girl. He has married for a third time, again without the benefit of a divorce. He subsequently abandons this untimely union, forcing the young, now tainted and unchaste girl to seek public assistance for herself and her as yet unborn child. It is at this point that the polygamy charges are filed, with Mr. Hughes sentenced to a year in the House of Corrections. It is reported that he also faces a neglect of family charge.

A mighty high price to pay for a smooth-talking man.

Alone, overwhelmed, and grieving the loss of her marriage, Mrs. Hughes' mental health begins to deteriorate. Deeply depressed, her behavior becomes increasingly erratic. "It is reported that the mother has been seen knocking on the neighbors' doors late at night begging for food for her children." The agency is sufficiently concerned for the children's welfare to remove them from their mother's now inadequate care, placing them in a series of foster homes throughout the city.

In referencing Grace Ann's initial placement, the social worker notes: "Grace Ann is doing very well at the Francis' home. They are extremely outgoing, permissive, and accepting foster parents, and are giving her a great deal of loving care."

It was just as Grace Ann remembered....

Having lost her husband, children, and home, and alienated from her family of origin, Mrs. Hughes, no longer able to cope, is hospitalized in a state mental facility. Records indicate that she is diagnosed with "Dementia Praecox, Mixed Type, necessitating continued hospitalization and electro-shock treatments."

During the summer of 1951, scribbled letters are received by the agency, each reflecting a mother's worry for her children and her desire to come home.

July 21, 1951
...please come to take me out of this hospital. Try to get my wedding ring...and my blue coat. I miss the children very much. Please try to get my yellow pocketbook, and my kirchief. I got to go pay my rent. I haven't paid it since April.

August 1, 1951
I got to get home. I have been hear long enough. I got to get home. The children been away from home since April or May. I got to get home. Please come for me. I've gotter go home and pay my rent and bring the children home. I would like to go home. All the people go to homes. I want to go home too.

August 10, 1951
I have been hear for four months, and it's been about time I went home. Don't you think so. Cause I want to take care of the three children myself.

Within a few short months of hospitalization, Mrs. Hughes is declared "to be insane." As a result, her children, forever lost to her, become permanent wards of the court.

"Little has been heard from the children's relatives"; therefore, upon receipt of the insanity decree, the children are removed from their temporary placements and located, as a family unit, in permanent foster care. They are reared as devout Catholics, as notations of catechism studies and first communions are scattered throughout the now altered document. Grace Ann scoffs as she sarcastically reads such accolades as,

> ...the children's medical, dental, and clothing needs have been met. They continue to receive excellent, close, and loving care in [their new] foster home...we have helped each of these fine young people to achieve their goal and supplemented their earnings when necessary with some financial assistance, and they always knew of our care and psychological support for them in their endeavors.

I scan the document for anything that hints of abuse. The only insinuations that all is not well are references to Grace Ann's broken ankle (alleged by the client to have occurred when she was forcibly tied down), a large bald spot on the left side of one brother's head (purported to be the result of the bat-wielding incident), and eerily, a 1963 notation which states, "Because of an emergency situation, _____[whited out] had to move to another home."

That's it! Someone had to move to another home?

Grace Ann sobs as she reads: "Each child regularly receives a card with two dollars for his birthday. It is always signed, A Friend."

Oh, my God, how sad! I want to cry, too.

My eyes focus on one brief paragraph, apparently the impressions of the social worker assigned to the case. The unobtrusive notation reads:

> ...much of the trouble began when she [Mrs. Hughes] became pregnant with Grace Ann who is now a year old. I wondered about her feelings for this child. Mrs. Hughes talked about _____[whited out] as the favored one. She stated, 'Grace Ann doesn't count around our house.'[65]

"Grace Ann doesn't count around our house?" I can't imagine such a statement being made about a tiny, innocent child!

Inwardly, I am horrified that Grace Ann *must* have read this, but she does not comment and I do not ask! I wonder if some part of her, someone from her inner family, is protecting her from a reality she is just too fragile to digest. If so, I surely hope he, or she, continues to cast that protective veil over the truth, whatever the truth might be. Grace Ann's mission to make sense of her past has only added an additional layer of mystery to an already perplexing drama. It is increasingly clear to me that I may never know what happened to Grace Ann, but that whatever did occur was horrific and altered her life forever.

I remind myself, reluctantly, that her healing lies not in the details of an abusive past, but in a faith, a conviction of a promising, light-filled tomorrow. To allow myself to be pulled too far into this tale will not only undermine Grace Ann's recovery, but my mental health as well.

The Surviva

"What is REAL?" asked the Rabbit one day when they were lying side by side near the nursery fender before Nana came to tidy the room.

"Does it mean having things that buzz inside you and a stick-out handle?"

"Real isn't how you are made," said the Skin Horse.

"It's a thing that happens to you. When a child loves you for a long, long time, not just to play with, but REALLY loves you, then you become Real."

"Does it hurt?" asked the Rabbit.

"Sometimes," said the Skin Horse, for he was always truthful.

"When you are Real you don't mind being hurt."

"Does it happen all at once, like being wound up," he asked, "or bit by bit?"

"It doesn't happen all at once," said the Skin Horse.

"You become. It takes a long time. That's why it doesn't happen to people who break easily, or have sharp edges, or who have to be carefully kept. Generally, by the time you are Real, most of your hair has been loved off, and your eyes drop out and you get loose in the joints and very shabby. But these things don't matter at all, because once you are Real you can't be ugly, except to people who don't understand."[66]

Margery Williams
The Velveteen Rabbit

CHAPTER FIVE

Defiantly, Grace Ann orders a new license plate, emblazoned with SURVIVA. A purple velvet bow, attached to the tarnished hood emblem, now adorns her faded, aging vehicle.

"I will survive, Deborah! I will! They can never hurt me again. They didn't destroy me then, and they can't destroy me now! You just watch me. You'll see. I'm going to get my life back. Nothing's gonna stand in my way!"

"I have no doubt you'll get your life back, Grace Ann, absolutely no doubt at all! I understand the plates, but what's the deal with the purple bow?"

Perplexed, even somewhat perturbed that I don't already know, she responds incredulously, "Because, Deborah, purple is Strong Man's color, and he protects us. He's always protected us. You know that!"

I guess I should have known that. Purple is indeed the symbol of royalty within the Christian faith, and Strong Man does wear a purple shirt. I pause to consider this internal self-helper, this Strong Man. Could he be something more? Could he be the illusive internal self-helper I read about at the beach last summer? Hmm...I have always assumed he was just another altered state of consciousness, just one more splinter of a fragmented mind. Now I'm not so sure, not at all assured of my earlier conviction. I don't know, I just don't know.

An Angry Surviva

The eternal debate continues. Middle-aged folks from Grace Ann's home town band together, men and women alike, forever cemented by memories of tainted trust, of unholy transgressions silently, shamefully endured, inequities inflicted upon their childhood bodies, their child-hood minds, by the very soul whose charge was their safekeeping. Many choose to testify at Father Stafford's trial. Most attend his sentencing.

Christening themselves *Victims No More,* they persist in their advocacy, even after the penitent priest is safely locked away. Their focus, and their criticism, is now redirected, projected upon a growing contingent of individuals who are vocally proclaiming the inaccuracy of the survivors' memories, maintaining these intrusive recollections of sexual violation *must* have been implanted by unscrupulous therapists, and encouraged by equally unscrupulous attorneys. They mobilize, determined to refute the opposing camp, the encroaching False Memory advocates. As a first order of business they undertake a nationwide search for lawyers claiming to have an expertise in ritual/ multi-perpetrator abuse. Once the listing is generated, it is forwarded to sympathetic individuals and organizations.

My client, a victim no more, is transformed into a 1990s version of a Norma Rae! Fueled by what she feels are corroborating testimonies, an incensed Grace Ann contacts female attorneys from coast to coast. She cross-examines every litigator who will take her call, determined to learn if she is friend or foe. I cringe as the phone bills again mount, and wonder, worry if I am truthful, how a single, disabled individual with no income continues to spend so freely with no apparent consequence.

It is on one particular spring day that she and her signature crutches hobble into the room. A video camera is dangling from one hand, a tripod from the other.

"Grace Ann, what on earth are you doing? Are we going to Hollywood? You didn't tell me. Look at me. I'm a mess!"

Grace Ann is in no mood for a joke.

"Deborah, we have been talking to an attorney who specializes in Ritual Abuse. She might take our case. We want to introduce ourselves."

"Well, O.K., I guess…"

I'm not sure what she means, but she's in no mood to chat. I sit, silently, as a focused Grace Ann proceeds to unfold the tripod, attaching the camera and checking and rechecking its position within the room. Satisfied at last that the appropriate camera angle has been achieved, she, or someone, I suspect a child, seats herself on the floor, faces the camera, and begins.

"We hope you can help us."

I realize that I, too, have a role in the unfolding drama, as she, perhaps they, pause, turn toward me, and ask, "The Big Lady can't stand them really bad switchin' headaches, Dr. Debbie. Can you help us? She don't need so much blue ice on her head if you count for us."

"No problem, guys!"

Anxious to do something, I count backwards, "Five-four-three-two, and one."

Not surprisingly, a jubilant Jessica appears.

"Take off your shoes, Dr. Debbie, bee's comfortable. I's a party girl. I never be hurted. I bee's the boss, 'cept Strong Man Jesus says he really, really, bee's the boss. I bee's the boss after him."

"Are you going to read us The Belbeteen Rabbit, Dr. Debbie? I luvs the Belbeteen Rabbit? Are you gonna make us real?"

She pauses, tilts her head, and listens. I can only assume she is hearing the advisement, or perhaps admonition, of an undisclosed member of her inside family.

"O.K., O.K., I ahave."

Then turning toward the camera, she squares her shoulders, and attempts, unsuccessfully I might add, to present herself in an adult-like fashion.

"I 'sposed to tell you 'bout me. I came about when Donnie bee'd born. You 'member Donnie, right, Dr. Debbie? You 'member, when our foster parents, the bad foster parents, had a baby boy. Grace Ann bee'd $6^{1}/_{2}$ and she not know how to take care of no baby, so I bee'd borned. Changed the baby's diapers, washin', washin', washin' the baby's hair."

I work hard to stifle a chuckle at her vigorous impersonation of washing an unfortunate Donnie's hair. Jessica couldn't be grown up if her life depended upon it. I visualize the inside family as a stone-faced jury, each head solemnly shaking in disapproval.

"Only one thing."

"What might that be, Jessica?"

"I not bee'd out as much as I like."

Oh, well. That will be it for Miss Jessica. Her fate has certainly been sealed now. She won't be 'out' much longer.

She points a now quivering finger toward the camera. "Is she gonna help us, Dr. Debbie, or is she gonna report us to the cult? Judith be really scared. She be scared of the movie pictures. She be so scared she ripped her skin off."

So a terrified Judith is here, too.

Jessica shakes her head as if to free herself from an unwelcome visitor, heaves an immense, aching sigh, then continues her self-appointed mission.

"I has to tell you about Baby Jenny and Baby Joann. Strong Man say that bee'd my job. They already telled their hurts. They be in a safe place in heaben with Mommy Francis, rockin', rockin', rockin'. Baby Jenny be hurted by her real daddy. He hurted her hot dog roll. Baby Joann, she getted hurt really bad. Her real daddy taked her to the hospistal. Habed [had] twelve, what you call them, Judith?"

"Sutures, Jessica."

"That be right. Thank you, Judith."

"Baby Joann habed twelve sutures. Her daddy blamed his brother. The policeman 'rested him, but letted him go. He didn't habe no ebidence."

Apparently the group has had enough of Jessica's testimony, for in a flash, it's someone else's turn. Wordlessly, Little Grace Ann pulls a pastel pink shirt on top of Jessica's darker pink one.

"Dr. Debbie. You telled me you was only goin' to work with me today. When I heared the Big Lady say we's gonna make a movie, I hided all the shirts. I hided them all over the Big Lady's 'partment— under her bed, in her craft bag, even in the 'frigarator. But Judith getted mad at me and maded me find them. I not like Judith no more, Dr. Debbie. I not want to make no movie, Dr. Debbie."

Uh, oh! I forgot. I did tell her she would have her turn today, since Jessica "bee'd a hog" during our last time together. Oh, well, apparently the family had other plans.

"I'm so sorry, Little Grace Ann. I completely forgot. Will you forgive me?"

"You know we luv you, Dr. Debbie. That bee'd all right. We know you forgits a lot. How old you be, anyhow?" she asks, grinning.

"Never you mind, missy. Now just what are we supposed to be doing?"

Her mood changes in a flash!

"What I do to make my daddy not like me no more, Dr. Debbie? Why he not be happy when I comed home from the hospistal? Don't daddies 'sposed to love their little girls?"

"Yes, Little Grace Ann, they are 'sposed to love their little girls," I sadly reply.

"Bad Little Grace Ann. I maked my daddy hurt me. I maked all the people at the bad foster parents hurt me. They taked me away from Mommy and Daddy Francis."

Pouting, "Little Grace Ann want Mommy to rock her. I be bad, bad, bad."

Anticipating a turn for the worse, I hurriedly chime in. "Bad things happen, but Grace Ann was never bad."

My attempt at consolation proves fruitless. The shaking begins. A hoarseness appears.

"Judith Brown, she died. They putted dead, black rose petals all over her. I try to help her get out. They say I killed her. They say it bee'd my fault. I killed her. I sorry. I berry, berry, sorry. I be so scared. I hided all the shirts. I hided them, Dr. Debbie. I be berry, berry sorry. I not want to make no movie, Dr. Debbie. Please don't let them get us! Please!"

"That's all right, Little Grace Ann. Take a deep breath. That's a good girl. One more time. Good for you."

"Thank you, Judith," she whispered, her breath raspy and labored. "I not know what I do without you, Judith. I luv you."

"I love you, we all love you, too. Now what are you supposed to be doing?" an invisible Judith inquires.

"I 'sposed to tell the lady that Mommy teached Grace Ann how to tie shoes, tie bow and everything. Mommy says she wishes she could 'dopt all of us. Daddy buyed Little Grace Ann ice cream."

Little Grace Ann fades away, as a shaking Jennifer places a peach shirt on top of the second pink shirt.

"Whew, Dr. Debbie, I's wheezin'. I didn't put that dead bird on the Big Lady's car seat. I didn't, honestly. I didn't put that book, that satanic book, between the doors either. One look at it and I came out. She couldn't handle it, Dr. Debbie. She was so scared. No, I'm smothering, 'cause I told. It makes me feel like I can't breathe."

"Slow down, Jennifer, big breath, that's right. Take a deep breath." Someone uses the inhaler. While I don't know who, it's clear it isn't Jennifer. She has gone back into hiding.

"We'll continue when you're ready. O.K. 5-4-3-2-1, when you're ready."

"Janice, slow down, take deep breaths, it's Judith. That's a girl, take deep breaths."

"Judith always helps me, Dr. Debbie."

"She does a good job helping you," I offer.

"I's Janice."

"I think we were speaking with Jennifer. Let's do that again. 5-4-3-2-1."

"O.K., Dr. Debbie."

"I's Jennifer. I's 9¹/₂."

"Good afternoon, Miss Jennifer. It's nice to see you again. What do you need to tell the Big Lady, I mean Grace Ann's attorney?"

"I need to tell her I didn't know how old I be 'cause we didn't never have birthdays. Strong Man Jesus told me. Strong Man Jesus has been with us all along, since Baby Jenny. This is my color, peach-orange [pointing to her tee shirt]. I comed about 'cause she couldn't take the pain they did to her on Halloween."

Do I hear Little Grace Ann again?

"That ritual on Halloween. Four times a year on the twenty-first of the month, they do the ritual. I get very scared. I'm scared somebody will be killed if we tell what happened to us. I usually cancel my appointments, but I didn't this time."

"You are very brave. I'm glad you didn't cancel your appointment."

"Dr. Debbie, can she help us get better?"

Turning to the camera, as if pleading her case to an invisible attorney: "Dr. Debbie's been helping us, but it costs the Big Lady all her savings money, and now we don't have enough money to buy groceries."

I hadn't heard that. Is it true? I'll need to speak with Grace Ann. Something will have to be worked out. She sure can't do without groceries!

I watch as Jennifer, in her mind's eye, leaves the room.

Regressing, voice tremulous, eyes darting: "It's dark, the only way you can tell if it's day is to look through the crack in the ceiling."

Leaning forward, I try to get her attention and diffuse a certain abreaction. "Jennifer, stop, look around the room. Look at the chair, the window. Where are you, Jennifer? Look in my eyes, Jennifer. Right here, in my eyes."

"Oh!" wiping perspiration and heaving a sigh of relief. "We're in Dr. Debbie's pretty room, the safest place in the whole world."

"Thank you, Jennifer, for sharing your story."

"I love you, Dr. Debbie. You have safe eyes.

An oversized purple shirt is removed from the canvas bag. Slowly, it is pulled over Grace Ann's head and meticulously arranged over the now shrinking frame.

"I've been helping Strong Man Jesus. I used to be Demon Judas; do you remember me, Dr. Debbie?" You know, I used to wear red. I hated that red but I love Strong Man's color."

"Yes, I do, Judas. I remember quite well."

"Is she going to help us, Dr. Debbie? Can we trust her? Is she going to cost us a lot of money? You know Jacqueline, she's going to be concerned about that."

"Someone needs to watch the Big Lady's money, Judas. Jacqueline has a very important job. How's she doing, by the way?"

"Not very good, Dr. Debbie. She tries. She tries really hard. But no one will listen to her. They just keep on spending. I think she's worried. The Big Lady won't tell you these things. She doesn't want you to know she's in trouble."

So the truth is finally out! I'm going to have to speak with Grace Ann about her finances. If she can't pay, she can't pay. We are not going to stop the work now. I want her to get well as much as she does, and if that means a pro bono, well, so be it. I'll make up the lost income somehow.

Then turning back to his original mission, Judas asks, "Do you want to tell her how I used to be bad and I'm not bad anymore?"

"No I don't, my friend, because you were never bad. Hurt maybe, but never bad."

"They put that fireplace poker…."

Judas, not to be confused with Demon Judas, removes a purple pen and pad from Grace Ann's canvas bag. Shaking, he draws a remarkable likeness of a pointed staff.

"They put it in Grace Ann's hot dog roll. She screamed and screamed and screamed. She couldn't take the pain, so I taked the pain.*"*

Little Grace Ann? Do I hear Little Grace Ann?

"I don't have to worry about it no more 'cause I told Dr. Debbie. Remember everyone, now that I told Dr. Debbie, I don't have to be

Demon Judas anymore. I am just Judas. I help Strong Man Jesus. I help everybody now. Dr. Debbie got to me first. You were smart, Dr. Debbie!"

"No, not smart, Judas. Just scared."

"I didn't mean to scare you, Dr. Debbie."

"Yes, you did, Judas. Don't you try that with me!"

He chuckles while shaking his head, for he knows who's telling the truth, and it's surely not him.

"Well, O.K., I did, but it didn't work."

"I don't know what we would do without you, Judas. You're very important to us—to all of us. You know that, don't you?"

"Yes, Dr. Debbie. I know that now."

"I was just trying to make you scared so you wouldn't talk to me. They told all of us, over and over, 'If you tell what they did to you, everyone that you love will be killed.' I tried really hard not to like you, Dr. Debbie. But, you were really nice to us, to all of us. And you have safe eyes. I didn't want you to be killed, Dr. Debbie. What would we all do if something happened to you?"

A speeding ambulance, sirens wailing, is heard through the office window. Judas shrieks, arms outstretched, as if preparing to fend off an assailant only he can see.

"Judas, Judas, look at me! That's an ambulance, an ambulance going to help somebody. No one is going to get killed, Judas. Everything is all right. Everyone is fine."

"Sometimes I forget, Dr. Debbie. Sometimes I still get scared."

"I know, Judas. Try to remember that no one can hurt you, any of you, ever again. O.K., Judas?"

"O.K., Dr. Debbie. I'll try. We love you, Dr. Debbie."

I watch helplessly as Judas, turning inward, takes direction from an inside voice. Fear turns to resignation, then to anger. Following an extended moment of uncertainty, I am again face to face with evil incarnate. A chill envelopes me as a hollow, disembodied voice declares:

"Grace Ann holds a lot of the programming."

"What does that mean?"

"If you tell what we do to you, everyone you love will be killed." With a shake of the head, Judas, I think it is Judas, continues, "They told each one of them—they would show them eyes—how they put eyeballs in everybody. Dr. Debbie, that's not true. It's NOT TRUE. They didn't put eyeballs in us. Do I have to show the lawyer the scars, Dr. Debbie?"

"No, no, Judas, you don't have to show her the scars," I hurriedly reply, in an attempt to stave off an unveiling before the camera.

Good Lord! That's all Grace Ann needs. She doesn't deserve to be filmed, half-naked, in front of her own camera. She would be horrified, and I don't blame her. Those scars will just have to remain another chapter in her story. Enough is enough. If she won't, or can't protect herself, I'll just have to do it for her.

A carefully folded royal blue shirt is removed from the canvas bag. After a great deal of preparation, I am greeted with a serenely lyrical voice, a voice unlike those of the previous presentations.

"These shirts certainly are big, aren't they? Grace Ann has lost a lot of weight. We used to weigh 489½ pounds. Now we weigh 274. We still have to lose a lot. We went to the restaurant with Nancy, and our pants fell down. We could have been on America's Funniest Home Video."

"Guess who got embarrassed?"

"'Barrassed Janice, I assume."

Nodding, she smiles, then pauses, apparently taking the time to refocus her thinking. The alter known as Jaqua then offers, "Dr. Debbie, the Big Lady's still drinking a lot of water."

"How much is she drinking now, Jaqua?" I ask.

"Well, if she's upset, she sometimes drinks 3½ gallons a day."

Three-and-a-half gallons? No way! I knew she drank water all the time, but 3½ gallons? No way!

"We used to take about twenty showers a day 'cause we felt dirty and shamed and bad inside. We drank a lot of water because of those men peeing in our mouths. But it never gets any better, Dr. Debbie. We still feel shamed and dirty."

"Dr. Debbie, I don't know how old I am, 'cause I came about when Grace Ann was just a little baby."

Uh, oh. When the babies arrive, we're in for a painful session. Rushing in to divert a certain de-compensation, I ask, "Your job is to help her feel clean?"

"Yes, Dr. Debbie, but she still drinks so much water. She says she feels dirty inside all the time. I try not to let her take so many showers. She's only been taking two a day lately.

"Really, that's much better. Every time she takes a shower, I have to wash all those clothes. Can you imagine how many clothes I washed when she was taking all those showers? It was unbelievable. One week she drank twenty-nine gallons of water. That's a lot of water.

"When is the Big Lady gonna stop feeling so dirty and shameful and bad inside, Dr. Debbie?"

"I hope very, very soon," is my feeble reply.

Hoping to gain some control over my own feelings of ineptness, I ask, in my most professional therapeutic voice, "Jaqua, the Big Lady asked that this session be taped. Do you mind?"

"No, Dr. Debbie, so long as no one gives it to the police or someone from the Big Hall, or sells it. People did that all the time. Someone always had a camera. I don't know what happened to the pictures."

"What would they take pictures of?"

"They would take pictures of Grace Ann on the grey marble table. She'd be tied with leather straps. The straps would cut into her skin and leave bruises. While they have you strapped down, the wife would hold your nose like this, and they would stick their (gagging)…in your mouth. It would make you sick and want to throw up. I tried to help her 'cause she would feel so dirty inside. She still does. Then they would pee all over you. Dr. Debbie, it's so gross. I feel dirty all the time, too, just like she does."

Hands shake once again. The gagging continues as she slurps water from the green plastic travel cup.

———◆◈◆———

"Who would like to talk next?" I ask, attempting to diffuse the potentially volatile situation.

"I guess Janice," comes the muffled reply.

"Janice? My 'barrassed friend, Janice?"

"She gets 'barrassed easily."

"Thank you, Jaqua. I appreciate your hard work."

"I just wish we could stop her from drinking so much water. I know it makes her skin look good, but she's drinking so much water. Dr. Debbie, will she ever stop drinking so much water?"

"Well, she's not drinking twenty-nine gallons now is she? And she's not taking all those showers?"

"Well, no. I guess not."

"Then she's already improving, isn't she?"

"I guess so, Dr. Debbie. I hadn't thought of it that way. Thank you for speaking with me," as she gently fades away.

Without warning, the regression begins. Jaqua, I think it's Jaqua, begins massaging the Big Lady's ankles. Sobbing, she cries out, "Oh, I shouldn't have told. I shouldn't have told. They're going to find out I told. Our ankles are bruising already."

I, too, see the bruising. *That's odd.* I hadn't noticed *that* before. Attempting to introduce an alternative explanation for the bruising, I offer, "That's what usually happens when Grace Ann has a nightmare and gets tied up in the bed sheet."

"Are they coming to get us?"

"Listen to me, Jaqua. No, no one is coming after you. Maybe you had a bad dream!"

"We didn't have no bad dream," she vehemently counters. "We been sleeping good the last two nights. We didn't have no bad dream. Love you, Dr. Debbie. Thank you for not giving up on us."

I watch as she drifts into the fog once again.

"5-4-3-2-1…I would like to talk to, let me see, I know, my friend Janice. Hi, Janice."

"Hi, Dr. Debbie."

I wait, for Janice rarely looks at me when we chat. As expected, she turns her back to the camera. I am surprised, though, as I watch her reach for Grace Ann's navy jacket.

"I'm too 'barrassed. I can't look at people," she timidly offers as she covers her head with the jacket.

"Well, Janice. What would you like to ask the Big Lady's attorney?"

"If she could help us," was her muffled reply.

"How would you like her to help you?"

"Help us to put our foster mother and father in jail, just like Father Stafford. And help the Big Lady get back some of her money that she took out of retirement…and…I want her to call the Child and Family Service and tell them, tell them they should never have left us with those people."

"That all certainly makes sense. What else would you like to tell her, Janice?"

"That when you have your monthly bleed, they do a special ritual. They take blood out of a hole right there (she points to her right inner arm). They put it in a gold chalice and they drink it. They say, 'Hail, Beelzebub, Hail Satan.'

"They ask you if you're ready to join. If you say no, they tie your feet and hands to the grey marble table. Then the men stick things in your hot dog roll. Sometimes even the women would do bad things you don't like."

"Thank you for sharing that with us, Janice."

I wonder how the unsuspecting attorney is going to feel about this unsavory bit of news. Am I getting immune to all of this, or am I just filled to my saturation point and unable to absorb more? Maybe it's time to take another short break. I never want to be dismissive of anyone, especially anyone who has lived through this much pain. My God, the very last thing I want to do is further traumatize her with my disbelief.

Then, regaining my composure, "Now take a big breath, Janice. Who needs to talk next?"

"I guess Judith," Janice sighs. "I'll take this off."

She pulls the jacket up and over her face, meticulously folds it, and places it in the canvas bag.

"Dr. Debbie, when I cover my head, 'cause I'm 'barrassed, the Big Lady Grace feels like she's smothering. I thought you might want to know that. When she says she feels like she's suffocating and doesn't know why, that means I'm covering my head. O.K., Dr. Debbie?"

"Janice, thanks so much for sharing that with me. That will be really helpful. You are very courageous! Did you know that?"

"No, but thank you for encouraging me, Dr. Debbie. I want to help you help the Big Lady. She's counting on you. Everyone else has let her down."

Whether the manipulation of a borderline or an adolescent truth, Janice's admonitions work. In less than five minutes I am again fully invested in this process. It's amazing how quickly one can recover when one feels, really feels in the depth of her soul, that she's needed.

"Dr. Debbie?"

"Yes, Janice."

"That's Judith's shirt. She likes Mickey Mouse."

Janice places the red Mickey Mouse tee shirt over her head. "We have an awful lot of shirts on."

"You certainly do. O.K., are you ready Miss Janice?"

"Love you, Dr. Debbie. I'll try not to make the Big Lady feel like she's smothering."

"She would appreciate that, Janice. Thanks so much for your help."

"5-4-3-2-1, I would like to speak with Judith."

I am greeted with a heavy, labored breathing. Judith scans the room suspiciously, eyes darting to and fro. Her eyes lock onto the camera. Stuttering with fright, she asks, "Are you going to sell that, Dr. Debbie? I think they sold the pictures they took of us."

"Of course not, Judith. You know I wouldn't hurt you like that. Besides, it's not mine to sell. It's Grace Ann's. Don't you remember, she wanted to film this session for her new attorney?"

"I remember, Dr. Debbie, but I don't like it. I don't trust this lady. We don't know her. She might be one of them. She might hurt us all over again. I don't think we could take that, Dr. Debbie, to be hurt all over again. Dr. Debbie, we almost didn't get her here."

"Really? What happened?"

"Little Grace Ann wanted the whole time today. She's ready to work, Dr. Debbie. She was so angry at us, she hid all the shirts. It took me forever to find them."

I laugh out loud at the mental picture of one alter hiding twelve tee- shirts, while another tears the house apart to find them. Just imagine the heated conversation they must have been having. Poor Grace Ann. It's no wonder her head hurts. I guess she does feel as if she's losing her mind. This is a special woman—incredibly, undeniably, unbelievably strong, she has had to be, to be able to deal with all of this. I must remember to tell her, once again, how proud I am of her.

Turning my attention back to the alter at hand, I notice, for the first time, the inflamed red abrasions.

"Judith, can you, will you tell me about your arms?"

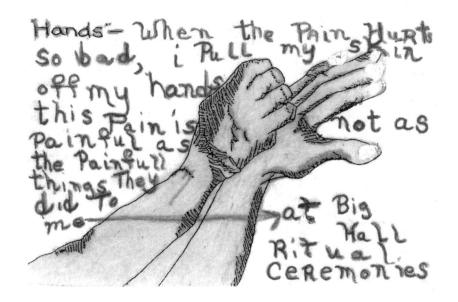

Hands - when the Pain Hurts so bad, i Pull my skin off my hands, this Pain is not as Painful as the Painfull things They did To me → at Big Hall Ritual Ceremonies

Tucking her head, as if crippled with embarrassment, she glumly whispers, "When we hurt, we pull the skin off, Dr. Debbie."

My first instinct is to yell at her, to ask why she would do something so stupid? Hasn't she, haven't they, hurt enough? Slow down, Deborah, breathe, breathe.

"I'm sorry, Judith. You must have really been hurting."

Chin still tucked in shame, she nods her head.

"Can you tell me what you were hurting about today?"

"I was scared someone was coming from the Big Hall to tape us, Dr. Debbie."

"Judith, let's think about this. Has anyone from the Big Hall ever come to this office?"

"Never!"

"Has anyone ever hurt you in this office?" I challenge.

"No, Dr. Debbie. This is the safest place in the whole world," she replies.

"And have I changed since the last time you saw me, Judith?"

Judith scans me from head to toe. Then, resting her gaze upon my smiling, hopefully welcoming face, she smiles as well. "No, Dr. Debbie. You still have the safest eyes."

"Then you, my doubting friend, have nothing to fear."

"I know, Dr. Debbie. Strong Man picked you special to help us. Sometimes I just forget. I'm sorry, Dr. Debbie. I know in my heart you would never hurt us. I really do. Strong Man Jesus has been protecting us, too."

"Dr. Debbie, somebody knocked three times last night. You told us to take a picture if we were suspicious of someone, but the Big Lady was stubborn-headed and wouldn't go to the door. They kept on knocking, three times…three times. Big Lady wouldn't go to the door."

"Judith, I'm glad she didn't go to the door. I didn't mean for you all to take pictures in the middle of the night. Please, I don't want you to be unsafe in any way."

"You want me to talk to that lady?" she asks.

"What lady, Judith?" *I have forgotten about the taping.*

"The Big Lady's attorney, Dr. Debbie. The one she wants to send this tape to—the one who's going to help us."

"I'm sorry, Judith. For a minute I just forgot. Let's see. Why don't you tell the lady what it is you do."

"That's easy. I help Dr. Debbie with everybody." She smiles as she states, "We have been on our own since we were 14^1/$_2$. We stayed in a bowling alley for three days."

"Can you tell her why you did that, Judith?"

"We just came out of the hospital. We were in the hospital for over two months. They never came to see us."

"Can you tell her why you were in the hospital? Remember, Judith, she doesn't know you."

"Because they told us that we had a baby and they took the baby with a coat hanger…they told the hospital that we fell on a picket fence. The social worker told the Big Lady that we needed thirty-seven stitches."

Jesus, No! I haven't heard about any coat hanger! I feel nauseous. The room is spinning. I'm not going to be able to fake it this time.

"You all right, Dr. Debbie? Dr. Debbie, Dr. Debbie? Can you hear us, Dr. Debbie? I'll get the Big Lady. She's a nurse. You don't look too good."

Regaining my composure, I feel dissociated myself as I mouth, "Do you remember exactly what she told the Big Lady?"

"Told her, Dr. Debbie? We don't remember what we were talking about. You scared us, Dr. Debbie. Are you sure you're O.K.?"

"Don't worry, Judith. I'm just fine. I thought I was getting a headache, but it went away. I'm just fine, really."

"Do you remember what the social worker told the Big Lady, I mean Grace Ann, about the vaginal tears?"

I immediately regret the question, for I can see Judith, our Judith, leaving the safety of the day, returning to a time long past, a time she did not wish to revisit, a memory that was better left alone. The combination of my swimming head and questioning has proved to be too much.

A seemingly unabashed Judith recalls: "That's when I took over. The Big Lady had to work. She could work 'till six if she kept her grades up. We worked at the five and dime and lived at the YWCA. We got out of school at twelve. I helped the Big Lady study. I helped her 'cause she was tired. I helped her study to go to L.P.N. school. I helped her study for four years of college. She worked full time and went to school full time. She was so tired, Dr. Debbie."

Then remembering the hospitalization.

"They threw away the records. It had been thirty years. The hospital social workers came every single day and asked what happened. I told them I fell on a fence. They said, 'You don't get vaginal tears from falling on a fence.' "

Judith begins to sob.

"Is there anything else you would like for us to know right now?" I redirect in a strained effort to thwart the inevitable abreaction.

"I just want us all to get better. I would like to see the lady from Child and Family Services put in jail…she should not have put us in that foster home…I feel so dirty sometimes that I could just rip off my skin."

Anxious to move on, I ask, "Who would like to talk next?"

"I guess Jacqueline," someone of an unidentifiable origin offers.

Grace Ann removes a green shirt from the slowly dwindling supply.

"When I think about those things the men do, it makes me sick. I think I'm going to throw up. They should put our father, our biological father, in jail and leave him there! We called him one time when he was seventy years old. He couldn't keep a job and was married for the tenth time. He is so disgusting! I'll keep trying to help you. O.K., Dr. Debbie?"

"Whenever you're ready," I instruct the nameless entity. "5-4-3-2-1."

"Dr. Debbie, Judith's taking some deep breaths," is the rasping response.

"Whenever you're ready, that will be fine."

"Hi, Dr. Debbie!"

"Hi, Jacqueline. Jacqueline, we're taping this," I cautiously inform the alter.

"I know that, Dr. Debbie. I've been watching," she indignantly responds.

"Well, Jacqueline, if you've been watching, you know everyone is telling the Big Lady's attorney something about her situation. So what would you like for her to know?"

"I would like for her to know that I have helped the Big Lady manage her finances since she was $14^{1}/_{2}$. I did a very good job until recently. When we started therapy, our insurance company punished us the first year and only paid for five sessions."

I, unfortunately, also remember that fiasco!

"We have had to use our savings and our retirement. And it wasn't just the therapy. We also have a little problem with Jessica ordering everything she sees that's free. A sample comes, she and the little ones love it, of course. What child wouldn't love a book, or puzzle, or stuffed animal, or a Beatrix Potter set of videos? So, they order again. They keep sending things, and we keep sending them back. It's really exhausting. I would like to get my hands around the neck of whoever it was that taught Jessica how to use the Big Lady's Master Card. That was one big mistake!

"I know we owe you a lot of money, Dr. Debbie. The Big Lady hates to owe anybody. She is used to *giving* money, not *owing* money. Now, she doesn't even have enough to live on. We're going to have to move in with Nancy if we don't get some money soon. She would be really angry with me if she knew I told you, but she took cash advances on her Master Card to pay her rent. I know she was feeling desperate, but I don't know why she did that. She can't pay any of the advances back."

The finances are much worse than I thought—paying the rent with a charge card? I can't avoid this any longer. I must speak to Grace Ann, and soon.

"How can the lawyer help?" I ask.

"I hope this lady will help us to put our money back in savings, and pay off our therapy bill. And help the Big Lady to have money again. The Big Lady used to save a lot. I still help her as much as I can. I'm not going to desert her, but the money will only go so far."

"You're doing the best you can, Jacqueline. Please remember that. Something will turn up," I weakly console, for I, too, am at a loss at what to do to help. "Thank you for your hard work. I expect you will always help her."

"She needed my help, Dr. Debbie."

"Jacqueline, she still needs you. Remember that. You've been a very important part of her life."

"Thank you for telling me that, Dr. Debbie. I don't feel very important right now. I know how the Big Lady feels when she's hurting and she says, 'I'm a failure, failure, failure.' "

"Jacqueline, the Big Lady is anything but a failure. I admire her strength and courage. She is a success just because she keeps on, and each of you, each part of her, is a part of that success. I'm really sorry, but our time is running out. Could you slip on Strong Man Jesus' shirt, please?"

"Sure, Dr. Debbie. This is Strong Man Jesus' shirt," she reminds me as she removes the violet shirt from its hiding place at the very bottom of the bag. "He helps everyone."

"You know, I don't think you told us why everyone's name begins with "J."

"Strong Man Jesus will have to tell you that," she chides. "That's his job, not mine."

"Boy, we have a lot of shirts on."

"Love you, Dr. Debbie."

"Bye, Jacqueline, and thank you."

"5-4-3-2-1, may I speak with Strong Man Jesus?"

There is a surreal metamorphosis within the room. A peaceful countenance appears; a soothing, tranquil voice emerges.

"Hi, Deborah. They've really worked hard, haven't they?"

"Yes, Strong Man. I must admit it has been an interesting session. I hope the lawyer sees it and agrees to help. I just don't know, Strong Man. I just don't know. I don't know a thing about this lady. I hope she's trustworthy and respectful. Anyway, what can you add to this, this unusual session?"

"I would like for the attorney to know that I have been with Grace Ann since the beginning; actually, I knew her before she was born. I'm still with her today, even though right now she doesn't think so. She's very angry with me. That's O.K. I understand."

"I don't really understand why she's so angry," I respond.

"She doesn't understand why I let her go through all that pain. She doesn't realize I was with her, that I've never left her, that I would never leave her. I've been with her since the beginning, holding her hand, protecting her. I never wanted her to be hurt so badly. That was never my choice. I understand why she is so confused," he sighs. "Everyone she has ever loved has abandoned her—her mother and father, Mommy Francis, Jim."

Jim?

"You asked about the names. All the alters have names that start with 'J' because I, Strong Man Jesus, have been with them before they were born. I have been both father and mother, the only constant force in their lives. Some of the 'J's' are from the first foster family—Jennifer, Jacqueline, Jessica—from the happiest time of her life. Judas, Demon Judas, of course, was the result of her earliest spiritual teachings, and came about after she was violated by Father Stafford, someone she was supposed to be able to trust.

"I'm helping you every day because I know this has been hard on you, too. It's been hard on you both. Remember that I'm always with you, too. I hope one day, one day soon, Grace Ann will know in her heart that she has never been alone.

"You're doing a very good job, Deborah. Thank you for not turning your back on her. It would have been very easy to walk away from all this. No one would have blamed you if you had."

"Is there anything you would like from the attorney?"

"Only for her to help Grace Ann get some of her money back— at least enough to pay off her therapy bill. And perhaps enough to put money back into her savings and retirement. She's worked very,

very hard. I don't want her to have to work ninety hours a week again."

"She's worked very, very hard the last two years, too," I offer. "She just hasn't been paid for it."

"You've worked very hard, too. Mommy Francis asked me to pick you special," he serenely extends.

"You never told me that, Strong Man. Please tell Mommy Francis I'm doing the best job I can."

"She knows, Deborah. I don't have to tell her. She already knows."

I do not understand!

A bit of something is peeping from the supposedly empty bag. A closer look reveals yet another shirt, this one in neon yellow.

"What is this yellow shirt all about? Yellow is not one of your colors!"

"No, Deborah, yellow is not one of our colors, not yet, but someday soon Grace Ann will have sunshine in her life, perhaps for the first time. Everybody, all her separate parts, are going to heal and be healthy and whole. Grace Ann is not going to stuff her feelings anymore like she has for so many years. And Little Grace Ann is not going to rip off her toenails, and Judith is not going to tear her skin, and Janice is not going to be 'barrassed, and Jaqua is not going to take all those showers, and drink so much water, and wash all those clothes. And Grace Ann is going to have a new knee. Yellow is for sunshine, and she has never had sunshine in her life. But she will, soon."

"Well, with your help, Strong Man, we're on our way," is all I can think of to say.

I am comforted that I am not alone.

Grace Ann sends a detailed letter, several journals, the Child and Family Services records, and the tape to the lawyer she believes will be her savior. I also consult the lawyer, attempting to explain this strange and tortuous case as best I know how. In the end, she will only take the case if Grace Ann agrees to forward $5000.00 for an initial retainer. I attempt to intervene, but am told in no uncertain terms that I am guaranteed insurance reimbursement for at least a portion of my services, and that she deserves nothing less. Once again, one more time, Grace Ann feels betrayed by individuals in whose hands she has placed her fragile trust.

My Safe, Free Place

Several weeks following the futile taping, Grace Ann hands me a small pencil drawing and the following journal entry.

> i have realized that i have been escaping to my safe, free place on the prairie, with the green grass, sun shining, the pretty mountain. i escape and i am free. i have to tell Deborah. i am doing this all the time now. Why am i escaping to my safe, free place so much?

I wonder if there's room on this prairie for me?

The coming months usher in a bevy of internal activity. The mind's walls, previously cast of inpenetrable stone, crack, then crumble, and are at long last carried away by the warmth of freedom's healing winds. While not unhappy, Grace Ann, the Big Lady Grace Ann, is thoroughly perplexed. She is escaping to her safe, free place because the children, imprisoned no more, are having the time of their lives.

I prepare an audio tape of their favorite stories. *I Like Me* is the story of a persevering pig who likes her curly tail, round tummy, and tiny little feet, who greets the mirror each day with, "Hi, good-looking,"[67] brims with self-esteem and is relished by the younger children. *God Cares For Me When I'm Thankful*, (one of the "library books" purchased by Strong Man Jesus and Judas and inscribed with purple ink) typically reminds everyone of how far they've come. *United We Stand: A Book for People with Multiple Personalities* (donated by the shopping queen, Jessica) covers such topics as "Am I Crazy?" "Do I Have to Talk to My Inside People?" and, "Who Can I Tell?" *Stories for the Third Ear: Using Hypnotic Fables in Psychotheray* ("The Seedling: The Story for a Client Who Has Been Abused as a Child;" "Journey From A Frozen Land: The Story for an Obese Client;" and "The Little Elephant Who Didn't Know How to Cry: A Story for a Client with Borderline Personality Disorder") are read for Big Lady Grace Ann. However, the favorite, by far, is Adams' *The Silver Boat*, the story of a little girl with dissociative disorder and the lady of the blue light who teaches her, and us, to face the uncertainty of our own forest by reaching for the inner self-helper, the inner light, that resides within, and among us all.

As she sat crying under the tree, the little girl heard a very soft voice,

"Little Girl, why are you crying?"

The child looked up shyly and saw next to her a beautiful lady dressed in blue light. The lady seemed to be floating, for her feet did not quite touch the ground. While the little girl was surprised to see such a sight, she knew somehow that the lady was not a total stranger...I am a part of you, and I will always be with you. Any time you wish, you may wrap up in this light and rest. . .

"You must think of what you want rather than what you fear..."

At first the forest felt friendly. The child could hear little birds chirping in the trees, and the ground made funny noises as she went along her way. She was somewhat frightened, but she kept thinking of the bright and sunny land where the people were friendly. She thought of the mysterious lady who promised to help her through this difficult journey....The deeper the little girl went into the woods the darker it became. No soft blue glow lighted the path for her. Nevertheless, after some time in the dark, the child began hearing strange and scary noises. The girl became very frightened.

What am I going to do? she thought.

The words which the lady had spoken came back to her:

"You must think of what you want rather than what you fear..."

The children quietly made a circle, closed their eyes, traveled deep within, and wished for a plan. The blue light became brighter and brighter....The little girl quietly stepped into the the silver boat. She no longer saw the lady in the blue light, but she knew that she lived within her wise, strong self. [68]

Ann Adams (1990), *The Silver Boat*

Everybody wants to be out, all the time. Attempting to quell the din of confusion, to quiet the noises in Grace Ann's head, I contract with each alter for thirty minutes of "out time" each day. Judith sets the timer—Jessica regularly hides it. The Big Lady no longer loses hours on end. She can now schedule her day around the needs of her inside family. Everyone wins. Jessica, at last banned from the Master Card, is content with her coloring. Jaqua and Jacqueline begin with play dough, graduate to modeling clay, and eventually turn the kitchen oven into a makeshift kiln. Judas chooses to paint. Judith, fancying herself a budding artist, spends her limited time with a sketchpad. Each child recognizes her own blue light, her own inner-knower who is Strong Man, and works hard for the strength and wisdom hidden deep within.

Unfortunately, at least for Grace Ann, each alter loves coming to "Dr. Debbie's safe room." Time is precious. As trust grows, everyone wants a turn. Every session runs over its allotted time. While I try to spend a few minutes at the close of each session informing Grace Ann of the day's events, she often returns home more confused than ever, sometimes with fragmented memories, occasionally without a clue of ever having been to the office at all.

> Let's see, where has this day gone? [she writes, as she reclines in bed listening to Jessica's 'alaxation' tape, the pages of the beloved coloring book spread among the Mickey Mouse comforter's folds.]
>
> Well, I feel at peace, yet exhausted with a very bad headache. Let me see what I can remember about my session with Deborah today. I left my journal and three tapes for Deborah on the chair. Then there was a fourth tape I didn't remember putting in my book bag. It said, 'To Dr. Debbie's Professers.' It was printed in a block print, in pink ink. That puzzled me. The next thing I remember, Deborah was reading my journal. It seemed like she was reading forever, yet I knew I hadn't written very much....I asked Deborah what she was reading, because I knew I hadn't written much. She said, 'Jessica has written me a lot.'
>
> I told her I still don't understand all this. What happens to me when all these other parts of my personality take over?

Why can't I just go to my safe and free place without creating all these different names for different parts of my personality? Sometimes, actually most of the time, I just don't
understand.

Deborah told me she talked to Jessica. She has the big
job of keeping her 'aformed of everyone else's needs.
Deborah said, 'Jessica is just 6½, but she has never been
hurt, and she tries to help all the others out.'

I, Grace Ann, don't understand, but i'll trust her for now.
i just don't want her to send me to someone else. i'm so
scared she won't want to help me to heal anymore, because
i've been such a headache to her. i trust her more than
anyone….She's the only one I feel free to ask or tell her
things and she won't hurt or judge me.

The next thing I remember Deborah telling me is that
she spoke with Janice and that she is really shy. Deborah
said that she spoke with Demon Judas, I think he's just called
Judas now. I have no idea what that means. Anyway, she
said she is even going to help him heal . . .I hope she can do
that, but I don't even know who he is.

The next thing I remember her saying is that everyone
did a good job talking to each other during the session. She
told me it might help if I would get a bulletin board, put it
in the hallway, and give each alter or different parts of my
personality permission to leave notes to each other. She says
to give them permission to continue to talk to each other in
my journal, too. I have to trust her, even though I don't
understand any of this. I am so confused, I just want to go
to my safe place and stay there until this whole nightmare,
this insanity, is over. I wish I understood MPD, but I don't
and it frustrates me. I guess when I am ready to handle
things, Deborah will let me read as much as I can about
it…But i am scared…i am very confused.

*I note the mixture of the upper (underlined for emphasis) and lower
case I's, and am encouraged that Grace Ann is beginning to understand, at least intuitively, that the ability to dissociate, the condition*

that originally kept her from losing her mind, is no longer needed or even helpful, and is now pillaging her life.

The Town Crier

Jessica, the pseudo-self-helper and resident "Town Crier," presents for most sessions ready and willing to report on the group's most recent clandestine affair.

"I's be here, Dr. Debbie," is the familiar beacon call.

I am 'aformed of The Big Lady's whereabouts between our twice weekly meetings, whether she has 'ahaved or "bee's really, really bad." I hear of Little Grace Ann's midnight freezer raids, of the *half-gallons* of Breyer's ice cream, the *loaves* of bread, and the *boxes* of cereal she inhales in a futile attempt to alleviate the relentless pain of a desecrated childhood. I am told of Judith's night terrors, the bruises, blisters, and mouth ulcers that mysteriously appear after she has survived the latest sieved memory of events long past. I discover that the Big Lady "be really, really, shamed," because her now familiar financial insufficiency doesn't allow her funds to pay, or pay-on, the mounting therapy bill.

At this point, the mounting therapy bill is the least of our worries. I'm a great deal more concerned about basic life expenses. Is she able to afford the essentials? Is she going without and too proud to ask for help? I must be more aware of her life outside the treatment room. Heaven only knows what is really going on!

We enjoy stories of Janice's budding sexual curiosity, of the "berry cute boy she see'd," and the unexpected blush that steals its way across the Big Lady's bewildered cheeks at the chance encounter with an oblivious (thankfully) teenage boy. We hear of Little Grace Ann's exploits at the Mall, of her attempts to simulate Dumbo's ears by wildly flapping her crutches in the air while running in and out of the toy store. A sophisticated Judith attends a book signing, the object of which is to obtain a book for the Big Lady's birthday. Well, Judith is unfortunately not alone, for when her turn arrives at the author's desk, the internal family insists that the book be dedicated to them as well.

I can only imagine the look on that poor soul's face!

Judith opens the book cover, and sure enough, the book is dedicated to "Big Lady Grace Ann, Judith, Jessica, Judas, Jennifer." *What must he have been thinking? What did they tell him, the truth?* I surely hope he's not prone to panic attacks!

Jessica shuffles in with a video of The Big Lady's 'zaleas [azaleas] in tow. Popping the day's entertainment into the VCR, she proceeds to narrate, first to me, and then to the others who, though beyond the scope of my earthly vision, are evidently watching from within.

"…one color for everybody. See, Baby Joann, see Little Grace Ann. Here's a red one for Judith—two purple 'zaleas for Strong Man Jesus. Janice, this be your color. Janice be scared, but that be all right.

"Look, Janice, Strong Man Jesus be all around you…he be protecting you…you be all right. You can't be hurted no more if Strong Man be with you. You hear me, Janice?" She hands over the journal, as the chatter continues.

"Dr. Debbie, I underlines the big I's. Don't you think that's progress for the Big Lady? Doosn't that mean that her self-esteen is better?"

"I sure hope so, Jessica."

I fluff up the chair's cushions, open her journal and am amazed at the ceaseless drama within.

> Dr. Debbie, the Big Lady has a new feeling that she wants to ax you about. But she is 'barrassed to ax you. So maybe Janice can ax you…the Big Lady has the feelings and she not understand the new feelings. How you spose to talk to the Big Lady and splain what she needs the answer to, when she be to 'barrassed to ax you? Janice wants to talk to you to. How you gonna talk to both of them at the same time? You the therapiest, right? You hav to figure that out. That not be my problem, no ma'am, not be my problem at all.
>
> Dr. Debbie, Big Lady put the new tape that you readed to us in her little walkman with the ear phones. Well, the minute, the second, Little Grace Ann heared you reading to all of us, she says, 'I heared Mommy reading the storybook to me. I heared her voice reading to me but I not see her. Where she be? . . Where my Mommy be?'

Judith, copresent with a now annoyed Jessica, takes over the story.

Dr. Debbie, you should have seen her. She gets so excited that Mommy is reading to her, she runs all over the house looking in drawers and boxes, looking everywhere for her beloved Mommy. She's not crying anymore—that hurts our hearts so—but now we have a new problem. Little Grace Ann thinks that your voice is Mommy's voice. She is really excited. She kept telling us to play the tape of Mommy reading to her. She keeps asking to have it played over and over and over and over. Each time she asks to have it played, all of us together, including Jennifer, say, 'Little Grace Ann, Dr. Debbie wants to talk to the Big Lady.'

We tell her this over and over. All of us together tell her Dr. Debbie wants to, needs to talk to the Big Lady. We are all really worried about the Big Lady's leg. Little Grace Ann's knee does not hurt. She is a very active 3½-year-old with endless energy. She doesn't even use the Big Lady's crutches. She just runs throughout the house looking for Mommy. Finally, we get her to sleep at 4:47 a.m. We are all exhausted.

Then we really have a serious problem, Dr. Debbie. We cannot get Big Lady Grace back…Little Grace Ann is as stubborn as Big Lady Grace. She asks, 'Where Mommy be and who all those other names on the tape? Do they be the bad people? I not know them. Who they be?'

Dr. Debbie, it was us, but Little Grace Ann is so excited to hear what she thinks is Mommy's voice that she does not recognize us at all.

Big Lady is in her safe place the whole time…Little Grace Ann is so excited she gets herself wheezin' and has to use her inhaler…WE still cannot get Big Lady Grace back. Can you believe that, Dr. Debbie?

Every other time since you taught us how to get her back it has worked, but not this time. Little Grace Ann is out from 2:00 p.m. to 4:47 a.m. I thought I was going to have a nervous breakdown, chasing her all day and all night like that. Thankfully, she is not crying, just excited to hear your voice… I give up, and ask for Strong Man's help. He must know how tired I am, we all are, because he says, in a deep, firm voice, 'Little Grace Ann, this is Strong Man Jesus talking to you. We, Judas and I, need for you to go to sleep. It is Grace Ann's turn to be out now.'

I struggle not to burst out laughing as Jessica attempts to mimic Strong Man's directive.

I couldn't believe it, Dr. Debbie, but she doesn't listen to him either. I don't think she even hears him, she's so excited about hearing Mommy's voice.

After fourteen hours of this endless energy, bundle of joy, we tell her, 'Now listen, Little Grace Ann. Mommy is in a safe place called heaven, and one day you will see her again, but for right now, Strong Man Jesus and Judas, and all of us, are taking care of you.'

Finally, we are all very firm with her, because we are getting tired and we know when we finally get Big Lady back, she will have a terrible eyeache and a lot of pain in her hurt leg. Fourteen hours of Little Grace Ann's endless running around…She finally goes to sleep. Thank the Lord! We all do. We hope when she wakes up, we will have the Big Lady back. Guess who is awake and running to the bathroom, dragging the Big Lady's crutches behind her? You guessed it. Little Grace Ann. We all tell her while she is sitting on the toilet, 'Little Grace Ann, Dr. Debbie wants to talk to Big Grace now. RIGHT NOW!'

Wait a minute! Don't get me involved in this! For once I'm innocent!

No such luck. She's not listening to us. She is determined to find Mommy. Jessica tells Little Grace Ann, 'Little Grace Ann, you have GOT to take a shower, because you have to go and see the doctor today.'

Little Grace Ann asks, 'Are we going to see the nice lady doctor?' She thinks we are coming to see you, Dr. Debbie. So we tell her, 'No you are not going to see the nice lady doctor today. You will see her on Thursday.'

Grace Ann says, 'When Thursday be? I like that pretty lady.'

Dr. Debbie, Little Grace Ann is finally starting to trust you. Amen…Hallelujah! Well, Jessica has no luck with getting Little Grace Ann to take a shower. So Jaqua tries, because she has to be at the leg doctor's at 9:50 a.m. Little Grace Ann doesn't want to take a shower, she wants to take a bath. So Jaqua fills the bathtub for her, and puts the Mr. Bubble in the way she likes it. Well, she hops into the tub. Just hops in, Dr. Debbie! Just like that! We all cringe, because we know what is happening to Grace Ann's leg. She doesn't even sit in the Big Lady's tub chair. She doesn't even hold onto the tub rail. Remember, Dr. Debbie, she doesn't have a bad knee, the Big Lady does. Jaqua helps her wash her hair. She wants to play bubbles in the bathtub. She says, 'What this chair doin' in the bathtub? What this monkey bar doin' on the side of the tub? You not get yoos legs through that little bar! What that for?'

Well, Dr. Debbie, we all want to kill her, well, not really kill her, you know what I mean, but she has us all laughing so hard. She doesn't understand that Big Grace has a hurt left knee. It's not really her fault. So there she is, cute as she can be, sitting in the bathtub while Jaqua washes her hair. We try again to get Big Lady Grace back. No luck. Jaqua gets Little Grace Ann out of the tub, drys her off, and dresses her so we can go the doctor's office. Well, Dr. Debbie, you're not going to believe this. Jennifer and Judith take Little Grace Ann and dry and fix her hair pretty to go to the doctor. Then Jaqua helps her brush her teeth. While they are all doing these things to get her ready to see the doctor, Jessica is trying desperately to call you to ask you what we need to do to get the Big Lady back. Remember, she has to drive us to the doctor, because she is the only one who can drive.

What are we going to do? Judith asks.

So everybody has to get really firm with Little Grace Ann. She's had her bath, she's dressed and her hair is fixed, so now all together we say, 'LITTLE GRACE ANN. DR. DEBBIE NEEDS BIG LADY GRACE BACK RIGHT NOW TO DRIVE US TO THE DOCTOR'S OFFICE. LITTLE GRACE ANN, WE MEAN IT, RIGHT NOW!'

Good Lord, I never thought of that. Who drove anyway?

We're all getting really nervous, because we think Little Grace Ann is going to drive. We're not riding anywhere with Little Grace Ann driving, no way! I had to drive once, Dr. Debbie. I was really scared, but I did O.K., at least I think I did. I didn't wreck the Big Lady's car, so I must have done all right. I didn't tell her. I don't think she knows.

I make a mental note to contract with the group about the driving. It never occurred to me that Grace Ann, Big Lady Grace Ann, wasn't doing the driving. Yipes! That's downright scary!

Anyway, Little Grace Ann is standing by the door with her coat on when we finally get the Big Lady back. We all hear her say, 'Boy, do I have a terrible eyeache. Where are my crutches? My leg is killing me.'

Big Lady finds her crutches, and drives us to the doctor's office. We get there at 9:30 a.m. The waiting room is full of people. Big Lady Grace doesn't get called to see the doctor until 12:45 p.m. We have a long wait. All the time, Little Grace Ann keeps trying to come out, over and over. We cannot let her get out in front of all those people. We can't let her come out in front of the leg doctor either. She would throw those sticks, as she calls them, and what would he think. We are so tired, Dr. Debbie. All that babysitting is exhausting.

Dr. Debbie, we all keep the Big Lady out until we see the doctor, thank heavens. Whew! Then she drives us to the drug store to get some leg medicine. She asks the young man at the register (he was really cute, Dr. Debbie) where the leg medicine would be, because her leg is killing her, and she doesn't think she can walk all over the store.

We know why her leg hurts so badly, but we're not going to tell her. We sure don't want her mad at us! Anyway, he is really nice, and goes to get it for her.

Well, you're not going to believe this, Dr. Debbie. Hold on! Then she asks that young man where the sanitary pads are. The sanitary pads? Do you believe she did that, Dr. Debbie? He's not even old enough to know what sanitary pads are. But he says, 'I'll go get them for you so you won't have to walk over there.'

She is the only customer in the store and he has the time to help her. Well, guess who has been listening. Janice, 'barrassed Janice! When he comes back to the counter, Big Lady's face is red as a beet because Janice is so 'barrassed. Jacqueline tries to help, to get him away so he won't see how red Big Lady's face is. So, she asks him where the Silly Putty is, and when he finds that, she sends the poor young man to look for the Hershey's Hugs. We need to take the Hugs to Dr. Debbie, so she can have them to give to all the children. We like to take them to her office, since she taught us, most of us anyway, the difference between good warm hugs and bad touches.

Finally, Jacqueline pays the bill. You remember she always pays for us, don't you, Dr. Debbie? Then, FINALLY, none too soon for me, we get the Big Lady to the car and SHE (not me, Dr. Debbie) drives us all home. What a day!

Not to be outdone, Jessica fights her way through the fog, determined to add her impressions of the evening's events.

It be berry, berry dark, cold, berry windy out. Brrr! Dr. Debbie, we has a serious problem. Big Lady is laying on her bed with the blue ice on her eyes, 'cus her eyes hurted real bad and she not understand why they hurted so bad, 'cus she not amember what she did in therapy. She just not understand why she be so tired. Big Lady getted scared and her hart be beetin' realy fast. She really getted panicked. She be shakin' really bad. I maked her split so I can runned in the livin' room so I can get the new tape you maked for us. Now she be so scared she be wheezin.' I keeped telling her to take slow deep breaths, but she be wheezed so bad she has to use her 'nhaler. She put on that alaxation tape with the blue ice on her eyes. She listens to the alaxation tape five times afore she stopps shakin'.

My hart hurted so for her, Dr. Debbie. She be so scared. She not understand.

She starts to go to sleep on her bed, so I put the new tape in the 'corder. Well, the first story you readed, guess who we get? Little Grace Ann! Dr. Debbie, we has a serious problem, not bein' able to get Big Lady back. Judith says, 'Little Grace Ann, go lay on the bed so you can hear the new stories Dr. Debbie readed us.'

Then Little Grace Ann say, 'I not no Dr. Debbie, but I listen to Mommy readed the stories. Where Mommy be? I heared her, but I not see her. Where Mommy be?'

She keeped axin' the same question over and over, so we all tell her, 'We be taking care of you, Little Grace Ann. Just listen to the tape.'

Since we not getter Big Lady, we all asided to tell Little Grace Ann just to listen to the new stories. Finally, Dr. Debbie, she felled a sleep. She never cried, thank goodness. We hurted for her when she cries so hard. But now we has a new problem. She thinks Mommy readed the stories. She keeped saying, 'I wanna hered Mommy read more stories. Where Mommy bee'd? Where my special Mommy bee'd?'

So Strong Man Jesus and Judas says, 'Little Grace Ann, we all be takin' care of you. Mommy be in a safe place called Heaven and one day you will get to see Mommy again. We promise.'

Parently, Little Grace Ann doosn't bleve them, 'cause she says, 'I no that be Mommy readin' to Little Grace Ann, I want to hear Mommy readed the stories.'

Sitting back, I attempt to absorb the evening's events. Little Grace Ann thinks she hears Mommy Francis' voice on the tape I prepared before our last session, gets excited, and insists on "being out." Everyone else spends the night trying to run her down! I'm trying, unsuccessfully, to get a visual image of this fiasco in my mind! Jaqua washes her hair? Jennifer and Judith fix her hair? Jaqua brushes her teeth?

Shaking the cobwebs from my befuddled mind, I decide just to give up, for I will never fully understand this dissociative process. I choose, instead, to take the high road, to thank Jessica for taking the time to tell her version of the evening's events.

"Miss Jessica, I really appreciate you helping out with the story. I know how you hate to write, since Judith is constantly correcting your spelling. You did really well! There are only a few words I don't understand."

Foiled again!!!! Ever-compliant, Miss Jessica presents for the next session with none other than "Jessica's Dishunary."

Jessica's Dishunary

This Bee's the Personal Dishunary of Jessica, the Boss, 6$\frac{1}{2}$ years old. Judith and Big Lady, keep your Paws off. Judith, I is usin' your red pen. Just cus you always telled me to use the Webster's dishunary. I Not like Webster's and I telled you and telled you I not like Webster's, so now I goin to right my own dishunary agin cus you keep hidin the one's I rite. This deafineitly not bee'd for Judith and Big Lady to read, specially not you Judith. You always say to look it up in Webster's. He so stupid. He not nos how to spell the words. So now I even goin' to use your pen to git back at you Judith! So there!

Dishunary—a place where Jessica keeps the meaning of her words cuz i spells them the ways theys be sounded. This not be readed by Big Lady or Judith.

Alongs—this means it just alongs to the rite person who owns it. Anybody who owns somethin of there very own. It alongs to themselves.

Ahave—this bee's when bossy Judith yells at us "Be good, ahave." The opposit of being bad is to ahave.

[Alphabetical order appears to be out of the question!!!]
<u>Zalyea</u>-my pretty pink one that I planted with everbody is so bootiful. We hav our own colors that Judith help us all plant. Judith can be nice sometimes, cept when it comes to doin our home work and helpin Good Little Grace Ann 3½ to print neatly. Sometimes Judith is so bossey.

<u>Professors</u>—this bee's men and women whoo's goes to skool for one hundred years. They wares white startched shirts, black and grey suits. Some of them getted kind of old. They combes there hair from there left ears over there balled heads to there rite ears. It looks stupid. They look better balled. *[I can't wait for the folks at school to hear about this. There goes my doctorate right down the tube!]* Professors be berry smarted and use hugh words that you not no how to say let alone not no how to spell. I wanna bees smarted like Dr. Debbie one day, but to hav to go to those stiff, starchy professors scares me. I glad Judith will hav to bees the first one to goes. We watch how she doo's, then we acide *[decide]* if we gonna goes to Dr. Debbie's smart skool. Big Lady be smarted to. She be smarted in the medical field. I not wanna take care of people who throw up all over me. Yuh! *[yuck?]* I gonna be like Dr. Debbie who helps people to tell theys hurts and tells people it not be their fault, not they not be bad. I wanna help put sunshine in peoples life like Dr. Debbie doo's to all of us.

<u>Behive</u>—a ladys high hair do.

<u>Aleve</u>—to aleve someone when they bee's tellin' the truth bout someone or somethin. Like when we's tell the truth and Dr. Debbie aleves us.

<u>Pictshunary</u>—a game Judith and all smarted peoples play.

<u>Embelopes</u>—white thing what you mail bills in.

[It seems that Miss Jessica has decided to play nurse.]

<u>Artery</u>—the study of a nice paintin in a museum.

<u>Barium</u>—when someone dies and you put them in a box and put them in the ground.

<u>Benign</u>—what you bee's after eight.

This Bee's the PERSONAL

Dishunary of
(dishonary)

Jessica the Boss
6½.years old.

Judith and Big Lady

Keep Your Paws
off. Judith, I is using
(using)
your Pen. Just Cus.
you always tells me
to use The Websters.
Dishunary. I NOT

Cesarean Section—a city in Rome.

Colic—a sheep dog.

G.I. Series—baseball games between teams of soldiers.

Hangnail—a hook to hang your coat on.

Minor Operation—diggin' for coal.

Grubbs—thing you putted on in the winder times to keep peoples hands warm when it bee's cold out. *[Judith says:] Jessica you spelled it wrong. Look it up in Webster's.* How I posed to look up things when Webster's doosn't hav the words that sound like you say? Webster be stupid!

Begetables—things like peas, carrots, broccoli, tatoes, beets, onions, amatoes. There be bunches of them when you throw everythin together and make soup. We all like begetables.

Nosey—when you keeps your nose in other peoples stuff.

Stupeid—Anybody not a smarted as Judith and Dr. Debbie bee's. Like Webster's.

Doosn't —opposite of you doosit.

Noffin—when you gets noffin cuz you bee's bad.

Skool—a place where little people goes to learn bout thins in life. Then like Judith, Big Lady, and Dr. Debbie goes to big skools with big professors who havs lots of letters next to they name. They also bee's berry, berry smarted. I bet some of them bee's smarted but they doosn't hav common sents. Sometimes Dr. Debbie doosn't hav no common sents. *[I heard that!]*

Morbid—a higher offer to buy somethin.

Organic—a church musician.

Outpatient—a person who passed out.

Post-operative—a person who carries mail or letters.

Urine—opposit of your bein out.

Secretion—when you hide or keep anythin a secret.

Varicose Veins—veins that beee's berry close together.

Bra-ce-let—what you wear on your wrist.

Ba-zard—a big black bird.

Bandaid—when you brings aid to a band.

Agetted—when you doosn't amember somethin.

<u>Dairy Queen Ice Cream Cake</u>—what Jessica feeds to Little Grace Ann when she bee's cryin'.

<u>Hilfiger</u>—a figer of somebody standin on a hill. *[Where did that come from?]*

<u>Abreaction</u>—it bee's when the Big Lady gets a bruise, blister, 'cus one of us tell Dr. Debbie our therapiest somethin we's not sposed to tell.

<u>Therapiest</u>—a berry berry SPECIAL lady who bee's kind of like our Dr. Debbie. You luv your therapiest cus she bee's smart to help children whos' bee's sexually, verbally 'bused, ritually 'bused, bye the witches at the Big Hall. *[I note the script is becoming larger and disjointed. Someone else is with us.]* I not like mean people like them whos' hurts good little children.

I not like that office. It has not windows. It bee's too small. It stinks. It be berry, berry dark. We all hate the dark...

I getted off. A therapiest is the bestest people in the whole world.

Jessica, use your spell master, [chides Judith].

Mind your own business, Judith.

Back to my meanin of a therapiest. A therapiest is (Ha! Ha! Judith, you missed a word!) a nice person who teaches us the difference tween bad touch and good touch. N she teaches us the difference tweeen bad hugs and good warm carin hugs. The good hugs makes me feel all warm and fussy inside. I like gettin good warm hugs from Dr. Debbie and Dr. JoAnn, Dr. Delores, Dr. Sarah, and Dr. Nancy.

Back to my meanin of a therapiest. She bee's a person who reads children story's...nice story's, not bad witch type stories. I not like those witch stories. They be grosse. I like Dr. Debbie's stories that she putted on the tape so we can go to sleep at nite. Dr. Debbie's stories keep Little Grace Ann quite *[quiet]*. Back to what a therapiest bee's. She has to go to smart school to get smarted. Professor teacher's are even smartered than she bee's. She doesn't make me do lots of jobs like Judith.

Jessica, it's 8:00 p.m...Time to go to bed. After you read Little Grace Ann a story I'll read you one, [writes Judith.]

I not want you to read to me. I will read to Little Grace Ann, but I wants Jennifer or Janice or Strong Man Jesus to read us another Bible Story. Not you Judith, you always bee's so bossey.

Good night. I will rite tomorrow after I say my prayers. Strong Man Jesus alway says we hav to say our prayers afore we go's to sleep. Good night Strong Man Jesus, Judas, Jaqua, Baby Jenny, Baby Joann, Jennifer, Janice, Jacqueline, Big Lady, and you, Judith. I luv Dr. Debbie better'n you, Judith. Good night Dr. Debbie, Dr. JoAnn, and Dr. Debbie's professsers at the smart skool.

Dr. Debbie. Doo's you know (see Judith I spelleed no's rite) what agape luv bee's? Agape luv is unconditional luv. Like how Dr. Debbie bee's to us.

Signed, Jessica The Boss 6^1/$_2$

Jessica's Dishunary also includes a developmental chronology.

The Ages

<u>Baby</u>—Birf to five year old.

<u>Pre-teen</u>—6-12 years old.

<u>Teenager</u>—13 years old to 19 years. These bee's the worstest cus P.M.S. Whatever that bee's.

<u>Young Adult</u>—20 years to 30 years. Get married, hav a mad passion night of sex (Whatever that bee's).

<u>Antique Years</u>—31years to 50 years. This bee's where Dr. Debbie, Big Lady, Dr. JoAnn bee's... antiqued!

<u>Old Age</u>—51 years to 70 years. This bee's where Big Lady's friend Nancy bee's.

<u>Prehistoric Age</u>—This bee's where Miss Madeline and Mr. Hall [my parents] bee's...

<u>Monkey Age</u>—101 years to 200 years. I not no anbody [this] age.

The dishunary includes a bill as well. . .

Dr. Debbie, we all asided to send Big Lady a bill for us cus we coudn't get hold of you to help us getted Big Grace back. We all asided to charge Big Grace and Little Grace Ann. We worked hard. We aserve it.

To Little Grace and Big Grace:

Strong Man Jesus $65 x 29 hours	$1885.00	x	2
Jenny $65 x 29 hours	1885.00	x	2
Joann $65 x 29 hours	1885.00	x	2
Judas $65 x 29 hours	1885.00	x	2
Jaqua $65 x 29 hours	1885.00	x	2
Jacqueline $65 x 29 hours	1885.00	x	2
Janice $65 x 29 hours	1885.00	x	2
Jennifer $65 x 29 hours	1885.00	x	2
Jessica $65 x 29 hours	1885.00	x	2
Judith $65 x 29 hrs	1885.00	x	2
Grand Totals	$ 37,700.00		

Thirty-seven thousand, seven hundred! I would be willing to settle for the five thousand (and counting) unpaid therapy bills I don't expect I'll ever see!

Dodging the Details

Throughout our work together, Grace Ann and I begin to gather momentum, only to be set back, once again, with another tale of woe. Countertransference, simply defined as "my getting caught in Grace Ann's stuff," is my constant, if unwelcome, companion. It is only when I have been able to rise above the details, true or not, that meaningful change takes place.

First, there's Jim, the tale of love lost. Then we're bombarded with the False Memory Debate, accusations of dishonesty opening wounds not likely to heal.

Jim

Judith, beginning to trust, writes of an engagement to a hometown boy killed the week before his discharge from Vietnam.

...he was killed when [a] land mine blew up. I didn't want to believe it, three days before he was to come home. Why? I wouldn't believe it when Jim's mother told all of us. It hurt so bad, I couldn't even cry. I believe even then I went to my safe, free place. Then I stuffed the hurt with food and tried to make myself believe it wasn't true—but no more letters came. Two months later, two men dressed in uniforms came with a box wrapped in brown paper with his parents' name on it. They handed the box, a small box about the size of a shoe box, to Jim's parents. The men said, 'This was all that was found of his belongings.'

His mother opened the box with all of the family in the living room, including me. All that was in the box were his dog tags and an I.D. card. I was numb. I would not admit to myself that he was dead. But I never got another letter from him. I just packed it away in my closet. I kept telling myself maybe he was a P.O.W. The longer it got that I didn't hear from him, the more I worked and stuffed the lonely disbelief feelings. I gave back all the shower gifts. I sold my never worn wedding gown. We canceled everything. The hall where we were going to have the reception, they wouldn't give us back our money. Nor would the caterers give us our money back. The florist hadn't done the flowers yet. We had to call everyone and tell them the wedding was off and why. Everyone was so shocked. Many people told me Jim and I were made for each other.

After the memorial service, I worked longer and longer hours and kept eating. I packed away the whole experience. I never discussed it or dealt with it until today when Deborah asked me about it. I just packed it back in the back of the closet with all the rest of the hurts in my life. Today I cried over it for the first time since I packed it away. My diamond is at the bank. One day if I need the money I might sell it. But I guess there's still a ray of hope that he might be alive.

Deborah said, 'I've been working with you for a long time, and you never mentioned this to me.'

It was me, Dr. Debbie, me, Judith. I was the one who was engaged to Jim. The Big Lady hardly knew him. The Big Lady doesn't like boys, but I do. It hurt my heart.

It hurts my heart, too.

The False Memory Debate

A consult is arranged with Dr. Gentry. This is just too much. No one person could possibly have gone through this much abuse. First her father, then her foster parents, then, of all things, a cult? And don't forget the priest, Father Stafford. I'm beginning to think she relishes her victim role, and wears her pain well. Dr. Gentry, incredulous as well, agrees. I discuss with her the emerging theory of the False Memory Syndrome, and agree to forward the most recent research into the "syndrome." As usual, her parting words are, "Hang in there, Deborah!"

I never remember feeling so lost, or so sad.

The phrase False Memory Syndrome is permeating the dissociative literature. Hopeful at last that I can couch this God-forbidden tale within some sort of theoretical framework, I search for data on this enigmatic syndrome, and settle upon the following:

In an apparent attempt to quell the "Kafkaesque eeriness" enveloping trauma and memory, *The Family Therapy Networker* devotes a significant portion of its September/October 1993 edition to the False Memory Debate. "The Seductions of Memory" cautions the trauma therapist to stay clear of "suggestive procedures," insistent questioning and encouragement to "confront your past." "Facing The Truth About False Memory," presents an opposing view of the "syndrome,"[69] as it has now come to be known. It defends the therapist *(thank God someone does!)*, insisting the controversy has surfaced due to a basic misunderstanding of the nature of therapy. There are bad therapists who practice bad therapy, but they are far from the norm. What would be the purpose in implanting memories? There's no economic pay-off! There's nothing special about being a trauma survivor. There's always pain and often shame—a stigma they wear like some misguided badge of honor.

I certainly agree with this perspective. I see no benefit to this work. It is nerve-wracking, tedious, never-ending, and catastrophic finan-

cially. No one in his right mind would choose to spend his days doing this!

The Shadow of a Doubt introduces the False Memory Syndrome Foundation (the grass-roots organization comprised of accused family members and disbelieving professionals), and presents the current theories surrounding the debate. While included are Gardner's references to alleged victims as angry paranoids, and Ganaway's view of the accuser as an individual involved in a delayed adolescent rebellion, it is the reference to Loftus' work that catches my eye. Loftus rises above the issue's emotionality—she does not become embroiled in the debate. I'm impressed! As an authority on cognitive processes and eyewitness memory, she suggests that memory, like anything else, is subject to "inaccuracy, fabrication, confusion and alteration." She cautions that in accepting "all repressed memories as literally true," professionals inadvertently harm those who have been the victims of childhood sexual abuse.[70]

I can understand Loftus' view. I breathe a sigh of relief, for I have not *even once* introduced the concept of abuse or persisted in a line of questioning regarding Grace Ann's allegations. Frankly, I am pleased to find some, even remotely plausible, explanation that will extract me from the emotional hot seat. Hearing these stories, session after session, has taken its toll!!! I ceremoniously (and sanctimoniously?) prepare my conversation with Grace Ann. This is logical. This makes sense. This will help her to feel sane.

Our next session arrives. Grace Ann listens politely to my stammering explanation. I'm troubled, for I fear she will assume I'm challenging her credibility. She contributes no alternative interpretation, so I believe she agrees with my assessment.

Then, two days later…

Ever the underdog, I am presented with an exquisite, but unusually cut diamond (alleged by the client to have been purchased by her fiancé in Thailand), a yellowed McCall's sewing pattern of a wedding gown, circa 1968, and a series of wedding cards inscribed, "To Grace Ann and Jim."

She then produces (from the bottomless, now dreaded canvas bag) a baptismal certificate and a newspaper clipping, and proceeds to cross-reference the date and diocese of her confirmation with the dates and service location of the now convicted priest. And finally, to my utter and scarcely contained horror, she presents me with a photograph, dated the previous month, taken outside of my office. The snapshot is of a black hearse, equipped with the license plate, "To Die 4," issued from a state some one thousand miles away. Staring malevolently into the camera is a straggly-haired, grey-bearded, unkempt man with a scornful countenance and cold, cold eyes. As the icy chills run up and down my spine and nausea shrouds my now hypervigilant body, I appreciate, within the eye of my understanding, what it means to have "safe eyes."

Within the week, I contact the local police. This photo is just too much. I'm not willing to risk Grace Ann's safety, nor mine, if the dark side is indeed lurking. A plain-clothes officer arrives at the appointed hour, bearing a large cardboard grocery box filled with "evidence." I am shown the journal of an alleged satanic worshiper, along with a satanically emblazoned jacket of a young man purported to have been mysteriously killed the previous summer. I'm informed of two local cults under surveillance by the authorities, and am shown Polaroid photographs of ritual gathering sights. The dreadful box also contains police photos of dismembered animals arranged in sacrificial patterns. I am told by the officer that he himself has ceased "this work" due to physical threats (phone calls, beheaded birds placed on the hood of his car, satanic literature postmarked from distant addresses) to his family and himself. I'm advised to be cautious, not only of those unknown, but of the client as well, as individuals "programmed" at an early age generally report back to the cult. I'm admonished to install an office security system, to arrange for an unlisted number, to move my locked car to a lighted area as dusk descends, and to be careful.

A friend brings a key chain with pepper spray, insisting that I go nowhere without it. Emotionally torn, I reluctantly entertain the possibility that a dark side really does exist, that I may indeed be bargaining with evil.

A Turning Point

Upon reflection, I realize that I have "known" Strong Man for a very long time. He has never officially introduced himself as Grace Ann's Inner-Knower or Spiritual Center. I, in my naivety, assumed The

Party Girl held that distinction; after all, she did call herself The Boss, and I believed her! That stinker!

Since the day of our first meeting, Grace Ann has emphatically declared, "Deborah, I need to work on my spiritual journey!"

I dismissed her request as inconsequential in the light of her severe pathology. I only followed Strong Man's lead begrudgingly, primarily because he obviously knew far better than I the needs of the internal band. Without even being aware of it, I have learned to defer to his wisdom and guidance. I find myself looking forward to his presence, ostensibly due to the therapeutic information he can convey, i.e., the details of the day's happenings or the level (and origin) of someone's pain. In all honesty, I am comforted by his support and encouragement for my struggle, and feel a sense of peace when he "appears." As if intuiting my discomfort, my own sense of abandonment, Strong Man's letters begin to arrive.

Dear Dr. Debbie,

Grace is very scared. She's received seven phone calls from one person and two from another reminding her that October 31st is the feast of All Hallows. She, Grace, will not answer anymore calls when the caller ID says "unavailable." She's been doing her Spiritual Journey. She reaches deep within, and says, 'Strong Man Jesus, Mommy and Daddy, please just hold me.'

She does this every time she doesn't know how to handle a situation. She's trying to create a safe place by asking me and Mommy and Daddy just to hold her...She doesn't understand anything that's going on. She is so fearful. She hates this month and just wants it to be over. She wants to go forward and get healthy. Please, Dr. Debbie. Help her! I have so much planned for you.

                                   Strong Man Jesus and Judas

To Dr. Debbie from Strong Man Jesus and Judas,

What is ritual abuse?

Betrayal is too kind a word to describe a situation in which a father says he loves his daughter, but claims he must teach her about the horrors of the world in order to make her a stronger person, a situation in which he watches his own daughter, and he participates in rituals that make Little Grace Ann feel like she is going to die. Little Grace Ann experiences pain so intense that she cannot think, her head spins so fast she cannot know who she is or how she got there.

All Little Grace Ann knows is pain. All she feels is desperation. She tries to cry out for help, but soon learns no one will listen. No matter what she does the pain will not stop. No matter how loud she cries, Little Grace Ann can't stop or change what is happening. [They] order her to be tortured and they tell her that she needs the discipline, or that she has asked for it by her misbehavior. Betrayal is too simple a word to describe the overwhelming pain, the overwhelming loneliness, and the isolation Little Grace Ann experienced.

As if the abuse during the rituals at the Big Hall [wasn't enough], Little Grace Ann experienced similar abuse at home on a daily basis. When she tried to talk about her pain to Father Stafford, she was told she must be crazy. He told her, 'Nothing bad has happened to you. You must have had a bad dream or watched a horror movie.'

Each day as the pain and torture gets worse, she begins to feel more and more like she doesn't know what is real. Little Grace Ann stops trusting her own feelings because no one else acknowledges them or hears her agony. Soon the pain becomes too great. She learns not to feel at all. She is robot-like. This lonely, desperate Little Grace Ann starts to give up the senses that make all people feel alive. Little Grace Ann begins to feel as though she is dead. Sometimes she wishes she were dead or that Mommy [or] Daddy would come and rescue her. For Little Grace Ann there is no way out. She soon learns there is no hope. As Little Grace Ann grows older, she learns to do what she is told with the utmost compliance. Little Grace Ann forgets everything she ever wanted, except the loving, nurturing care Mommy [and] Daddy gave her. No one could take those very precious memories and the love they gave her and showed her through their eyes. They loved her dearly. When the social worker took Little Grace Ann from their house, she and they cried much. They always wondered what happened to her. She was daily in their thoughts and prayers.

Little Grace Ann never let go of those precious memories. Her biological father took her virginity from her when she was just eleven months old. The painful life she lived still lurks, but it is easier to pretend it is not there than to acknowledge the horrors she has buried in the deepest parts of her mind. Any friends or relationships are overwhelmed by the power of her emotions. Little Grace Ann reaches out for help, but never seems to find what she is looking for. The pain continues to get worse. The loneliness sets in when any feelings return. She is overwhelmed with panic, pain, and desperation. She is convinced she is going to die. Yet, when she looks around her, she sees nothing that should make her feel so bad. Deep inside her she knows something is very, very wrong, but she doesn't remember anything. Grace Ann thinks, Maybe I am crazy.

Grace Ann creates a safe place within her mind. She goes to the prairie where the grass is green. There are mountains that reflect the cloudless blue sky. She is running free....

A cult is a group of people who share an obsessive devotion to a person or an idea. Many cults use violent tactics to recruit, indoctrinate, and keep members. Ritual abuse is best defined as the emotionally, physically, and sexually abusive acts performed by family members and by other cult members. Most violent cults DO NOT openly express their beliefs and practices, and they tend to live separately in non-communal environments to avoid detection.

Little Grace Ann, like some other victims, was abused outside of the home by non-family members….Little Grace Ann needs to tell what [they] did to her….Some adult ritual abuse victims often include grown children who were forced from childhood to be a member of the group or cult. Some other adults and teenagers are people who unknowingly joined social groups or organizations that slowly manipulated and blackmailed them into becoming permanent members of the cult. ALL cases of ritual abuse, no matter what the age of the victim, involve intense physical and emotional trauma.

Violent cults, such as the one our biological father and foster parents belonged to, performed sacrifices as part of religious rituals. They used torture to silence Grace Ann and others unwilling to join or participate. Ritual abuse victims like Grace Ann feel they are degraded and humiliated and are often forced to torture, kill, and sexually violate other helpless victims. The purpose of the ritual abuse is usually indoctrination. This cult intended to destroy these victims' (like Grace Ann) free will by undermining their sense of safety in the world and by forcing them to hurt others.

A number of people have been convicted on sexual abuse charges, such as Father Stafford and her biological father. In most of these cases of sexual abuse, there were also reported elements of ritual child abuse. Grace Ann could and needs to tell about being raped by groups of adults who wore robes, costumes, and some even masks. She was forced to witness religious type rituals in which animals were tortured or killed. Grace Ann was told she killed other children. She did not, yet they brainwashed her into believing she did.

The Big Hall had secret tunnels etched with upside down crosses and pentagrams. There were stone and marble altars and candles in a make-believe cemetery where rituals occurred.

Some people suggest that the tales of ritual abuse are just myths and mass hysteria. However, what Grace Ann lived through was no myth. She survived it with my help, Strong Man Jesus, and all the other alters who took the pain of the different rituals. It was so painful, physically, emotionally, and spiritually for her, that these alters were created within her mind. Her first alter is Jenny, eleven months old, the next is Joann, fifteen months old. Her biological father raped her and stole her virginity from her. I kept her fighting to live. I have great things in store for her once she is whole and healthy. However, she has much to tell, as do all the alters, before I can use her for my glory.

Along came Jessica $6^{1}/_{2}$. She was never hurt. Her foster parents had a baby boy thirteen years after their daughter was born. They were very disappointed that it was a boy, as they wanted a girl to use as a breeder. They made Grace Ann $6^{1}/_{2}$ care for the child. She was only $6^{1}/_{2}$ and knew nothing about the care of a baby. So Jessica took over and helped her care for [the new baby boy]. Jessica is the part of Little Grace Ann who is happy-go-lucky, playful, loves to meet new people. She is a joy and the very fun-loving part of Grace Ann. However, her heart hurts and she will cry when Little Grace Ann, Judith, or any of the other alters relive something painful in therapy.

It appears he, or He, turns to address the system within, as if to reassure the younger children.

Dr. Debbie has taught the older ones to screen. Little Grace Ann does not understand how to do screening. Sometimes some of the other alters start to relive the pain. However, Dr. Debbie is sensitive and has the wisdom to discern this and will stop them so they don't have to relive the pain. Dr. Debbie is very good at knowing how far to push each alter and when to stop.

There is another alter that came about before Jessica. It was Demon Judas. He was always told how bad he was and believed it. He took the pain for Little Grace Ann when [they] took a very hot fireplace poker and put it up her vaginal area. Until Dr. Debbie told him he was never bad, and it wasn't his fault, he tried to scare Dr. Debbie. At first she was even scared of him, but she had the wisdom to work with him and now he is just Judas. Since Demon means bad, he knows now he was never, never bad. He helps Dr. Debbie and me.

Judas, not Demon Judas, continued to take a lot of the physical, emotional, [and] spiritual pain for Grace Ann until Halloween of 1957, when they performed a special ritual done only on Halloween to young girls to get them to join. Grace Ann could not take the pain. It was so excruciating that Jennifer was created. She absolutely hates Halloween. Well, they all hate Halloween. They put their little legs up in stirrups and scrape[d] out their vaginas with serrated spoons. They all hate Halloween because of the different rituals that were performed before a young lady started her monthly menstrual cycle. Once she starts her menstrual cycle, another type of ritual occurs. It is very painful; they take blood from the vagina and put it in a cup and all drink it. To backtrack a little, when infants are given their bottles, they mix formula milk with blood so the children will get accustomed to the taste of blood. This started with her real birth father and aunt who lived with her parents to help with the children while her mother worked in the garment factory.

Dr. Deborah, I want to tell you I will be there with you helping Grace Ann through those horrible hurts. Watch her eyes and all of her body movements. Keep pushing her until she tells you about all those hurts. She needs to tell at least one person about them so those earliest hurts can start to heal. Once she works through those hurts, she'll then have to tell you the rest. She has many hurts she has stuffed inside and told no one. She'll try many times to change the subject. Just keep her with each hurt. I know at times she has been frustrating for you, but she is a fighter, and you and she will win. This will be your most rewarding patient. At present, she is very confused and frustrated. She has a big fear you will send her away. Keep re-assuring her no one will ever hurt her again. She fears people touching her, except, when you taught her the difference between a warm good feeling of a good hug from a bad touch. Later when you think she's ready, maybe send her to a massage therapist, but make sure she is ready for it.

I am with you always when you work with your patients, not just Grace Ann, but all your patients. She named me "Strong Man Jesus." If you will notice, she named each member of her inside family after me. Everyone's name begins with a "J." That is because I have been with each of them all along. I held each child's hand at birth, granted, it was a horrible birth, but a birth nonetheless. Each child knows me personally. Grace Ann knows me, too, but she has just forgotten. She cannot feel me because of her pain. She thinks I abandoned her. I never did. I never will.

Strong-Man Jesus
Holding 11 Month old

The Handiwork
of God

Grace-Ann's hand
When her real father raped her

I've just finished reading letters from someone who calls himself, or Himself, Strong Man Jesus. Strong Man Jesus! I can't wait to share this tidbit with my colleagues. What will they think of me then? They are already wondering about my sanity. I have no doubt this will push them, and me, over the edge.

I attempt to hide in humor, but it provides no refuge.
I'm lost.
I look outward for answers. There are none.
I'm desperate.
I have no choice but to turn within.
No choice at all…

Lost and Found

Wasted Time?

The world tells me I'm wasting my time,
      watching these children grow.
But anyone who has ever
      tied a shoe,
      or wiped a tear,
      or shared the wonder of nature with a child
      knows,
      in a way the world can never comprehend
That this
      wasted time,
These days of self-discovery,
Are the very foundation upon which all future
      accomplishments draw
          for strength,
             direction,
                and purpose.

Deborah Berkley
1981

CHAPTER SIX

Have I been wasting my time? I remember thinking I had, many years ago when, although conflicted, I chose to leave a career I loved to become a full-time mom. I asked this question then. I'm asking it again now. Am I choosing well? Can the world comprehend this, this strangeness? Are these, once again, days of discovery? Will this experience with Strong Man, whomever he, or He, may be, provide "…the very foundation upon which all future accomplishments draw,

for strength

direction

and purpose?"

Have I been wasting my time?

———◦·▪◦◦———

Who, or *what*, is this Inner-Knower, this purveyor of veiled wisdom? Is he, Strong Man as we have come to know him, just another fragment of a demented mind, or the gateway to a transcendent Presence behind the mystical veil?

The case of Anna O. portrayed this internal self-helper "as a clear-sighted and calm observer [who sat], as she put it, in a corner of her brain [looking] on at all the mad business."[71] Some attribute the internal self-helper with an exceptional intelligence, while others suggest it, whatever *it* may be, possesses both a transcendental capability and a capacity to heal. Some doubt it even exists. The truth is, no one knows. I find myself mulling over this concept of the illusive self-helper as I embark upon my daily walk, for I am learning to take walks, lots of walks. Our tiny office is located on The Boulevard, a majestic sweep of pavement meandering through the heart of the city's mimosa-lined historic district. A visitor strolling through its idyllic setting is greeted with vistas of noble verandas on splendid turn-of-the-century homes, verdant lawns, and tranquil, soul-sweetening secret gardens. Early morning strolls are the best, for these undisturbed, as yet uncluttered, early hours serve to *ground* the troubled thinker. It is on days such as these that I struggle to find a semblance of order in this most unordered chain of events. Psychology tells me that as individuals we seek to categorize our experiences in an effort to give them meaning. Well, this *experience* has no meaning. How can this be? *Am I just wasting my time?* I have an alter, a gentle, welcoming soul, guiding the therapy. When I am willing to step aside, to suspend my well, perhaps overly, developed ego, I can *hear* his wisdom and *know* his peace. On the other hand, when I plow ahead, certain that I know what is in Grace Ann's best interest, I fall fully upon my now much bruised and wounded face. I am not scolded by Strong Man, but softly chided, gently reminded that if I would only listen, only trust, discernment would be mine.

My rational mind will simply not support this mystical encounter. I have no category for a Strong Man Jesus. It, or he, just does not fit. I reluctantly acknowledge that I am faced with a challenge far greater than any I have ever known. I can't *think* my way out of this one, heaven only knows I've tried. I have no choice but to turn within, no choice but to surrender. I have no choice but to let go....

All paths lead to a deeper, more profound center. The contemplative walks are soon to be augmented with a long overdue return to the daily practice of meditation. As I gaze inward, the world, the world I have known, takes on a sublime value, an unlikely hue. The scarlet-throated daffodil, the blazing sunset, and even the subtle wind whispering through the lacy branches of the beloved weeping cherry tree are somehow brighter, more radiant, more alive. An ethereal glow, for I do not know how else to describe it, surrounds the strangers I meet. I *experience* Strong Man's "peace that passeth all understanding," recollect similar instances of this *celestial comprehension*, and ponder upon my own circuitous spiritual journey.

In my mind's eye, I *see* myself in the white clapboard church of my youth, a gawky, shapeless adolescent with unsightly braces and unfashionably wavy, shoulder-length hair. I observe this insolent teen, sparring with her junior high Sunday school teacher, who just happens to be my Uncle Harris, over the New Testament's relevance within the chaos of a 1960s world. I like going to church, because I like to debate—and I almost always win. *Thinking back, I wonder if I really do win, or if Uncle Harris, far wiser than I, just lets me think I do. Was there an inner-knower, an internal source of wisdom in him, too?* I, like the others, partake in the sacrament of Christian baptism. I, like the others, receive a leather Bible *(mine red)*, which, upon high school graduation, I promptly place on a shelf, out of sight, and most certainly out of mind.

As the inner journey continues, I discover that not all awareness is bliss. I am, in *the eye of my understanding,* now a young mother, torn between the love of a child and a world that tells me *I'm wasting my time*, that I should return to the fast track, the world of achievement and competition, my world. My *celestial comprehension* takes on a decidedly hellish chill, as I am unwillingly drawn back to my own period of unabashed despair, a time, now long ago, when I, as Grace Ann, knew endless days of darkness. I *feel* those days of hopelessness, days when I seek solace in the teachings of my childhood, the only certainty, or truth, I have ever known.

I search for that old Bible. In the dusty cobwebs of my mind, I recall when in the midst of my own life-altering depression I had, in a dire attempt to retain my own hastily unraveling strand of sanity, scribbled within its pages what were to become well-worn affirmations of encouragement and faith. In fading, age-splotched ink, I find testaments to my own fear and discouragement, and feel as if I am returning to the embrace of an ever-present but long-neglected friend. Once again, Barclay speaks to me:

> …when Christ is there, the storm becomes a calm, the tumult becomes a peace, what cannot be done, is done, the unbearable becomes bearable, and men [and women] pass the breaking point and do not break. To walk with Christ will be for us also the conquest of the storm.[72]

The tattered, gold-embossed end page reaches out to comfort my hollow soul. I find from Philippians:

Have no anxiety about anything, but in everything by prayer and supplication with thanksgiving let your requests be known to God. And the peace of God which passes all understanding will keep your hearts and minds in Christ.[73]

An excerpt from the Gospel of Luke offers:

Ask and it will be given to you, seek, and you will find, knock, and it will be opened to you. For everyone who asks, receives, and he who seeks, finds, and to him who knocks it will be opened.[74]

And, written in a bold, determined script, as if emanating from the depths of my unconscious, from the wellspring of all knowing, I read from John: "...and you shall know the truth, and the truth shall set you free."[75]

The back cover of this now pitiful volume is attached by a single thread of a twine-like binding. Once positioned, upright if not intact, I discover a remnant from *The Confessions of St. Augustine*, and *feel* the mystic's presence as I once again devour:

What is man?

Can any praise be worthy of the Lord's majesty? How magnificent is His strength! How inscrutable His wisdom! Man is one of Your creatures, Lord, and his instinct is to praise You. He bears about him the mark of death, the sign of his own sin, to remind him that You thwart the proud. But still, he is part of Your creation, he wishes to praise You. The thought of You stirs him so deeply that he cannot be content unless he praises You, because You made us for Yourself, and our hearts find no peace until they rest in You.[76]

Why do I feel so calm?

Etched along the margin, an unlikely Tolstoy offers, "Where love is...God is."

Jung declares, "I don't believe in God...I know God."

And from Dante, "His will is our peace."[77]

I realize the words that sustain me come not from my own ego, but from a source far greater than I, for like Barclay, Luke, John, St. Augustine, Tolstoy, Jung, Dante, and countless others before me, I, too, struggle with the appropriateness of my path. It is only in surrender that my answers come, never from an intellectual knowing, but from a higher consciousness, an as yet undiscovered realm. I have no choice but to relinquish the *illusion* of control, no choice but to get out of my own way. Continuing my reluctant mission, I search through yellowed, mildewed boxes, testaments to an earlier life. My memory is jogged as I unearth early literary attempts, autobiographical pieces, poetry, and children's stories, some published, some not, most from this *era of darkness* I have chosen not to remember. Unsuspecting tears stream down my cheeks as I read from my first article, "Neither Forsaken Nor Forgotten," when, in the utter depths of despair, I question, as Grace Ann must, where God hides when we're in pain.

I peruse a second aging magazine, only to uncover a poem written in an apparent tribute to both my young son and my hard-fought understanding.

O Child of Mine

O child of mine,
If only I could stop your pain
The pain of insecurity,
    awkwardness,
    inferiority.
The pain of forever measuring your worth,
   your abilities,
    through someone else's eyes.

O child of mine,
Let me tell you of God and His love.
You will never conquer your fears, but
    His love in you can—will.

O child of mine,
Live for God, not for man.

Then, only then, will your accomplishments,
        whatever they might be,
            be worthy of you and your potential.
Only then will you find peace.

O child of mine.

I knew this then. What happened to my knowing? When did I lose my way?

———◆›❀‹◆———

The meditations continue. Along the path of my inner wanderings, I encounter an immense shimmering silver cord, an ambiguous strand whose singular purpose seems, at least to my mind's eye, to link one life event to another. At various points along the free-floating cord, I am rewarded with fleeting snapshots of past moments which, upon review, I *understand* categorize my life in such a way that I am afforded a clarity of spirit. I pause to reflect upon the curious wonder of "a mother's intuition," that uncommon genius for insight we women treasure in the depths of our soul. What is its source? Our individual humanity? Jung's "collective unconscious?" A latent but ever-present wisdom that resides within, and among us all? We *know* when our child is approaching danger. We *know* when he is in need of our nurturing care. *Nothing* can convince us otherwise. I smile inwardly as I reflect upon all those times I have said, "I don't know how I know, I just know," only to be met with "You're weird, Mom!"

I remember instances of long distance awareness, someone in pain, a loss, a death, a feeling of dread that something, somewhere, is not as it should be. I shake my head as I recall *seeing* my younger son lose his wallet while on an elementary field trip, some two hundred miles from home. Upon meeting the tired youngster at day's end, I ask, without a second thought, if he made it O.K. without money, for I am genuinely concerned that his stomach may be empty, and this much anticipated outing ruined. Perplexed, he tilts his little blonde head in a show of exasperation and exclaims, "Who told you? It wasn't my fault, Mom! Honestly it wasn't."

I *observe* that I seem able to wordlessly intuit others, especially my clients, often *knowing*, at some level, the issue at hand prior to entering the therapy room. What is this higher level awareness? This subjective comprehension? This world of multi-sensory perception? Am I, as my son has suggested, *really weird?* These questions lead me through yet another gossamer portal, into, or rather back to a time of dis-ease, when guilt-plagued over a senseless life choice I had foolishly made, I begin to suffer from debilitating migraines. Desperate to find relief, for the well-intentioned medical community has not been forthcoming and I can no longer subsist on a diet of Fiorinal with Codeine, I seek out our area's only alternative healer, a Buddhist chiropractor. While I relish the stress-relieving manipulations, the real blessing comes in his teachings, for during our brief time together I am introduced to both the healing art of Reiki and the natural world of Edward Bach.

I recall driving the forty-five minutes to his office, my head pounding so badly my vision is distorted and nausea threatens to turn me back. Sensing my unrelenting pain, he closes the blinds as I struggle to lie down, now dizzy and disoriented by the throbbing anguish. Silently, he cradles my head in the palm of his hand, while, in the stillness of the room, he bows his head and waits, simply waits. In a matter of minutes I am pain-free, and feel as if I am suspended in mid-air as I experience healing warmth embracing my head and radiating throughout my neck and shoulders. It is much later before I am to understand his position as a Reiki Master, that he has directed the healing energy of the universe through his hands and into my pain. At the conclusion of the anonymous Reiki treatment, a chiropractic assistant enters the profoundly tranquil room and proceeds to "do a Bach reading." I watch with mounting skepticism as four of the thirty-eight remedies are prescribed. Examining the small brown apothecary bottle, I notice the handwritten label, which now reads, "Centaury, Gentian, Oak, and Walnut." I am advised to place three to four drops of the personalized prescription under my tongue at six-hour intervals. The assistant then hands me a list of affirmations, which I am instructed to repeat throughout the day. The "homework" consists of:

"My task is only to be found within myself."

"I believe in an ultimate success."

"Everything has a deeper meaning."

"Joy will yield strength."

"I am only following my own inner guidance."

As strange as this all seems, I still have no pain. On the way out of the office, I notice *Bach Flower Therapy: Theory and Practice*, and purchase a copy for no other reason than to soothe my burgeoning curiosity. Settling in with a mug of hot chocolate, I learn of Dr. Bach. As an English physician, Bach presided over a lucrative medical practice. Disenchanted, at the age of forty-three, he leaves the world of traditional medicine to explore the relationship between spirituality and disease. Believing divine healing to be our birthright, Bach writes:

> Disease is solely and purely corrective; it is neither vindictive nor cruel, but is the means adopted by our own souls to point out to us our faults, to prevent our making greater errors, to hinder us from doing more harm, and to bring us back to the path of truth and light from which we should never have strayed. [78]

Dis-ease, in Bach's view, is the consequence of disharmony. Healing occurs, not through external applications, but rather through reversing internal energy blockages. Therefore, Bach practitioners do not diagnose on the basis of physical symptoms, but on the disharmony in the patient's soul. *I find this an utterly foreign concept, the antithesis of all I have been taught.* Confused, I forge ahead, and am consoled to read that I am not alone in my disbelief, for to date no one knows how the Bach Flower Therapies work. I discover it is accepted that the remedies, the distilled essences of flowers, increase the subtle energy vibrations and open the individual to his own, ever present, but unrecognized, spiritual self. I am told the essences address the negative soul states which, if not treated, will result in physical illness. *(In my case we appear to be too late!)* In referencing the essences, Bach writes:

> They are able, like beautiful music or any glorious uplifting thing which gives us inspiration, to raise our very natures, and bring us nearer to our souls and by that very act to bring us peace and relieve our sufferings. [79]

I'm curious about these essences. Why were these *prescribed* for me? Scanning the text, I find Centaury, and learn it has been incorporated to strengthen my will, to lessen my overreaction to the wishes of others. *Interesting! Now how did that chiropractic assistant know that?* Gentian, an essence of faith, is offered because I am "unconsciously refusing to be guided by [my] Higher Self and to see [myself] as part of a greater whole."[80] I am at first startled, then oddly uncomfortable, as I read that Oak, too, is related to an individual's refusal to be led by a Higher Power, that the "Oak Person" is lost in a world of achievement and winning. This sounds hauntingly familiar, maybe even too close for comfort! Walnut is prescribed for persons who are immersed in the uncertainty of life changes, for those who "have decided to take a great step forward in life, to break old conventions, to leave old limits and restrictions, and start on a new way."[81]

Several months pass. I still do not understand the logic behind someone holding my head while I sip a tincture of distilled flowers. I'm an open-minded person, but this truly makes no sense to me. How could these alternative healing practices possibly be beneficial? How did that assistant know, or *know*, so much about me? Yet, interestingly enough, I remain pain-free, so I decide not to protest too loudly, and continue with Bach's program throughout the rest of the year.

Cosmic Consciousness

As I continue my trek along the silver cord, I see myself poring over *the slightly used* section on the back wall of my favorite musty bookstore. Curious about a somewhat bedraggled volume, definitely more than slightly used, I paid my three dollars and devour it while sipping iced tea in Louis's garden. *(Louis, a scrawny, mottled grey stray cat had been rescued from a construction site sixteen years earlier, and was my best buddy and confidant until he left for his much deserved rest.) Cosmic Consciousness* was written by Bucke as a tribute to a deceased son. The author had lost his child, his spirit was broken, and he wanted, *needed* to know why this unfathomable tragedy had befallen his family, and why, as a man of medicine, he had been unable to stave off death. Crying out, flailing in a darkness of his own making, he hears nothing. It is only in surrender that he is led to first study, then chronicle the lives of "enlightened men," i.e., Buddha, Christ, Paul, Mohammed, St. John of the Cross, Pushkin, Emerson, Thoreau, and the like. It is in the surrender of these lives that he finds his answers, and his peace.

I am struck that he, as does Bach, references a higher form of consciousness, a state of "illumination." Bucke describes this higher plane of existence as an eternal understanding, a joyful and morally stimulating awareness which can only be *learned* through experience. Believing cosmic consciousness to be the inevitable legacy of us all, this hurting father writes:

> In contact with the flux of cosmic consciousness all religions known and named to-day will be melted down. The human soul will be revolutionized. Religion will absolutely dominate the race....It will not be believed and disbelieved. It will not be a part of life, belonging to certain hours, times, occasions. It will not be in sacred books or in the mouths of priests. It will not dwell in churches and meetings and forms and days. Its life will not be in prayers, hymns, nor discourses. It will not depend on special revelations, on the words of gods who came down to teach, nor on any Bible or Bibles. It will have no mission to save men from their sins or to secure them entrance to heaven. It will not teach a future immortality or future glories, for immortality and all glory exist in the here and now. The evidence of immortality will live in every heart as sight in every eye. Doubt of God and of eternal life will be as impossible as is now doubt of existence; the evidence of each will be the same. Churches, priests, forms, creeds, prayers, all agents, all intermediaries between the individual man and God will be permanently replaced by direct unmistakable intercourse.... Each soul will feel and know itself to be immortal, will feel and know that the entire universe with all its good and with all its beauty is for it and belongs to it forever.[82]

Each soul will feel and know itself to be immortal....

Bucke speaks of his own cosmic understanding, of a glorious spring evening spent with friends reading Wordsworth, Shelley, Keats, and Browning, an evening when he,

> All at once, without warning of any kind, found himself wrapped around as if it were a flame-colored cloud. For an instant he thought of fire, some sudden conflagration in the great city; the next, he knew that the light was within himself. Directly afterwards came upon him a sense of exultation, of immense joyousness accompanied or immediately followed by an intellectual illumination quite impossible to describe. Into his brain streamed one momentary lightning-flash of the Brahmic Splendor which has ever since lightened his life; upon his heart fell one drop of Brahmic Bliss, leaving thenceforward for always an aftertaste of heaven.[83]

Images are now appearing at a frenzied pace, so fast and furious that my conscious mind can capture only fleeting impressions. My life is swirling around me. Now and then it slows, blessedly, to allow me to experience, once again, moments of higher level awareness. It is as if a giant celestial computer is sorting mortal experiences from those of my soul. I recall my own "aftertaste of heaven," when, in the midst of a weekly trek to graduate school, I, most uncharacteristically, depart from the beaten path to explore a place called "Swannanoa." I question the wisdom of my impulsive act as I attempt to dodge the potholes of an unkempt mountain road. Upon reaching my destination, I sit in awe of the majestic Italian Renaissance dwelling; I am bathed in an aura of astonishing serenity, yet remain skeptical of my judgment. *This isn't me! Have I taken leave of my senses? Is this what happens when folks have their head in a book for far too long? This, too, at least on the surface, appears to be wasted time. I'm going to be late! What will my professor think? How will my tardiness affect my grade?* But, even with all these misgivings, I choose, again uncharacteristically, to throw logic to the wind.

Upon entering the towering carved door, I discover that Swannanoa was the home of Walter and Lao Russell, and formerly was the headquarters of their legacy, the "University of Science and Philosophy," a foundation dedicated to "self-transcendency." *(I do not know the meaning of the word, "self-transcendency.")* I'm drawn to the energy in the cavernous dwelling and am mesmerized by the Christ of the Andes that resides, arms outstretched, ever welcoming, ever patient, amidst the neglected garden of a distant time. I don't understand the magnetism, the force that pulls me here, yet I know in my center, in my being, that my coming is not by chance. My few moments *in the light* confound, yet impress me greatly, for when called upon to engage a speaker for an Advanced Counseling Theories class, my thoughts immediately return to Swannanoa. I write the gentleman who had, during my brief visit, introduced me to the Russell's teachings, and receive the following correspondence in return.

> Hi Deborah,
>
> I was pleased to make your acquaintance and to meet a soul who resonates to the ideas of Oneness and Wholeness expressed in the Russells' teachings. I have been mulling over the questions you posed and the intent you have to incorporate these teachings/philosophies into your counseling and psychotherapy. *(I have no memory of discussing this concept with him, or with myself, for that matter!)*
>
> I believe the root word "psyche" means spirit or soul which gives an excellent lead-in to the Russells' perspective on who we are and what is real.
>
> First, I would emphasize communication through meditation with the Divine presence within. In the Stillness within is the source of all knowledge, power, presence, and healing…. By bringing your desire for healing into the Stillness the process is energized with Divine force, guidance, and action. Constantly seeking communication with the Divine presence within will gradually activate the true nature and character of the soul into the personality/ego/sensed environment. I would add here, Deborah, there is an abundance of research literature available on the benefits and effects of meditation to support this idea.
>
> In conjunction with meditation *(or if necessary apart from using it),* I direct you to the universal truths espoused

in Lao's Code of Ethics. Practice of these simple principles of behavior will gradually reap the bounty of so-called "fruits of love," or any quality of character a person may want to have can only come from within him, he will learn to take responsibility for his feelings and thoughts.

When I give love, love fills my life; when I give recognition of worth I receive it; and as an extension, as I give time, money, feelings, things, so I receive them. I give anger, hurt, jealousy, disdain, hate, etc., I will receive like back. I have found my own inner sense of love and self-esteem to be ever increasing. The fears, dysfunctions, uncertainties, guilt and sense of separation gradually melt away as I continue to go within and express my desire for wholeness (mental, emotional, and physical health) to the inner point of Light or Stillness which I am. Slowly a sense of well-being, trust in life, and connection with my Creator and creation evolve....

In service and Light, God Bless You,

James

It is a time of questioning—

Overwhelmed with thoughts of Catholicism, Satanism, and the seemingly *purposeful* disappearance of a *supposedly* loving God, I find myself embroiled in a quagmire of existential yearnings. What do I do with this case? Where do I put my recent discoveries about abuse? Am I to place them on a shelf, pretending I have no knowledge at all, indeed, that no knowledge exists? Am I to incorporate them into the therapy itself? *What therapy?* All I am doing is white knuckling an oversized arm chair while Grace Ann recounts, weaves, or both, a nightmarish tale of abandonment and despair. *How do I go on?* I dread checking the voice mail! I search for her car as I pull into my parking space, praying for a few precious moments of respite before the bombardment begins! Fran, a woman of impeccable qualifications, informs me, "I don't think I'm the person for this job."

Hell, I don't think I am either, but it doesn't seem that anyone is listening.

"Hang in there, Fran. It'll get better, I promise."

I hope!

In sheer desperation, I seek out my long-time refuge, the cherished, family-owned bookstore of whose blessings I too frequently partake. Even if I fail to find the gem of the day, just being in this place makes me feel better. I suppose I have always felt that if I allow myself to be surrounded by the knowledge of the ages, some of it will, in due time, rub off on me.

Who knows, but on this particular springtime day, a day only to be fully appreciated by those fortunate residents of the southern Blue Ridge, I find, unearth, am led to, I don't know, a book that is to give direction to both my work and my life. I see *(again?)* with the eye of my understanding. My work takes on a spiritual path. Who I am and what I do are no longer at odds. It is as if I have been a great Vidalia onion, whose layers, once peeled away *(they rarely peel without splintering)*, reveal an unbelievably sweet core which feeds the bulb throughout its lifetime, without its even knowing. There is no more work and me. *There is just me.* I am once again transported back in time to my youth, and am again sitting in my Uncle Harris' Sunday school class. No longer debating, I am instead listening, absorbing, understanding. At last his words have meaning. My newfound knowledge has led me to the most remarkable place...*home.*

The Women Mystics

I have heard of Carol Flinders. Her vegetarian cookbook, *Laurel's Kitchen,* has been lauded as a classic. I do not, however, know *this* Flinders, professor of Religious and Women's Studies at U.C. Berkeley, and now author of a no less than inspiring *Enduring Grace: Living Portraits of Seven Women Mystics.* I buy first, the book, then a tape, then a second. Flinders admits finding herself immersed in early feminist writings, when, as a doctoral student, she chooses to compare the earlier "showings" (visions) of the fourteenth century recluse, Julian of Norwich, with the "long form" drafted by the Anchorite during the latter years of her life.

Sifting through the patriarchal language of medieval Europe's "chaotic, holistic, multidimensional world," Flinders is convinced the voices of the women mystics have become "marginalized" due to the canonization process, i.e., the Catholic Church's elevation of an individual to sainthood. This "kiss of death," as she terms it, has resulted in history remembering these women as pious and unapproachable, to be worshiped from afar, entrenched in the church of the day and void of all humanity. Their misrepresentation, and ultimately their absence, has left "a deep hunger that [has been] felt across the whole imbalanced culture. . .[for] every human relationship finds its perfect fulfillment in the mystical experience." These women offer a unique spiritual perspective, for they speak of transcendence while fully grounded in the reality of their medieval world. "The God that [is] encountered in isolation must also be encountered in the world."[84]

*The God that is encountered in isolation must also be encountered in the world! Is this what is happening to me? I know the God of isolation. Am I now confronting the God of the world? Is Grace Ann a lesson in a **lived** spirituality?*

Flinders' mission, as she sees it, is to "paint a living, hands-on portrait of these women," vividly detailing their imperfect stories, their wanderings towards Christianity's Council of Perfection, their horrible suffering, and their ultimate joy. She portrays each as the mortal, infallible creature she is, diverse in perspective and voice, oftentimes responding "willy-nilly" to her call, but united by a "genuineness for inwardness...[a] seeking [of] her own deepest self."[85]

I know "willy-nilly," for I, too, have followed a circuitous route to my own awakening. I also understand "horrible suffering." Grace Ann has certainly shown me that. But, will there be an ultimate joy?

I learn of Saint Claire of Assisi, and her "pure, spotless, gleaming, radiant path." As a member of the austere Franciscan Order, Claire refuses the traditional, often lavish, convent holdings of the day, insisting instead that she and her sisters subsist only upon whatever God provides. Claire's vow of outward poverty leads to a holy trust, an abandonment of all worldly attachments, a forsaking of self-serving behaviors, and ultimately, to an inner letting go.

A holy trust. How many times during my work with Grace Ann has she spoken of trust?

"Dr. Debbie, how do we know we can trust you?"

"Strong Man Jesus says we have to trust you."

"We trust you, Dr. Debbie. All of us do. You have safe eyes...."

It is only after trust is established that Grace Ann is willing to suspend her fractured ego, to let go.

———◆◆◆◆◆———

Two hundred years have passed. Upon finding herself betrothed to an undesirable man, Catherine of Genoa, overcome with despair, prays for three months of sickness, just enough sickness to confine her to her room. Catherine's intuitive self recognizes her need for isolation *("just enough sickness"),* and senses an inner movement towards a spiritual awakening, for the biographers of the day write that she emerges from this purgative experience with "her mind...clear and free, and so filled with God that nothing else ever entered into it."[86] Catherine provides an opposing view of the sainthood, for unlike the serenity of a Claire, she turns her back on convention, leaves her life of privilege among wealthy Geonese society, and, of all things, establishes a hospital for the disenfranchised, lepers, plague sufferers, and the like.

Flinders' insightful work leads me to Catherine of Siena, a very different soul, a "high-visibility, charismatic, spirit-filled" saint who heals plague victims and performs exorcisms. *Where was she when I needed her?* While her historical claim to fame has been her uncanny ability to influence a pope (she does, after all, persuade him to return the Papal Court to Rome), her biographer, Raymond of Capua, suggests her true gift to be the capacity to construct within her being an invisible cell of self-knowledge. This "secret cell...inner cell which no one could take away from her"[87] provides Catherine with a marvelous inner awareness, a continuous intimate dialogue with Christ.

Of this Catherine, Flinders writes, "Everyone [is] astonished at the quality of her listening...[she can] see the beauty of the soul despite the wretchedness of the container...."[88]

...the beauty of the soul despite the wretchedness of the container. Once again, I am reminded of the inner goodness of Grace Ann. Her pain has been ungodly, yet her soul's generosity has shone through. It seems that nothing has been able to *permanently* extinguish her light.

I learn of Teresa of Avila, the brilliant saint with "a genius for mental prayer." Though her adult life is filled with sickness *("twenty years of the pain of continuous vacillation")*, Teresa is eventually, through what she terms "raptures," to experience "delights and favors from God." These "raptures" allow her to see the beauty of God, satiating her hunger and instilling within her the gift of detachment.

> She…moves beyond the need for raptures, but she remain(s) grateful always for having had them because they [have] given her the detachment that her work would require, detachment from all things, including the admiration and affection of others she [has] always needed so desperately. She would never again look outside herself for joy or security because she [has] found the source of all joy and security within.[89]

I question if the experience of "raptures," defined by Webster, *not Jessica*, as "extreme joy, ecstasy, bliss, exultation," would constitute pathology in today's medical model society? What would be the treatment of choice, *Brief Therapy*? Which antipsychotic drug would most likely be prescribed? On a less sarcastic note, I wonder if, in cases of dissociation, a rapture could be synonymous with the internal self-helper, the inner-knower, the God that lives within. *Are we diagnosing these unfortunate folks as psychotics, when they are in the throes of a spiritual emergency? A communion with God? Oh, Lord! I don't even want to think about it!*

It seems that Teresa craves a mentor. She fully acknowledges the church's discouragement of her mental prayer *(the Inquisition is in full swing)*, and is indignant that there is no one to direct, what seems to her, to be this "wholly unconventional journey from awareness to understanding." Chaffing at the perceived dearth of direction, she couches her pilgrimage in the only way she knows. Teresa may have thought she was on a *wholly unconventional journey*, but I wonder if hers was any more *unconventional* than mine. I *know* her frustration. I, too, crave a mentor. I, too, chaff at the *dearth of direction.*

Hmm!

Perhaps no one can *mentor* another through a spiritual awakening. Perhaps this *dearth of direction* is how it needs to be. Perhaps we *must* write from our souls, from our own experiences.

Perhaps....

Teresa outlines her ascending levels of mental prayer by likening them to a garden, insisting, "the soul [is] a garden [that] we must cultivate." The physical body becomes fatigued, and we will only succeed if we remain committed to pulling the weeds. Flinders writes:

> The garden of the human soul, she explains, is on barren soil and full of weeds, but 'His Majesty' pulls up the weeds and plants good seed. God plants the seeds, she emphasizes; it falls to us to water the plants.[90]

Likewise, the beginning stages of mental prayer require a determination of will, and an acknowledgment of the certain weariness of the intellect. At this level, mental prayer, like gardening, is simply hard work. Teresa's next stage, the *Prayer of Quiet*, is compared to turning the crank of a cistern. While continuing to require effort, the work itself is less laborious and increasingly effective. With the rising water comes an intellectual clarity, as one is closer to the light. Teresa writes that although she does not know Latin, she is now able to decipher the message in Latin prayers.

Amazing! By turning within, she is able to access the collective knowledge of the universe! Now that's an intellectual clarity!

In her third stage, later known as the *Prayer of Contemplation*, the nurturing life force flows, instinctively, into the garden through a river or spring. The gardener's only job is to direct the flow. In so doing he will receive the fruits of the garden. The will and intellect slumber, inviting the tremendous bliss of a soul giving itself over to God.

The last stage of mental prayer, the *Prayer of Union,* is compared to rainfall. As the heavenly water saturates the garden, the soul, too, becomes immersed, free to become increasingly "courageous" in its quest for the ultimate freedom.

It is Teresa who insists that young women be granted, as Julian will so eloquently state, "a room of [their] own with a door [they] can close."[91] She wishes to spare them the frustrations of her lifetime, and seeks to provide the guidance and support she has found so lacking. In what later is to be known as the Benchmark Prayer of Saint Teresa of Avila, she encourages her fellow travelers to:

Let nothing upset you,
Let nothing frighten you.
Everything is changing;
God alone is changeless.
Patience attains the goal.
Who has God lacks nothing;
God alone fills all her needs.[92]

Is she speaking to me?
I marvel at how closely this Bookmark Prayer resembles O Child
of Mine, my own admonition to a hurting son.

Live for God, not for man. . .
Only then will you find peace.
O child of mine.

Julian of Norwich is now my guide as I continue this trek toward understanding. Recognizing that contemporary scholars are often uncomfortable with the medieval concept of visions *(as are contemporary psychotherapists)*, Flinders describes Julian's expanding consciousness as "deep down truths that she can feel in her bones." (Interestingly, the male clerics of the day don't seem to experience these feelings, these *deep down truths [they] can feel in [their] bones,* for they have been forced to walk a scholarly path, their minds cluttered by a university education. They are less receptive to God's truths, not through fault of their own, but because they have not been afforded the luxury of contemplation, of communion with God. Amazingly, *they,* not their counterparts, are responsible for instructing the masses. *It doesn't appear that much has changed at all!*

Julian dialogues with God, asking Him questions that have burdened her heart. God not only accepts, but *encourages* her questions, a concept foreign to women in medieval Europe. She brings to Him her conflicted self—the church teaching her of a wrathful God, her "showings" revealing yet another. A perplexed Julian offers, "For I saw not wrath except on man's side, and He forgives this in us."

Julian inquires about the nature of evil, asking how it is that the "great prescient wisdom of God" has not prevented sin?[93]

A respectful God replies that sin has no ultimate reality, for it simply represents "all which is not good." Ever the teacher, He shares that man falls into sin, not because of his wicked nature, but out of ignorance and naivete. He suggests that sin is necessary, for it is instructive rather than punitive, leading one to self-knowledge and to a humble seeking of God. He chides his willing student to remember:

> All will be well,
> All will be well,
> And every kind of thing
> Will be well...[94]

Julian believes it is our *separation from God*, not our shortcomings, that create our pain and suffering.

> The Lord sits in state, in rest and in peace. The servant stands before his Lord, respectfully, ready to do his Lord's will. The Lord looks on his servant very lovingly and sweetly and mildly. He sends him to a certain place to do His will. Not only does the servant go, but he dashes off and runs at great speed, loving to do his Lord's will. And soon he falls into a dell and is greatly injured, and then he groans and moans and tosses about and writhes, but he cannot rise to help himself in any way. And of all of this, the greatest hurt which was in him was lack of consolation, for he could not turn his face to look on his loving Lord.[95]

I bolt upright as I read of Julian's encounter with a "fiend," much like my old friend, Demon Judas, no not Demon, just Judas.

> And as soon as I fell asleep, it seemed to me that the devil set himself at my throat, thrusting his face, like that of a young man, long and strangely lean, close to mine. I never

saw anything like him; his color was red, like a newly baked tile, with black spots like freckles, uglier than tile. His hair was red as rust, not cut short in front, with side-locks hanging from his temples. He grinned at me with a vicious look, showing me white teeth so big that it all seemed the uglier to me. His body and hands were misshapen, but he held me by the throat with his paws, and wanted to stop my breath and kill me, but he could not.[96]

She faced the fiend, awakening "more dead than alive," understanding that even though he sought to kill her, "He could not…. my heart began to gain strength…and immediately everything vanished and I was brought great rest and peace."

God speaks, "Know it well, it [is] no hallucination which you saw today, but accept and believe it and hold firmly to it…and you will not be overcome."[97]

"…and you will not be overcome."

Grace Ann has questioned where a loving God is hiding when a mother leaves, or dies, or is simply unable to care for her children. Julian seems to be listening to her plea. "…as truly as God is our Father, so truly is God our Mother."

Julian attributes to God a mother's love for her child, calling this ever-present love "one-ing." Our love of God brings us to that "natural place, in which we were created by the motherhood of love, a mother's love which never leaves us….No one ever might or could perform this office fully except Him." Julian is assured, according to Flinders, "the mother we long for, and the mother we long to be, is with each of us. We can meet her there."[98]

I must remember to share this with Grace Ann.

Julian reminds us she does not *ask* for these showings, for she has no natural desire to understand the great mysteries of life. Flinders offers:

Not intellectual curiosity, but desire, was her starting point….Withdrawn from ordinary objects and focused intensely, her desire to grow closer to God has finally pierced the veil between this world and the other.[99]

It is quite likely that Julian's writings were suppressed due to the vast difference between her showings and the teachings of the Catholic Church. She comes to *know*, in the "eye of my understanding," that nothing obscures healing more than one's *perception* of a wrathful God. Because of fear or anger at this *perceived* wrath, he *willfully* separates himself from his Creator. He moves. God doesn't. Our healing, and ultimately our freedom, lies in our trust of His abiding love.

I sigh as I, too, *understand* I can neither change Grace Ann's past nor her perception of her past. Her healing lies not in my hands, but in a union, or more aptly stated, *reunion*, with a God she is convinced has forsaken her. I humbly recognize that I am merely a vessel, a conduit really, nothing more. My *understanding* of a loving God, the God of,

> And all will be well,
> And all will be well,
> *And every kind of thing*
> *Will be well...*

is all I have to see me through.

Reflecting upon our work together, I recall Grace Ann's university teachings had been of an external god, a vengeful, wrathful god of repentance and shame. I remember her stories of the Catholic Church of her youth, and recognize that, based upon her childhood recollections, she is not likely to once again place her trust in any institution. My mind ricochets as I recall Nancy's version of the exorcism. Grace Ann is declared demon possessed, and once again, is turned away, held captive, by the very faith that she prays will set her free.

I remember the children, the heart-tugging children, and recollect the day when I had vaguely, ever so vaguely, suggested that if I couldn't help them, I would find someone who could. They, through their self-appointed representative, Miss Jessica, plaintively cry out, "But we luvs you, Dr. Debbie. Please, please don't send us away. We gots nowhere else to go...we promise we be good. Strong Man Jesus told us he gonna help you help us....We luvs you bunches, Dr. Debbie. Please don't send us away!"

It's time for another walk....

Mechtild of Madgeburg's honesty touches me most deeply. I *understand* Mechtild. I have *lived* Mechtild.

Mechtild is never even considered for the sainthood. She receives no accolades. Catherine and Teresa and Julian are revered. She is not. It is only through her *jottings*, her writer's notebook, that we come to know of those who hold heaven's hand while treading earthly paths.

Mechtild is brutally honest, for while she freely admits she has never regretted her union with the Divine, she never pretends it's easy. She is, perhaps, more of an everyday mystic, more of a working woman's mystic, a wide-open kind of gal! She writes simply, from her heart. She possesses none of the serenity of a Claire or a Julian, nor the eloquence of a Teresa. She is forced to leave her home, and is then exiled from her newly adopted family. She is betrayed by trusted spiritual companions and is barred from the rite of Holy Communion, although in the church's defense, this refusal is likely the result of her reference to the cathedral clergy as "stinking goats."[100]

Oops!

When in despair, Mechthild seeks out the convent life, but is refused entrance due to her insufficient social stature and absence of dowry. With nowhere to go, she joins a Beguine community, a women's movement right in the middle of medieval Europe. While the Beguines lead Christlike lives, they are neither authorized, nor acknowledged, by Rome.

So unimpressed is she with her own jottings that she doesn't even bother to pull them together until the age of sixty-three, near the end of her earthly life. She writes of flow of wine, mother's milk, honey, and tears, the "love [that] flow[s] from God to man without effort, as a bird glides through the air without moving its wings." She speaks of an everlasting connectedness, a "deep reciprocity," a sense that "God is as hungry for union with the soul as the soul is for God." Of this hunger, she writes:

> Before the world I longed for thee.
> I longed for thee and thou for me.

When two burning desires come together,
Then is love perfected.[101]

Mechtild counsels that we must be open if we are to receive God's grace. She describes God's love as only flowing into the low places, flooding our souls when we empty ourselves of pride and anger and arrogance, and become, as do the women mystics of the day, "poor and naked." Sighing, she states, "Ah Lord, even in the depth of unmixed humility I cannot sink utterly away from thee...in pride I so easily lost thee, but now the more deeply I sink, the more sweetly I drink of thee."[102]

Mechtild writes of dualities, of light and dark, grief and joy, separation and union. She courageously addresses both sides of the mystical journey. She speaks of humility and acknowledges that it is our *desire,* and our desire alone, that leads us toward God. Once again, Mechtild reminds us that our union with God is the result of flow, not force, and cautions the seeker not to over-intellectualize his spirituality. After all, if faith is a *gift* from God, we must accept it as the *gift* it is...undeserved, unearned, free.

She states:

Fish cannot drown in water,
Birds cannot sink in the air,
Gold cannot perish in the refiner's fire,
This has God given to all creatures!
To foster and seek their own nature.
How then can I withstand mine?[103]

How then can I withstand mine?

I consider the lives of these extraordinary women as I snatch a precious few early morning moments in my garden. The peace that I encounter here is so unlike anything Grace Ann, in her fragmented state, has ever known. Strong Man, Grace Ann's own inner-knower, her own spiritual core, has extended his loving hand, offering solace and rest to this tormented soul. Serene and ethereal, he has served her well, as protector, guide, healer...the Source. It is to him that each member turns for guidance and reassurance. It is he who comforts them, *and me*, as they tell of their hurts. The alters aren't burdened with turmoil and doubt. They gleefully, without reservation, acknowledge the presence of this *purveyor of veiled wisdom,* this inner divine. If the upcoming integrations are to be successful, if there is to be any healing at all, it will be the result of Strong Man's loving direction, not mine.

Why can't Grace Ann see? Is she going to remain angry and distant from God to the bitter end? Would she rather self-destruct than forgive? Does she intend to ceaselessly spiral, knowing no grounding, no peace?

How I wish she would visit her own "invisible cell of self knowledge" as did Catherine of Siena, and experience her own "secret cell... [the] inner cell which no one [can] take away from her." If she would only heed the instruction of Teresa of Avila to abandon her will and permit her intellect to rest, she might know the unequaled joy of a soul in step with its God. If she chose, she, as did Catherine of Genoa, could emerge from her own cathartic experience, with a mind "clear and free, and so filled with God that nothing else ever entered into it."[104]

If only Grace Ann could know Mechtild, could possess but a small measure of Mechtild's desire. She, too, was humiliated, cast aside. How different Grace Ann's life would be if she could or would just let go of the guilt, the self-deprecation, accepting that a union with God always *flows*—is never *forced*.

Julian of Norwich experienced her own inner-helper, her own Strong Man, that deep down wisdom, the truths she could feel in her bones. Grace Ann could, too. If she were willing, she could know, as Julian before her, that it is she, not abandonment, nor neglect, nor even abuse, that willfully separates her from her creator. Grace Ann would see that she alone is the source of her ungodly pain.

The Healing

And the giant's heart melted as he looked out. "How selfish I have been!" he said. "Now I know why spring would not come here. I will put that poor little boy on the top of the tree, and then I will knock down the wall, and my garden shall be the children's playground forever and ever!" He really was sorry for what he had done....

And the giant stole up behind him and took him gently in his hand, and put him into the tree. And the tree broke at once into blossom, and the birds came and sang on it, and the little boy stretched out his two arms and flung them around the giant's neck, and kissed him.

And the other children, when they saw that the giant was not wicked any longer, came running back, and with them came the spring.[105]

Oscar Wilde
The Selfish Giant

CHAPTER SEVEN

The time of atonement has come. Thirty months have passed, thirty months of outrage and woe, disbelief and bewilderment, joy and resolution. Fear and loss have faded away, ushering in a new awareness, reconciliation for a greater good. Emotions, welcomed and unwelcomed, are embraced for the freedom and peace they are sure to bring.

"Dr. Debbie, Strong Man Jesus says to ax you, could you 'splain it to us all. Everybody listen up, give Dr. Debbie some 'aspect."

It is a time of giggles and twitter. The system has come alive, each facet having at last been released from the austerity of the mind's overbearing classroom. It is a happy time, a time of finger painting and bubbles, play dough and color crayons, Humpy Bumpy and Jessica Rabbit. Even the older alters, struggling to provide a voice of reason and restraint amongst the enchanting chaos of the elementary parade, are immersed in their own predictable adolescent endeavors.

The enthusiasm is contagious. Democracy rules. Each "child" has a moment. Each is begrudgingly respectful of his comrades craving to be free at last. Birthday parties, an enigma to the internal captives, are gleefully celebrated, with Judith, of course, providing her signature cake. We revel in everything—a daffodil peeping through the mid-winter's snow, a robin gorging on crusts of bread, the antics of "Mr. Squirrel." It is Strong Man who reins in the unlikely band. Always the director, he gently chides us all not to lose sight of our purpose.

"Aw, Strong Man Jesus, come on, haves some fun."

Ever the gentle overseer, Strong Man Jesus serves as comforter and guide. A child can simply announce, "Strong Man says," and the assembly lines up, little faces turned upward "in an attempt to gather instructions from the Master Planner." *I can almost see his knowing smile.*

"It Hurts My Heart to See Them Cry"

A vote is taken. Since the tiniest alters cannot give voice to their anguish, they continue to experience short-lived, but agonizing periods of pain. It is decided that they, Baby Jenny and Baby Joann, will be the first to be given "A Healing Day," the first to know long-denied freedoms. Jenny and Joann are to "be taken home to Mommy," for the memories of the good Mommy and Daddy have sustained them throughout their otherwise traumatic lifetime. They are reminded, by their big brothers and sisters, that happiness is a birthright—goodness can, and does, exist.

There is a flurry of activity. Jobs are assigned. I, as therapist, feel as inept as a first-year teacher in a faculty meeting. Strong Man, the resident principal, is calmly designating responsibilities. I, too, am accepting his instructions, for he is in charge, and EVERYBODY recognizes Strong Man knows best.

The much-heralded day arrives. A heavily-laden Judith ambles, stumbles, through the door, her garbage bag brimming with carefully selected props for the upcoming production. One by one, bears of every size and color are removed from their non-illustrious transport. A crutch, a bottle of rubbing alcohol, red and white paper, a sofa pillow, and even the office trash can are commissioned into service. The preparations continue, as each bear is first meticulously labeled with the name of a child, health professional, or alleged perpetrator, then thoughtfully arranged around the room. The crutch becomes an instrument of torture, while the trash can assumes the role of a toilet. The now-familiar red bat is carefully positioned within arm's length of the pink-shirted Judith.

I watch, at first perplexed, and then in horror, as oversized rubber bands, packing tape, and even a toy gun are produced. Judith seats herself on the floor and, ever the mother, senses my discomfort. Attempting to quiet my growing apprehension, she gently chides, "Dr. Debbie, the babies are going to do what you told us to do. They're going to feel their pain, and with Strong Man's help, let the pain go."

Strong Man Knows Best

Greatly relieved that Strong Man is still in charge, I accept my role as observer in the unfolding drama. Judith tucks her chin, closes her eyes, and fades into the indistinguishable infants. A strip of packing tape is yanked from its roll, and is forcefully placed across the mouth. Rubber bands are wound around the wrists and ankles. Struggling to lie down, she (or they) attaches the remaining length of each elastic band under the leg of the room's two overstuffed wingback chairs. Now prone and held captive by the innocent chairs, I first question, then understand that I am observing an infant being tied down. I watch as Grace Ann, a.k.a., Baby Jenny and Baby Joann, rails against the imaginary assailant. Breaking free, she points to, then slaps the "perpetrator bear" labeled Bad Daddy Hughes, all the while screaming, "Mama, mama, mama, mama, mama, mama...."

Still secured on three sides, the child (or children) grabs the pillow with the remaining free hand, places it over the face and simulates the act of smothering. The offending pillow is then cast aside. The tape is again affixed. Breaking free of the chair legs, Grace Ann pulls herself to the office trash can, the designated toilet. Grabbing a bear marked Baby Joann, she acts out an attempted drowning, repeatedly thrusting the bear, headfirst, into the invisible water.

Gasping, the wordless epic continues. Writhing and clutching her vaginal area, she simulates a forced penetration. Over and over she is violated, all the while screaming and wincing with pain. The bear marked Baby Joann is slapped, ostensibly because she is unable to stop crying. I am no longer an observer, but an unwilling participant, for I find myself providing a verbal commentary for the sickening mime, and am corrected by a violent shaking of the head if my narration has missed its mark, if it has gone astray.

Grace Ann frantically searches for, then locates, the red construction paper labeled "Blood." Assured that I have a full understanding, she places the child's construction paper under her vaginal area. She motions wildly, as if to indicate the presence of profuse bleeding. To my utter disbelief, she reaches for the alcohol bottle, then pours its imaginary contents over the affected area. I do not question, but cringe as my imagination soars. *Who would do such a thing to a child?* It is as if she hears my unspoken thoughts, as she screams, "No dada, no dada...bad medicine, bad medicine."

The carefully scripted mime continues. Red pieces of paper, the blood, are all around. The toilet becomes a bathtub, as a frantic attempt to stop the bleeding is undertaken. Unsuccessful, Bad Daddy wraps the screaming child in a blanket (Janice's peach blanket is whisked into service), Bad Auntie gruffly holds the hurting child as Bad Daddy drives to the hospital's emergency room.

The Doctor Bear caresses Baby Joann while the Nurse Bear forcibly throws Bad Daddy Bear out of the room. The Nurse Bear takes over, attempting to soothe the screaming child while injecting her with a pink ink pen labeled anesthesia. Quieting, the baby whimpers as one by one, twelve sutures are applied. The surgery completed, the baby is tenderly wrapped in a diaper (a piece of white paper) and is cuddled and rocked by the loving health professionals. Exhausted and sobbing, the child seeks a final retribution. Seizing the bat, she systematically selects a perpetrator bear, beats the hapless creature mercilessly, and then flings the surrogate abuser from the room while screaming, "Hate, hate, hate." She continues, bear after bear, wheezing and rocking to and fro, until faint, barely perceptible, cries are heard. "Mama, where's mama?"

Sixty-seven very long minutes have passed. The traumatic memories are at last felt, owned, and let go.

"No one can ever hurt Joann again," I soothe, while Grace Ann, now labeled Mommy, is rocking a tiny white bear named Jenny (bedecked with the customary pink bow).

"Mommy is rocking Baby Jenny?" I ask.

Grace Ann nods as she searches her bag, producing the little one's favorite book. She has chosen a story of growing older, intuitively aware of the need to leave this stage behind. Continuing to rock the whimpering child, she leans back on the carpeted floor.

I am the designated reader. The story has a calming effect upon the tiny alters, for as page after page is turned, the furious rocking slows to a gentle motion, and then to a peaceful slumber.

"Baby Joann rocked by Strong Man Jesus and Mommy," she sleepily says. "I need to say goodbye to you, Joann. No one will ever hurt you again."

"Bye, bye Joann....Bye, bye, Jenny."

And suddenly, the words of a children's lullaby enter my mind—strangely, I feel, since the simple lyric has not been sung, or even thought of since my own two children were small boys.

Lulay thy little, tiny child
Bye bye, lulee, lulay
Lulay thy little tiny child
Bye bye lulee, lulay.

The rocking ceases. The previously labored breathing, once fitful and erratic, becomes blessedly peaceful. Minutes pass. I tiptoe around the room, rearranging the furniture, rescuing the unsuspecting stuffed animals from their transgression. Finally, the resident town crier awakens, stretches and yawns, then states, in that matter-of-fact manner that is uniquely hers, "The babies be with Mommy. They bee'd rocking. They bee'd O.K. Thank you, Dr. Debbie, for not terminating us."

"No problem, Miss Jessica. No problem at all...."

Little Grace Ann

Two months have passed. The alters have pampered Little Grace Ann, 3¹/₂, sacrificing their "time out" for her, empowering her, granting her that to which every child is due, the gifts of joy and love.

The carefully chosen day is here. Ever the protector, Judith arrives wearing Grace Ann's pink shirt, tears streaming down her troubled face. "She went through a lot of things, Dr. Debbie. Are we going to have to tell it all? We're gonna miss her, Dr. Debbie," she hoarsely whispers, as she, ever maternal, grieves her impending loss.

"Before she leaves us to go with Mommy, I'm going to ask each of you to tell her goodbye," I less than enthusiastically offer, for I, too, am somewhat wistful. "I'll start. Thanks, Judith, for taking such good care of Little Grace Ann."

Anticipating the difficulty of this day, I have picked a red rose from my garden, and present this token of affection to Judith.

"Nobody ever brings us flowers, Dr. Debbie."

"You deserve flowers, Judith. You've done a good job. Now, 5-4-3-2-1. I need Little Grace Ann."

Before I draw a breath, I am greeted with "I din't mean to make Judith cry all night. She says she can't go with me to Mommy." Gazing down at her still ample abdomen, as if attempting to look within, she tearfully implores, "Judith, you happy for Little Grace Ann?"

A nodding Judith gazes upward. "She says yes, Dr. Debbie."

The session begins.

Little Grace Ann presents with her version of *The Hurt*, dated April 1952, neatly contained within the pages of a pink (of course), spiral-bound notebook. She begins:

> i not like the water pipe, [the] handcuffs—it be berry, berry dark in the closet—had to stay in closet all night—then he came to get me in the early a.m.—if you not cry, I'll take you out—he say—I going to make you feel better—he tickled me—telled me to rub his hot dog—remember not to cry or I'll put you back into the closet—i try not to cry, but i cry inside and go to my safe place. I told you not to cry—now you have to go back to [the] closet—he dragged me up the stairs and threw me back into the closet—you bad, bad girl...Jennifer, $9^1/_2$, takes the pain for me.

I hurriedly interrupt, for I see we're headed towards an old, old memory—an unnecessary pain.

"We talked a lot this week about all the bad things that have happened. You wrote to me in two notebooks. Do you remember? Is there anything else bad you need to tell me?" I ask.

"Just that they made my older brother hurt me when I was tied on the bed with the ropes. I love him, but why he have to do that to his sister?"

I can't think of a single, plausible response.

"You say I a good girl now, Dr. Debbie?"

"You've always been a good girl, Little Grace Ann. The things they told you were never true."

"You say I could go be with Mommy. I want to do like Joann and Jenny dooed. But, before I can go, Strong Man says I haves to do one thing. I haves to look in the mirror and not say, I be ugly, I be bad."

She removes Humpy Dumpy (alias, Humpty Dumpty) from her canvas bag. A Christmas present from her older siblings, she delighted in their thoughtfulness, but has been reluctant to play with the stuffed egg with its mirrored belly. Gazing into this, the most unlikely of all reflections, Little Grace Ann cries, "Grace Ann, you never be a bad girl and you not ugly. Strong Man be with you since you be borned. It not be your fault. Judith, thank you for taking care of Little Grace Ann like a mommy should. I thank you for always reading me stories when I had nightmares."

And now sobbing, "I love you, Judith. Keep the happy Little Grace Ann in your heart."

Then turning inward to an unseen Jennifer, "Jennifer, tell Dr. Debbie all your hurts. You feel better when you telled them. You has to tell. O.K., Jennifer?"

"Janice, you get 'barrassed all the time. I love you so much, but I want to go be with Mommy. I stay with you in my heart, O.K.?"

Placing Humpy Dumpy tenderly out of harm's way, she picks up the red bat and, looking around the room, declares, "I don't know which one to do first—don't know which one I hate most."

"I'm mad at you for…" she cries, as she gives voice to a lifetime of captive pain.

Furiously, without remorse or restraint, she beats and beats, beats and beats. Finally depleted and wheezing, she whispers, "Thank you Judith, Jessica, Jennifer, Strong Man, for giving me strength. Now I want to go be with Mommy. I don't want to hurt no more."

"Dr. Debbie, can you readed to Grace Ann?" she pleads, fatigue dripping from every pore.

"Of course I will, Little Grace Ann. I'm very proud of you."

The child within the very adult body struggles to lie down. She attempts, unsuccessfully, to cover up with the peach, satin-trimmed, baby blanket. A smile spreads from ear to ear.

"You look so happy. What do you see?" I ask.

"I see Mommy," she nods, as the smile widens even more.

"Will you give her something for me? Will you give her this yellow rose?"

"O.K., Dr. Debbie.…She sayed thank you, Dr. Debbie. She be very proud of me. She sayed she and Strong Man picked you special."

Eyes closed, she kicks off the worn, faded-around-the-edges, pink, summer flats.

"Why are you taking off your shoes, Grace Ann?" I question.

"'Cause I goin' to put on the white shoes Mommy buyed me. Dr. Debbie, she says keep pushing the Big Lady hard. O.K., Dr. Debbie?"

"Little Grace Ann, before you go we've got to see that pout, one more time!"

"O.K., Dr. Debbie," as her chin and bottom lip jut outward.

She is beaming, her angelic smile casting streams of light across the room. Positioning her arms across her chest, she lovingly mimics her long-lost Mommy.

"Come on honey, I rock you," she tenderly consoles.

And then, to me, "Strong Man say he always be with us, since afore we be babies. I sorry I gived you a headache, Dr. Debbie."

"That's all right, Little Grace Ann. I think I've recovered now."

Gently arousing herself, she removes *her* book from the ever-present canvas bag. Familiar with the drill, I proceed to read *The Hurt* by Doleski. Curling up, cradling Humpy Bumpy and Mommy's yellow rose, she resembles a contented cat in blissful repose.

"Grace Ann is going to grow up to be happy and healthy, and never has to go back to the bad people or think of the bad people, not ever, ever, ever."

"Is there anything else you need to say, Grace Ann?"

"Thank you, Dr. Debbie. Thank you, Strong Man. I love you."

"Bye, bye, Little Grace Ann," I tearfully respond, as I prepare to sing the soothing lullaby.

Incongruence reigns, for within the still-sleeping countenance, a familiar pixie-like voice can be heard.

"She looks peaceful, Dr. Debbie. No more hurts for Little Grace Ann," she whispers, reluctant to arouse the napping child.

Then, without a moment's hesitation, Jessica bolts upright, startling me, disrupting the surrealistic, ethereal calm of the room.

"Ooh, a yellow rose... it's bootiful. I glad I don't have to do that. Where the comb be? I need to comb my hair."

I just shake my head and smile. *When am I going to get over this, to learn to expect the unexpected?* Nothing in this case is as it's *supposed* to be!

"We bringed bubbles to celebrate, Dr. Debbie. She worked hard, Dr. Debbie. No more hurts for Little Grace Ann. Now you know whose turn it be?"

"It be Jennifer's," is my only reply.

I see the blushing cheeks, and wince as an unseen, *but very present,* Jennifer begins to cringe.

Jennifer

August 28th. Jennifer, wearing the trademark peach tee shirt and Little Grace Ann's tiny gold cross (the single remaining gift from Mommy and Daddy), arrives with a large shiny apple "for the teacher." She also hands me a journal, dated 1961, in which she has meticulously identified seventy hurts. Relieved that so much work had been done outside the session, I inquire, hopefully, "You've done such a good job of writing these out, is there any need to read them today?"

Grimacing while shaking her head, she replies, "No, Dr. Debbie."

"Is there anything else we need to remember, anything at all?"

"It just scares me if I see any symbols. When we go by the recycling place, I see the symbols. The symbols scare me. They scare me, all those symbols."

"That's called graffiti, Jennifer. I know you saw the symbols when you and the Big Lady went to the recycling bin. But after today, the symbols won't scare you anymore," I offer with as much optimism as I can muster.

"All these voices kept flashing in my mind and Strong Man said I could just write them out for you."

"Well, Jennifer, Strong Man has been right so far. I really don't expect that to change."

"Dr. Debbie, you said one time that MPD was a curable defense to a very extreme trauma. It is curable, isn't it, Dr. Debbie? I am going to get well?"

"You most certainly are, my friend."

"Thank you, Dr. Debbie and Strong Man, for showing me how to laugh and have fun. We are one, with Strong Man and Dr. Debbie's help. I want to get all the anger out. Strong Man Jesus asked me to look in the mirror. They all said we were ugly, ugly, born of a bad breed— that our real parents didn't want us. That's not true, is it, Dr. Debbie?"

"No, Jennifer, you were never ugly, and you certainly were not born of a bad breed. Your mother wanted you, really wanted you. Remember the letters. She was just too sick to take care of you all. She would never have left you had she been well. You know that, don't you?"

"Yes, Dr. Debbie, I know that in my heart." She caresses the small cross.

"What needs to happen today? How can we put this all behind you?" I ask.

"Get the anger out," is the now standard reply.

Locating Grace Ann's Humpy Dumpy, Jennifer squares her shoulders and defiantly gazes into the egg's mirrored belly. Oblivious to all that surrounds her, she, in a most proper and grown-up voice, solemnly states, "Strong Man says I have to look in the mirror. They all said I was ugly, ugly, ugly, and they all said I was born of a bad breed. They said that my parents didn't want me and my other foster parents didn't want me. They all lied to me. That's not true. Strong Man Jesus said that I'm not ugly, that my real mother really wanted me, but that she couldn't take care of me because she had a nervous breakdown. The other foster family that took care of Little Grace Ann really loved us. They loved us and wanted us. Strong Man Jesus kept us alive. He says I don't have to be hurt anymore."

Compared to the alters who preceded her, Jennifer spends a relatively short time pounding the perpetrator bears. At some point, Grace Ann is bound to reach what has seemed to be a bottomless pit of anger. *We must be nearing that point.*

The meticulous work in her journal has lightened her load and made today's release much less painful. She curls up, head resting blissfully on folded arms. The lullaby is sung. All is so beautifully quiet.

"Dr. Debbie," she whispers.

"What is it, Jennifer?"

"Dr. Debbie, can I stay awhile? I just feel drained, and I'm so sleepy. It feels so good to go to sleep and be all healed."

"Of course, Jennifer."

"Thank you, Dr. Debbie and Strong Man."

Fortunately I have chosen an unused, somewhat isolated office for this healing, since my officemates, while thrilled with Grace Ann's progress, have begun to comment (tactfully of course) that our "healing sessions" are wreaking havoc. I locate a full-size woven blanket, one much more substantial than the ever-present baby blanket, and leave her to regain her strength. The secretary and I alternate the afternoon vigil. We, too, are peaceful as we watch, for she remains in a gentle repose, a smile upon her sleeping face. Unfortunately, we can only afford her five hours of this uncustomary bliss, for the end of the workday has arrived and we, also exhausted by the day's events, must go home.

'Barrassed Janice

October 3rd is chosen for 'Barrassed Janice's healing day. Arranging the room to accommodate the now familiar production, Janice, in a private world of her very own, addresses the father and priest bears as they are removed from the hapless garbage bag.

"Dr. Debbie said I could set up for my healing. Today is October 3, 1964. You'll never put your hot dog in my hot dog roll ever, ever, ever again. You can't hurt Dr. Debbie either. You're so mean."

And to Mrs. Lang, the Social Worker bear: "I don't like you, I hope you get put in jail. You should never have taken us away from the nice foster family. They really loved us, they really did."

She locates the blue washcloth and wipes the tears that are now dripping from her chin.

"How many other children did you do this to? Not let children see their mothers and fathers! You can't ever put any other children into homes to be hurt, ever again!"

To the aunt bear, "I don't like you either, you won't let us see our mother! Dr. Debbie says it's O.K. to cry, that when you're hurting, it's O.K. to cry!"

Janice carefully assembles *her* books, those that have brought meaning and support to her pre-adolescent curiosity. Murphy's *God Cares For Me When I'm Thankful*; Carlson's *I Like Me*; Lobby's *Jessica and the Wolf*, and West's *Rainbow for Patti*, are among the treasured selections. Freeman's *It's My Body*, a children's book of empowerment, is allocated a place of honor.

"I will miss you, but thank you, Jessica, for always making me laugh, and for helping me play, 'cause we never could play…for teachin' us how to color and play bubbles. Jessica, pretty soon you can come to be with us…you make my heart so happy…but right now you have to help Judith. I love you, Jessica. You helped us all."

Then turning to Judith: "Judith, thank you most of all for helping me. You've been the strongest one. You've been like a mother to us.

Don't be afraid to tell Dr. Debbie. Thank you for taking us to Dr. Debbie's safe, pretty room where we weren't so scared. Thank you for always helping us in school and everything. Thank you for helping shy 'barrassed Janice."

And then to me: "Thank you, Dr. Debbie, for telling me it's O.K. to cry and for never giving up on us. Please help Judith to heal, too, Dr. Debbie. Please help the Big Lady. Teach her like you taught me. Judith, Strong Man, please take care of Dr. Debbie, O.K.? She can help a lot of children. I wish she could be our mother. . .that she could come live with us."

Sobbing, shoulders shaking, gasping for air, she gulps, "It's O.K. to cry," once again giving herself permission to grieve.

Presentations are made all around. A plaque, engraved with the alters' names and healing dates, is placed on the playroom door. Unwrapping a small package, I find myself holding a tiny, gold filigree crib cradling a smiling, sleeping child. Attached to either side of the crib's rails is a blue engraving. One side announces the babies' healing day, and the second, to my astonishment, tells of Jaqua's. (I had been unaware that Jaqua, too, was fifteen months old, and could spontaneously integrate once an alter with shared memories was "all healed.")

Jacqueline, recalling Janice's desire to have a birthday party, provides an assortment of balloons, color-coded plates and napkins, and a chocolate sheet cake *(we all like chocolate!)* decorated in purple, Strong Man's color. Pictures are taken to preserve the happy occasion. Once again, Little Grace Ann's Humpy Bumpy is called into service.

"Janice, you have to do what Strong Man told you to do with that mirror. Now don't you forget to do it," Jacqueline chides.

And to the rest of the gang: "Little Grace Ann, I'm going to come be with you soon. We love you, Little Grace Ann, but we know that you're with Mommy and you're tired 'cause you've been hurting for a long time, long time.

"Judith, you were so pretty and you were such a good nurse. You have safe eyes, too, like Strong Man and Dr. Debbie. Now remember, you must tell Dr. Debbie all your hurts. I know you're scared to death, but tell her all your hurts. Don't leave a single one out! Thank you, Judith, for helping Janice. You know she's so 'barrassed. You took such good care of her."

A blessed silence encircles the room.

"Are you ready, Janice?" I gently ask. "Since we have already gone over all the hurts, is there anything else that needs to be said or done today so you can be healed?"

"No, I don't think so, Dr. Debbie. I'm going to be able to see all the babies."

"You're going to have a very important job, Janice, taking care of all those babies."

Reaching into her bag, Janice retrieves a purple tee shirt and struggles to add this second layer to her color-coded ensemble. She halts in mid-stream, as she first tilts her head, then listens to the dialogue within. An exasperated look covers her face, as she indignantly addresses her internal adversary. "Judith, I is working. Strong Man said we can wear his color—we going to be with Strong Man and Mommy and all the little children that they hurt."

To the bad foster mother: "You were wrong. You told us if we looked at the mirror it would break. You were wrong. Strong Man says he doesn't make ugly children....I'm not ugly. We don't crack mirrors...."

And to Little Grace Ann: "Grace Ann, you'd better move over 'cause I'm gonna come and sit on Mommy's lap with you."

"You have an important job. We're going to need you to help us," I offer.

"When you see the Big Lady get 'barrassed, you know it's me....Thank you, Dr. Debbie."

"You're more than welcome, Janice."

"Dr. Debbie, would it be all right if I lay on the sofa with the Big Lady's George, because only good people can sit on the sofa and Strong Man says we were never bad."

"You know you're welcome to sit on the sofa," I reply. "No more stomachaches, no more nightmares, no more bruises. My goodness, I think I'd like to come with you, Janice!"

"No, Dr. Debbie. It's not your time. You're needed here. When you're done helping others we'll be waiting for you. You can sit on Mommy's lap, too."

"That's a nice thought, Janice. Thank you."

"You're welcome, Dr. Debbie."

Clutching George in one hand and a picture of Mommy in the other, the soon-to-be integrated alter crawls to the couch, pulls herself up, and proudly positions herself upon the forbidden foe.

"Judith and Jessica, make sure you work as hard as you can," she encourages. "Strong Man and Mommy, I'm coming to see you."

I sit in a thankful silence watching as she peacefully sleeps, the multi-colored balloons floating overhead, the ever-protective George tucked lovingly under an arm. I feel as if I have exited reality, and have, without ever moving, stepped into an impressionist painting, where everything is muted and surreal. Her chest gently rises and falls in an unhurried rhythmic peacefulness. My own breathing calms as well. We share a tranquil smile.

"Who is with us?" I ask the sleeping soul.

"All healed Janice," is the serene response. "Thank you, Dr. Debbie, thank you for everything."

"Goodbye, Janice," is my heartfelt reply.

The "Aprise"

Blissful. Jubilant. Elated.

There are really no words to express our enthusiasm. Fran, the secretary, thrilled by the lessening interruptions, asks if I can do this with all our more challenging clients. Dr. JoAnn and Dr. Dolores, counselors in training, request updates at each staff meeting. Dr. Gentry, Grace's primary care physician, phones to share in the good news. Grace's friend stops by to thank us, offering that Grace has been exceptionally calm, has ceased stuffing food, and for the first time that she can recall, is sleeping restfully and well. We decide the final integration will take place on Grace's birthday, some $2^{1}/_{2}$ weeks away. Judith, $14^{1}/_{2}$, and Jessica, The Boss, have decided to join the others in the system, while Grace has requested that Strong Man, her inner self-helper, not take part in the final fusion. Still angry at God for "allowing me to go through this," Grace is honest in her unwillingness to forgive.

Judith and Jessica are joyful in their preparations, busily scurrying around, as if orchestrating an Olympic-caliber event. Judith, typically the voice of restraint and reason, appears resigned to defeat, and is only half-hearted in her attempts to rein in her mischievous friend.

Excitement mounts as together they smugly announce their impending surprise.

"I not tell Dr. Debbie. We has a aprise for you. Judith says I not tell."

I cannot imagine an "aprise" I have not already encountered.

The long-awaited day arrives, the culmination of three years of rewarding, but intensely draining work. Judith, attired in Strong Man's purple tee shirt and sporting Grace Ann's very precious Australian black opal ring, arrives early to prepare for the upcoming performance. Once again the animals are placed in a semi-circle, all within Grace Ann's easy reach. Another cake has been prepared, this time with yellow icing, "'cause Strong Man says we gonna have sunshine in our lives." Nancy has been invited, too.

Unable to contain her infectious enthusiasm a second longer, Jessica again blurts, "We has a aprise for you, Dr. Debbie," and hands me a slender box wrapped in purple construction paper. "Remember what you always sayed, Dr. Debbie, that the greatest gift we could give our therapiest bee's our own healing."

"Yes, I remember that very well, Jessica."

Inside the box is a lovely heart necklace, engraved with the initial, D. *I decide this is no time to resume my lecture on gifts.*

As I look upward to thank Miss Jessica for her kind gift, I find myself face to face, not with Jessica, but with Strong Man's unmistakable, omniscient smile. Holding a carnation tinted in purple, he lovingly offers, "Dr. Debbie, this is to remind you that I am always with you."

I am touched by their (her, his?) thoughtfulness, and make a mental note to place both gifts in a place of honor, in remembrance of this day. This has indeed been a wonderful aprise. After three years of being one step behind, I should have known better, for this is hardly the final act of the play.

As I gaze into the contented, peaceful, tranquil smile, I begin to understand the meaning of "Your Serene Highness." A pink rose appears. Since pink is neither Judith's nor Strong Man's signature color, I am at first perplexed, then dumbfounded.

"Dr. Debbie, I have something special for you." Lowering his head, he removes the purple name tag and selects from the garbage bag a small pink and white bear labeled Little Grace Ann. Eyes sparkling, a tiny voice is heard to say, "Hi, Dr. Debbie, I be Little Grace Ann. I axed Judith if I could come today."

Tears stream down my cheeks.

"I be sleeping for a long time. I sleep on Mommy's knee. Jenny and Joann be sleeping, too, and Janice be taking care of all the babies. Strong Man said I could come back and be with Judith 'cause that was her 'quest. That what Jessica sayed."

"I tell you what, Little Grace Ann, this is some surprise. I didn't know you could come back after you were all healed."

"Strong Man said I could," she humbly offers. "Strong Man can do anything he chooses. You knowed that, Dr. Debbie. Mommy be rocking, rocking. I don't even have to pout." She revives the all too familiar petulant pout. "She be helping Janice find other children."

I am given a small present, less than neatly wrapped in pink construction paper. Inside is a child's rendition of Humpy Bumpy, "all put back together again."

Little Grace Ann has two more roses, one for Baby Jenny, the other for Baby Joann. "Strong Man has to take Little Grace Ann back to Mommy," she says. No fear or discontent can be heard in her voice.

"Strong Man really surprised me."

"Were you aprised?" the uncharacteristically quiet Jessica chimes in.

"Yes, I was truly aprised, Miss Jessica."

"Little Grace Ann, in the future, how will I know that it's you? How will I know when you're talking to me?" I ask, for the events of today have opened up an entirely new realm of possibilities.

"You'll know when you're working with little children. I will come and help. Remember that picture of Mommy that we keeped with us? Remember Mommy's kind eyes? You'll know when you see my eyes, they be just like Mommy's."

"They're sparkling right now. You look so happy."

"I'm all healed. I love you, Dr. Debbie."

Heaving a Little Grace Ann sigh, she turns inward. "O.K., Strong Man, take me back to Mommy."

I, too, am turning within. My hand involuntarily grasps Judith's small gold cross, the gift from Mommy Francis before she is removed, once again, this time to the darkness of the second foster home. As I clutch this tiny memento, I recall Judith's account of how this precious token of better days was saved—that after one particularly dreadful evening, her supposed caretakers, sensing the significance of this, her single piece of jewelry, threatened to rip it from her neck. Hiding in her room, she removed the steam heater's drain cap, placing her cross and its chain in the damp chamber for safekeeping. The memories flood back, as I, in my mind's eye, look back on the day I answered a call from a sobbing Judith, devastated that she had lost her Mommy's cross, that it was gone again, this time forever.

I am unaware that Little Grace Ann is still with me and am startled as a hand gently reaches out and touches mine, as if to console me for my own unspoken loss. Pointing to the inexpensive, but ever so precious necklace, *all healed* Little Grace Ann explains, "It be Judith's cross, Dr. Debbie. Judith losed it, but Mommy helped her find it. Remember, Dr. Debbie, remember when Jessica taped it to her hand?"

"Yes, I remember, Little Grace Ann."

First a smile, then a drop of the head. Blinking, I am face to face with an old friend, Jaqua.

"Well, Jaqua, I haven't seen you for a while."

"Thank you for helping us and helping the Big Lady. Thank you so much for never giving up on us."

"How are you feeling now, Jaqua?"

"I'm wearing the Big Lady's opal, 'cause blue is my color. I like pretty things. We never had pretty things. Judith gave it to me and told me I could wear it as long as I wanted. I'm happy, Dr. Debbie."

I sit in hushed silence, observing as yet another old friend appears. A peach carnation is removed from green florist's wrapping. Familiar with its owner and, by now, the schedule of events, I ask, "'Barrassed Janice, are you still blushing?"

"Yes, Dr. Debbie." She smiles. The blush broadens to a rosy glow.

"Dr. Debbie, Mommy helped me find all the babies and they were all whole and happy."

"Jaqua tells me she's happy. How do you feel, Janice?"

"I feel very good, Dr. Debbie."

"I'm glad, Janice. It's so good to see you smile."

"Strong Man Jesus 'splained *[do I hear Jessica?]* it to us all, and Jessica is the only one who doesn't understand."

"Jessica will probably never understand," I remark. "What did Strong Man say?"

"Dr. Debbie, he sayed that when we all got rid of our hurts we would still be a part of Grace, not the Big Lady, we can't call her Big Lady no more. She doesn't like it. He sayed a lot of good things about us. He sayed we saved her life. He sayed the Big Lady, I mean Grace, needs a lot of help, 'cause she's going to have all these new feelings that we took for her, and she doesn't know what to do about them."

Attempting to inject a degree of humor into this suddenly somber occasion, I ask, "So Grace is going to be hard to get along with, huh?" *Little did I know that I would live to regret that statement.*

"I think so, Dr. Debbie," she responded, as if aware of the difficulty ahead. "Love you, Dr. Debbie."

"I'm so glad you're happy."

Lowering her head, she quietly, maybe even sadly, states, "Strong Man, you have to get whoever is next."

I watch as a beige stuffed bear, labeled Judas, is removed from the bag. This time I am presented with a purple flower.

"The first time I saw you, you looked mean, Judas. I almost ran from the room. You scared me so badly I wanted to cry. In all honesty, you scared me so badly I almost changed professions. The lesson you taught me was to go for the pain first, Judas."

"I wish you could tell that to Grace. She's not willing to get help," Judas offers.

"Oh, you don't know that, Judas."

"Yes, I do, Dr. Debbie. No more mean looks, Dr. Debbie...you remember that in your therapy. When someone gives you a mean look and tries to scare you, that means he's really hurting bad. You did the right thing. You wouldn't have been able to help the others if you hadn't gone for the pain first."

"I figure if it worked for you, it will work for someone else, too. You really taught me a lot, Judas. I need to thank you."

We have now resorted to using Snow White and the Seven Dwarfs. Judas picks up a dwarf, formerly Sleepy, now named Jennifer, and slowly fades away. A shake of the head, and my old friend Jennifer is back, same tilt of the head, same peaceful smile.

"I don't ever have to go through another bad Halloween, Dr. Debbie, not ever again." Handing me a pink carnation, she continues, "The Big Lady thinks she'll be healed by Christmas. She doesn't know she'll be healed by her birthday."

"Uh, oh, was I supposed to tell her that? I forgot. I'm sorry, Jennifer. I guess I messed up. It *will* be a surprise."

A green carnation appears next. Familiar with its owner, I remark, "Hello, it has been a long time!" Turning to Grace's friend, "Thank you, Nancy, for helping the Big Lady when she didn't have any money."

"Dr. Debbie, we're going to help you get organized."

"You're going to have a mighty big job there, young lady," I respond, as laughter breaks out in the room.

"The Big Lady, oops, I mean Big Grace Ann, has taken all her money out of savings, out of her retirement, too."

"I didn't know that, Jennifer. No one told me. Now I *am* worried."

"Don't worry about it, Dr. Debbie. Strong Man will provide for us. He always has. He's gotten us through a whole lot worse than this. It's just that it'll be hard for a while. We know everything will be O.K. We have Strong Man. You know, Dr. Debbie, that Grace Ann is still angry at God."

"Yes, I know."

With a nod of the head, Jennifer turns to the half-empty garbage bag, removing none other than the "Belbeteen" Rabbit, alias, Jessica, The Boss.

"Hi, Dr. Debbie."

"Guess who!" I reply, amazed that some things never change.

"How you bee'd?"

"I bee'd fine, thank you."

"Dr. Debbie, I din't tell the secret that Little Grace Ann was coming back. First time I keeped a secret!"

"You did keep a secret, didn't you? Now I'm really amazed!"

That familiar, oddly comforting, pixie-like grin lights up the room. "I be a party girl. Strong Man Jesus sayed I could still be a part of Grace, but not the Big Lady. Strong Man Jesus says, 'Jessica, you be getting a little stubborn-headed like Judith and the Big Lady.' Hurry up, open your presents, Dr. Debbie! We luv you bunches, Dr. Debbie. Twelve kisses and hugs to you. Dr. Debbie, you'll hear me 'casionally. We're going to all be together, and we're going to be Grace. I still rite in Jessica's dishunary. It not bee'd Grace's dishunary. I luv you bunches, Dr. Debbie."

"Judith, don't you be scared, now." Voice trembling, "You're gonna be all right, you hear me, Judith. Then you and me be with Strong Man. And you gonna be fifteen, not 14¹/₂. You not have no pain, no more, O.K., Judith?"

"Dr. Debbie, one last time, would you teach Jessica how to get Judith?"

"Not in this lifetime, Jessica."

"Oh, all right, Dr. Debbie," she huffily responds as she crosses her arms in mock despair. "I luv you anyways, Dr. Debbie."

And in a blink of an eye, the Party Girl is gone.

Jim

"Dr. Debbie, I'm scared. Strong Man told me I have to tell you one more thing."

Judith hands me a red rose, then, interestingly, a yellow rose as well.

"Would you give this yellow one to the Big Lady?"

"Of course I will, Judith."

"Balloons, Dr. Debbie?" she asks, scanning the room.

"I think they must be for you, Judith."

"That's the first time I got balloons. They have Strong Man's colors. Who got them, Dr. Debbie?"

"Who do you think got them, Judith?"

"Strong Man, Dr. Debbie. He can do anything."

Anxious, yet somewhat melancholy, Judith sighs, then tearfully states, "I want to get it over with, Dr. Debbie."

"O.K., Judith. You don't need to worry. Grace Ann's going to be all right."

"It's just that I always took care of her, Strong Man and I. If I'm not there to help her, and she won't listen to Strong Man, what will happen?"

"You've done a good job, Judith, no, not a good job, a great job! You have earned the right to be well. I'll tend to Grace, don't you worry!"

Little did I know those words would haunt me.

Reaching into the plastic bag, Judith removes a poster. I inspect the picture closely. Standing on a hillside is a young girl with braided hair, about Judith's age. Facing what appears to be a field, or maybe a prairie, the child stands, hands clasped behind her back, head hung as if in despair.

"This is the Big Lady's safe, free place, her prairie. No one could hurt us there. Now we don't need this picture. We're not alone anymore."

One by one she pounds the captive bears. Then, turning to me, "Strong Man is going to help you talk to people, Dr. Debbie." Turning inward to Strong Man, "Thank you, Strong Man, for letting everyone come to my healing. Strong Man, will you hold Judith and Jessica and let them be a part of the Big Lady, I mean Grace?"

And then, hearing Strong Man, her inner knower, she addresses herself, "Judith, you're not stupid no matter what they said. I need you to help Grace deal with all these new feelings.

"O.K., Strong Man. Dr. Debbie, I'm ready to be with Strong Man. Thank you, Dr. Debbie."

"Why are you crying?" I ask. "This is a happy time!"

"Promise me, Dr. Debbie, that you'll help the Big Lady. O.K., Dr. Debbie? She doesn't know how to sew, or cook, or do anything."

"O.K., Judith. You know I will—I promise."

"I'm tired, Dr. Debbie."

"It's time for you to get some rest—you've earned it, Judith.

I nod my head as she turns within.

"Jessica, we have to go to a party."

Always ready for a party, Jessica, one more time, springs into action. "I luv you, Dr. Debbie. Do you still know Jessica?"

"I'll always know Jessica. There is no way I could ever forget...."

"How're you going to write this in your paper, Dr. Debbie?"

"I have no idea, Jessica. I don't think I'll even try. No one would believe me anyway."

I am reminded of Dorothy in The Wizard of Oz, as Grace, formerly known as the Big Lady, situates herself on the office sofa. Lying down, she clutches Strong Man's balloons, the "Belbeteen" Rabbit, alias, Jessica, a picture of Mommy, and the rest of the garbage bag's toys. I half expect a tornado to rush in and whisk us all away to the safety of Auntie Em. Has this, too, all been a dream?

"I love you all very much. I'm still going to help you, Dr. Debbie."

Tearful once more, I begin the standard lullaby and am heartened as the internal chorus chimes in.

> *Lulay, thy little, tiny child,*
> *Bye bye lulee, lulay,*
> *Lulay, thy little, tiny child,*
> *Bye bye lulee, lulay.*

There are no words to describe the serenity of the room this day. And then, in the barest of whispers, I hear, "Dr. Debbie, I can see Jim, and he's whole. And look, Dr. Debbie, look at all the other soldiers. They're whole, too."

A smile adorns her beautiful face. "Thank you, Strong Man. Thank you all."

A Tremendous
Breakthrough

All come to the light in their own time,
and in their own way.
Make no mistake, and have no fear.
In God's time, *they all come.*

Deborah Berkley
They All Come

CHAPTER EIGHT

"Deborah, don't get me wrong. I'm not complaining, and I don't want to sound ungrateful, but I feel so stupid. I don't like feeling this dull, this dumb. One of my staff called yesterday. She said she called to check on me, but I think she wanted to ask a medical question—something about some sort of rash. I drew a complete blank. I was clueless! CLUELESS! It was like something fuzzy was blocking my brain. I just couldn't get to the information."

Once again, tears are streaming, as our supposedly "all healed Grace Ann" cries out, "I know Judith was the one who went to school—I sure don't remember any classes. But this is ridiculous! How will I ever go back to work? I'm a good nurse, Deborah, a good nurse! I can't live like this. I don't want to live like this! I think I want Judith back!"

Judith back? No, I don't think so, not after all we've been through. Nope! Not going to happen! There has to be a better way!

I know Grace Ann can't cook. All of those burned cakes are certainly a testament to that! But, I must confess it never occurred to me that Judith held all of Grace Ann's nursing skills, too. Good grief! What am I going to do now? She's right! She'll never be able to return to nursing like this!

What does she mean anyway? Something fuzzy blocking her brain? Is it like the haziness we experience upon awakening from a deep sleep? Or the fog of anesthesia? I guess it's back to Strong Man. It's always back to Strong Man!

"I know you're scared. And I know you're tired of all this. I'm tired, too. We'll find an answer. You know that, don't you? We *always* find the answer, Grace Ann. Just try to be patient a little longer. I don't know what to tell you right now. Give me a couple of days to think it over, and we'll talk about it next week."

I need to speak with Strong man.

Next week couldn't come soon enough for me. I can hardly contain my edginess as Grace Ann methodically settles in.

"May I please speak to Strong Man?"

I watch for the wordless nod, then the gleaming eyes that are certain to follow. Anxious not to waste any more time, I forge ahead, suspending the usual pleasantries.

"Strong Man, I think we have a problem."

"You mean YOU have a problem, don't you, Dr. Debbie?" he chuckled.

No offense, but this is no time for humor!

"I guess you don't like Grace Ann's cakes. To be honest, I don't much care for them either."

"I can live without the cakes, Strong Man. But Grace Ann can't live without her nursing skills. What are we going to do?"

"Why don't you ask Judith? I'm sure she'll tell you what to do."

"Ask Judith? Are you crazy?"

The words tumble from my mouth. I sheepishly peek from beneath my lashes, unsure of what's to come. I just asked Strong Man if he was crazy! Good Lord, Deb, why don't you dig an even deeper hole?

That ethereal smile appears.

"I'm sorry, Strong Man. I really am. But, do you really think I should ask Judith? I don't want to start this process all over again. No way! Isn't she happy with Jim?"

"Just ask her, Dr. Debbie. You won't know until you ask."

"You *really* think that's a good idea?" I ask, just checking to be certain I was hearing correctly.

The steady smile continues.

"O.K. O.K. If you say so. I really don't have any other options, now do I?"

No response. Just that smile.

"How will I get Judith? I've never read anything about speaking with an integrated alter."

"Just ask, Dr. Debbie. All you have to do is ask. You should know that by now."

"O.K. I hear you."

"Strong Man, may I please speak with Judith?"

"Certainly, Dr. Debbie."

A bare thirty seconds later.

"I knew she would need me, Dr. Debbie. I tried to tell you but you wouldn't listen. I told you I always took care of her. I told you she wouldn't listen to Strong Man. I told you! I protected her for so long."

"So you've been listening all along?"

"Yes, Dr. Debbie, I've been listening. I can't really be happy until I know the Big Lady is all right. I don't want to stay for very long, but I'll help if you need me. What do you need, Dr. Debbie?"

"I need for Grace Ann to get her nursing skills back. She won't be able to take care of herself if she can't work, and nursing is all she knows how to do. And, by the way, it wouldn't hurt any of us here if she could cook again, too."

"She's really awful, isn't she, Dr. Debbie? You should see her try to crack an egg. It's amazing. She didn't learn anything! When I took over she was putting water on her cereal. I was afraid she was going to starve to death!"

"Little Grace Ann would eat anything, but I don't think even *she* would risk the Big Lady's cakes!"

"All she had to do was ask, Dr. Debbie. She has such a hard head. All she ever had to do was ask. Come to think of it, Dr. Debbie, all either of you had to do was ask. Didn't Strong Man teach you anything? As Jessica would say, 'Dah, Dr. Debbie!'...I'll be glad to help with the cooking."

"Thank you, thank you, thank you, Judith. I could kiss your feet. How about her nursing skills? Can you handle that, too?" I ask, relieved that this just might be simple after all!

"I can, Dr. Debbie, but I'm not sure I want to."

What? Alarmed, I bolt upright.

"What do you mean, you don't think you want to?"

"Well, Dr. Debbie, it seems to me that I'm kinda important. What do I get in return? You don't expect me to help the Big Lady out for free, do you?"

"O.K., I see your point. Miss Judith, what's it going to take? How painful is this going to be?"

"We'll see, Dr. Debbie. We'll just have to see."

"I've just spoken with Judith. How badly do you want your nursing skills, Grace Ann?"

"I have to have them, Deborah. I won't be able to keep a roof over my head much longer. I have to go back to work."

"O.K., Grace Ann, I hear you. I guess you'll just have to go shopping."

"Shopping? You know I hate to shop. What am I supposed to be shopping for anyway?"

"You won't believe me if I tell you, Grace Ann."

"Try me."

"Judith wants you to buy her a red bra."

"A RED BRA!"

"That's what she said, Grace Ann."

"A red bra?"

"Yep."

"That's not going to happen, Deborah. I hate the color red."

"Don't shoot the messenger, Grace Ann. I'm just passing on what I was told. She says she hates your ugly white cotton underwear. I guess teenagers like pretty, feminine undergarments. Remember, Judith is 14$^1/_2$."

"A red bra. Imagine that. I wouldn't have thought of that in a million years. A red bra."

"Seems like a pretty simple request when you think about it. She gets a red bra. You get your smarts back. Think about it, Grace Ann."

"A red bra," she mutters under her breath as she readies herself to leave the room. "A red bra...."

Several weeks pass, uneventfully. I don't dare ask. She doesn't offer. Sensing the jubilant return of the post-integration Grace Ann, I cautiously inquire: "Wow, things seem to be getting back on track! You don't seem—what did you say—fuzzy, that's right, fuzzy. You don't seem fuzzy anymore. What's happened, Grace Ann? You seem to be your old self again."

"It's kinda simple, Deborah."

"Grace Ann, I don't believe you. With you nothing is ever simple."

"Well, this one is. I bought a red bra!"

—◆◆◈◆◆—

Dear Dr. Debbie,

Everyone has reminded me that your name is Dr. Debbie, not Deborah, so, if it makes them happy, Dr. Debbie it will be! I'm writing to tell you of Grace Ann's tremendous breakthrough. She had just taken a shower and was sitting on a stool in front of the bathroom mirror. As you know, her leg continues to cause her considerable distress, so she still has to sit down while toweling dry. You also know how she hates mirrors, going out of her way to avoid them at all cost. Well, Dr. Debbie, she was preparing to get dressed for the day when, looking up, she caught a glimpse of herself in the mirror and for the first time, *the very first time ever,* she was able to see me, Strong Man Jesus, within her. She didn't hide her face. A tear slowly crept down her cheek as she recognized me. She knew me! What a joyful moment that was! The longer she sat, the more of her inside family (I guess I should refer to them as her former inside family) she was able to identify. She saw Little Grace Ann, Good Little Grace Ann's happy face, not the sad, hurting little child who rocked and cried for Mommy. She saw Miss Jessica, with that pixie-like smile and those unmistakable dimples, and laughed out loud. One by one, she recognized them all! I even laughed when she came to Janice, remember 'barrassed Janice, Dr. Debbie? She was still toweling dry and had not yet dressed. When Janice appeared, Grace Ann blushed from the top of her head to the soles of her feet. I guess some things never change!

She has not called on me in a very long time. That saddens me greatly, for I am here, ready, wanting to help. As soon as she is willing to ask me back into her life, she will be complete. Thank you for your hard work, Dr. Debbie. Remember, I am with you always.

Strong Man Jesus

Ever determined, Grace Ann has been successful in ferreting out long-lost relatives and has wrangled herself an invitation to spend the holiday season with the daughter of Mommy and Daddy Francis, the *good mommy and daddy*. Not only is she joyously returning home healthy and whole, she will be spending Christmas as a part of a family, a part of the *only* real family she has ever known. She is beside herself with happiness! Thrilled to be normal, as she puts it, Grace Ann invests her long-denied energy and mounting enthusiasm into baking an assortment of her now renowned cakes: five-flavor pound cake, coconut, sour cream, and my favorite, the scoundrel responsible for the ten extra pounds on my backside—chocolate. She works late into the night completing cross-stitch projects, barely putting the finishing touches onto one before beginning another, for upon healing, her creativity and love of needlework has returned with a vengeance. Everyone is to receive a present, from the adopted family she barely knows to friends she has not met. Several therapy sessions are scheduled only to be canceled (*unheard of for Grace Ann*), for between the baking and the sewing and the wrapping and the packing, "I'm sorry Deborah, I'm so busy. I just don't have the time!"

These are glorious moments. It is a very happy time.

The early winter passes uneventfully. Grace Ann attends one hour of therapy per week, a far cry from the six hours and countless phone calls of several years back. She has long since exhausted her insurance company's *mental health allowance* and has amassed an enormous bill which I have willingly accepted is unlikely to ever be paid. I am also concerned for her still excessive dependence upon me. I remind myself frequently of the many extraordinary experiences we have shared; I have been one of the few constants in her life. Each part of her being extended its fragile trust to include me. Still, I'm uncomfortable that I might be setting her up for a fall if I don't continue to set, and then enforce, some pretty strict boundaries. After all, the goal of good therapy is for Grace Ann to grow away from me—to no longer need me—to be free of her haunting past and its oppressive burdens.

I encourage her, once again, to embrace *her* life.

"Grace Ann, for heaven's sake, look at what you have been through! You've paid your dues, my friend! This is *your* time!"

She joins AMAC, an Adults Molested As Children group, altruistically sharing her story, and her healing, with those in need of hope. She makes new friends at Weight Watcher's. And then, lo and behold, who comes to town but Richard Simmons himself! Arriving at the mall early to snag a front row seat, she flails her arms wildly *(Jessica?)* to draw attention to herself. Hard to miss, he calls to her, asking if she has a story to share. *Does she ever!* God bless him, for, upon hearing of her dogged determination, he warmly extends, as only Richard Simmons can, a heart-felt congratulations for her success and support for her continued struggle. She *relishes* the moment, basks in the glow of his encouraging words, and, as we have all heard many, many, times, even gets a kiss!

These are joyful days, yet a nagging uncertainty persists. There's a sense, a foreboding, an indiscernible, yet unshakable doubt that all is not as well as it might seem. Grace Ann has always been strong in her faith, or at least I thought she was. Now I'm just not so sure. Was it just lip service? She, *or someone inside her*, graduated from a Christian college, served as a missionary nurse, and was *always* loyal in her church attendance. *(Who was that?)* During our early days together, *someone* insisted that we embark upon a spiritual journey. *I assume it was Grace Ann!* Yet, when asked if she, Grace Ann, is ready to return to the life of prayer and supplication she professes has brought inner peace and fulfillment, her mood changes instantly, a darkness descends, and she haughtily, even fiercely protests, "No, Deborah! I don't think so! I'm not ever going back to church. And, I no longer read my Bible! I still haven't made my peace with God, and I don't intend to! Where was God when I needed Him? Don't ask me again!"

No problem, ma'am!

"Grace Ann, I know you're not attending church any longer. But, what about Strong Man? He's your final alter, the last one. I can hardly believe it myself! Once he's integrated, you'll be whole—complete. Imagine that, Grace Ann! All of this pain will be over! You'll be free!"

My query, admittedly a tad manipulative, is met with an angry defiance—arms folded protectively across her chest—a vehement shake of the head. Rocking once again, she defends herself against my words, as if they wore talons capable of piercing her scarcely mended heart.

Then, suddenly still, she sits, staring ahead towards the nothingness of an empty chair, and does not utter another word.

Aftermath

A battle of the wills begins. I'm determined my reluctant client is going to invite Strong Man back into her life. She's determined she's not. *(Is this what happens when spirituality is crammed down someone's throat?)* An awkward truce takes shape. Unspoken tension permeates the room. The air is thick with uncertainty. Dread rears its ugly head, as I wait in anxious anticipation. Turning dejectedly to my old friend, I inquire, "What's going on, Strong Man? I *feel* an enemy, but I have no idea *who* or *what* it might be. It seems she's slipping back, losing ground. Is there any way to stop this, this disintegration?"

"I'm trying to help her, Dr. Debbie, but she is so angry with me! She cannot hear my voice. She has shut me out. She still thinks I abandoned her, so she's turning her back on me. This is all so unnecessary. Pray for her, Dr. Debbie. It breaks my heart to see her in so much pain. It breaks my heart to see her *choose* so much pain!"

Another March arrives, and with it, the spring equinox.
Oh, Lord! I thought these days were over!
The phone calls, long-since ceased, return with a vengeance. The arrogant, demanding, obnoxious caller identifies herself as Grace Ann, yet I begin to wonder whose finger is pressing the redial button.
Why? If I could only understand why.
Startled, I leap from my chair as our harassed secretary, frazzled and clearly out of control, repeatedly slams the hapless receiver back into its cradle. She is angry! Grace Ann is angry! My colleagues are angry! We were almost there! Night after night, I lie awake asking, *"Why?"*
The combination of sleepless nights and frightful days weaken my resolve. Caught up in my own drama, I lose focus. My own boundaries soften, then grow fragile, finally collapsing in surrender to the former friend turned merciless foe. I'm angry, too. How dare she! Who does she think she is! I've lived through this once. I have no intention of

going there again—the constant calls, the plaintive wails, the threats, the accusations! No way! It's time for a referral! I have nothing left to give!

A session, *if I have my way, our final session*, is hastily arranged. I am distant, terse—*resolved.*

"Grace Ann, I need for you to hear me—for *all of you* to hear me. If you remember, we agreed long ago that I could only continue to see you if the rights of other clients were not violated. You are *not* my only client, Grace Ann! I'm trying to help others, too. You do not seem willing, or able, I don't know which, to stop these endless phone calls. We cannot work this way.

"I told you, in no uncertain terms, that if you did not respect others, I would have no choice but to refer you, at least for a few sessions, to another therapist. You have left me no other option! My staff is furious with me for letting this go on as long as I have. I've arranged for you to work with Ms. Stevens, an adult therapist who works with the local C.S.B.—Community Services Board. Perhaps she can help you stabilize yourself. I'll be following your progress carefully. I've asked her to stay in touch."

Shaking from head to toe, fury barely contained, Grace Ann, cursing *(cursing?)*, storms from the room, slams the outer door, and pounds the corridor's wall with her crutch as she exits the building. Unwilling to relinquish her stranglehold, the onslaught continues.

"Deborah, I thought you terminated Grace Ann," my colleague questions, barely able to mask her ire.

Please don't use the word terminated. Jessica would have an absolute fit!

She won't stop. We can't continue. A block is placed on her phones. The silence is deafening.

Grace Ann attends two sessions with Ms. Stevens, then refuses to return. A quick call from the C.S.B tells me what I already know—she cannot be contained in individual therapy, as she refuses to respect the boundaries established by her new therapist, and she is not suitable for a group. A quick call is placed to Grace Ann's psychiatrist, in hopes of gaining some sort of support. None is forthcoming. *He seems as angry as Grace Ann! His unspoken words ring loudly. Why have I let Grace Ann down?*

She's back....

Strong Man Jesus attempts to intervene, to interject reason, to deflect the predatory blows.

"Dr. Debbie, I know you are angry."

You're damn right I am.

"I'm trying to help you. Just be patient—she'll come around. Everything will be all right, you'll see! Remember, Dr. Debbie, she is in so much pain!"

I don't think so, Strong Man! Don't even go there! I'm through! I'm not the least bit interested in her pain! As soon as I can locate a referral source....

By now, Grace Ann is on a mission. She's determined to self-destruct. Incensed that "children are still abused every day," she, without my knowledge and certainly without my approval, places an ill-timed call to her eighty-year-old biological father, who, incidentally, has not been seen nor heard from in forty-four years.

Forty-four years!

My jaw drops in disbelief as I recognize the caustic voice on the tape. For, after introducing herself, she scarcely pauses to catch her breath before demanding that he, her grossly neglectful father, lend her the five thousand dollars needed to retain an attorney to, of all things, sue *him*! When *(not surprisingly)* he refuses, she proceeds to badger him with allegations of molestation. He hangs up!

The ever-escalating stresses continue their ruthless march! Grace Ann is informed, by letter, that she no longer has a job! Her facility, her home for twenty years, is shutting its doors. As of the end of April, she is unemployed...*unemployable.*

Dr. Johnson, her kind and empathic orthopedic surgeon, schedules a consult with his long-term patient, colleague, and friend. Tearfully, with as much consolation as he can muster, for he, too, is overwhelmed by the pain of impending loss, Dr. Johnson explains to an unbelieving Grace Ann that he has been diagnosed with a debilitating neurological disease. No longer will he be able to operate on his patients. He explains that he will remain in the area as an office physician until he can obtain a teaching position, and he and his family can relocate. Grace Ann is inconsolable! *He promised to perform her surgery!* Now he's leaving her, too! As a result of his misfortune,

Grace Ann is referred to a colleague, who, upon reviewing her medical history, *allegedly* informs her he is unwilling to perform surgery on "psychiatric patients."

I'm too tired to verify her accusations!

The mental free-fall continues. I am now the recipient of another barrage of angry attacks.

"Why did you integrate me? You liked my alters, but you can't stand me."

No joke! I'm beginning to agree with you there!

"Don't talk to me about no Strong Man Jesus!"

Deluge follows deluge. We're swirling about in class five rapids when the dam bursts. Grace Ann's father dies.

So?

The inner turmoil surfaces. Old wounds are laid bare. "How dare he? How *dare* he? He's dead, Deborah, and I *still* can't forgive him! I thought it didn't matter anymore, but I was wrong! He doesn't *deserve* to be forgiven! Look what he did to my mother! To all those other women! Look what he did to *us!* I hope he's roasting in hell!" The calls begin again, this time not to me *(thank God!)*, but to, of all people, her aging mother. "I just want to wish her a Happy Mother's Day, Deborah," an indignant Grace Ann declares, as my brows arch in disapproval.

She calls, then hangs up. Then calls, and hangs up again. Finally, her mother, not her aunt, answers the phone. Delighted, Grace Ann hurries to introduce herself, only to be interrupted with a clipped, "I don't have no children. Don't call this house again!"

Her world is once again the color of despair.

A Thwarted Hospitalization

We continue this tenuous, haphazard journey until June, when, in what has now become a typical encounter, Grace Ann delivers another volley from her toxic tongue. No longer her knight in shining armor, it seems I have been relegated to the ranks of a swiftly swelling enemy camp. *(Borderline?)* It is on a deceptively serene early June day that she artfully delivers the fatal blow.

"That's all right, Deborah," a venomous Grace Ann spews. "Soon everybody will know who you *really* are."

"I don't have a clue what you're talking about," I respond, aware that an all too familiar sensation of dread is suddenly upon me.

"I called that lady today, that lady at the licensing board. I told her what you did."

"What did I do, Grace Ann?" I ask, the dread wrapping its fingers around my now constricted throat.

"You know what you did, Deborah! You stole one hundred thousand dollars of my money!"

One hundred thousand dollars! One hundred thousand dollars! I haven't even gotten paid! Breathe! Breathe! One hundred thousand dollars? You've never even had one hundred thousand dollars! How am I supposed to steal it? I am absolutely incredulous! I can't breathe! I don't even want to look at her!

"Grace Ann, you may leave now!"

"You can't make me leave, Deborah! Who do you think you are? I'm paying for this session, and I'm not going anywhere!"

I'm not going to argue. I leave the room instead. I assume she will hobble off once she no longer has a captive audience.

Wrong again!

Closing the door tightly behind me, I paste a smile on my frozen face, stick my head *(with its frozen smile)* into the waiting room, and motion to my waiting client to join me, not in my room, but in the adjoining office.

"I have a client who's preparing to go home, and it's taking her a little longer than usual. We'll be using JoAnn's office today."

That sounds therapeutic, doesn't it?

I don't think she believed me, at least not the "preparing to go home part," for the obscenities, targeted at me, all but bounce off the unsuspecting walls. Excusing myself, again with a smile on my face, I leave the room, open Grace Ann's door, and, in a hushed, controlled, yet seething whisper, demand, "I told you that your session was up! I meant it! I'm not asking you to leave, Grace Ann. I'm *telling* you to leave!"

I attempt to resume my session as I return to my wide-eyed client.

The barrage continues, this time accompanied by a trash can banging against the closed door. The screams turn to wails, then to sobs. There's no way to continue my work next door.

"I am so very sorry. Obviously, we can't go on. I'm afraid I have no choice but to tend to this, this client. Please ask Fran to reschedule with you, *at no cost.*"

She all but trips over herself hurrying to leave the office, never to be seen again.

The walls are reverberating with the screeching tirade as I throw open the door and sail into the room. Refusing to sit, I stand, hands clenched tightly behind my back to quell my shaking.

"Grace Ann, I'm going to tell you one more time to leave. If you don't vacate the premises *NOW,* I'm going to issue an Emergency Custody Order and have you removed. Do you understand me? I said *NOW!* And I mean *NOW!"*

I must look pretty threatening, for Grace Ann hears me. Dragging herself off the floor, she hustles *(a Grace Ann sort of hustle!)* out of the office, spouting imaginative profanities as she kicks, then slams, the door.

Fran looks at me. I look at her. We both collapse in a fit of hysteria, laughing so hard we gasp for air.

"For God's sake, Deborah. What did you do to her?" Fran asks, pulling a tissue from the waiting room's box to wipe her streaming eyes.

"What did *I* do to *her*? You mean, what did *she* do to *me*?"

Fran sits, dumbfounded, as I tell her of the one hundred thousand dollars. Too numb to speak, she again erupts in a fit of giggles, not even bothering to console a still seething me.

"I'm sorry, Deborah, I really am. Really, really, I am. But, it was all so funny! You should have seen that lady. She looked like she'd been plugged into a light socket! Grace Ann was screaming—something about you! She was really loud! I started screaming, too, so that lady could hear me! I asked her if she wanted to reschedule, I *did*, I *swear* I did, but she just shook her head and ran out the door."

She erupts again!

"I'm sure glad you think it's funny, Fran. This may well go down as the worst day I've ever had!"

Not to be!

The phone rings. And rings. And rings.

Grace Ann has reported for duty. Fran's laughter turns to tears. My head pounds. All other sessions scheduled for the day are cancelled, as

I join my swiftly fading assistant, the two of us taking turns answering the phone that has again become our tormenter. Finally, the day, and my patience, are exhausted.

It's my turn to place a few calls!

Contacting the local magistrate, I first request, then *insist,* that an Emergency Custody Order be issued. She's never been *this* out of control! I don't know *this* Grace Ann, and am not at all certain what she might do! The police are dispatched to her home. Their mission: to transport the groundless, illogical, tantrumming client to the hospital for a mental health assessment. *She must be protected, even from herself!*

The police arrive. A now combative Grace Ann locks the door, refusing to allow the officers to enter her small apartment. The rescue squad is called into service, then members of the fire department. She threatens. They cajole. After several hours of this mindless banter, an angry Grace Ann flings open the door and, to everyone's dismay, must be cuffed and shackled before her still flailing body makes its way onto the cruiser's back seat. Anger escalates to rage. Rage turns to fury. By the time the vehicle pulls in under the hospital's portico, a bare seven minutes later, Grace Ann is so vicious in her verbal attacks that the staff has no choice but to issue a seventy-two-hour Temporary Detention Order. Grace Ann, and her *almost*-all-healed inside family, are ushered into a small, windowless, padded cell, not to punish her, but to provide a measure of safety. A commitment hearing is scheduled for the next morning. As is required by law, Grace Ann is to be examined by the emergency room physician. Her psychiatrist is informed of her involuntary admission.

This day will just not end, for I receive yet another call *(I hate telephones!),* this time in the evening, at home.

"Ms. Berkley. Your client's hearing will be held at 9:00 a.m. tomorrow. She sure seems angry with you! We will need for you to be here."

One more call must be placed, this one to my weary secretary.

"Fran, I really hate to tell you this after the day you've had. The hospital just called, and they expect me to attend the hearing tomorrow morning. I'm afraid I have to ask you to come in early. We need to cancel some more sessions."

She's hardly jumping for joy! I'm not certain if she's angry, or just very tired, for it is clear this is far from a welcoming call. I make a mental note to take her to lunch if the hearing wraps up before noon. No one, not Fran, not even me, should have to work in these conditions!

Nine a.m. arrives. I enter the padded detention room, along with the usual entourage—the transporting officers, Grace Ann's court-appointed attorney, the staff physician, emergency mental health consultant who staffed the case, hospital security guards, and the judge. A tearful, contrite Grace Ann sits, bed sheet tucked protectively under her chin. Remorse is written all over her face. The questioning begins.

"Ms. Hughes, I understand you had quite a day yesterday," the judge says. "Can you tell us what was going on?"

"Yes, sir, I can." *Who is this timid, mouse-like creature? That tiny voice?*

"Your Honor, I love my therapist. She's really helped me. I don't know what I would have done without her. I only wanted her to call me back. I wouldn't have done all that if she, if she would have just called me back! I just wanted, I *needed*, a phone call!" The tears begin.

All eyes turn to me. I feel my wrath rising as I confront her with this *most recent* ludicrous accusation! Her attorney crisply objects to my retort. His objection is sustained, and I am the one who is chastised.

"Ms. Berkley, you have not been asked to speak. If you continue to interrupt, you will be asked to leave this hearing."

Score one for Grace Ann! Is that a smirk I see radiating from those eyes? I don't know those eyes!

Next to testify is the staff physician. She reports no unusual findings and does not believe a hospitalization is necessary. She volunteers that Grace Ann's psychiatrist has been contacted. Once informed of his patient's status, *by her*, he, too, feels this hospitalization is unwarranted.

"I see," replies the judge.

By the time my turn finally arrives, I am *beside myself*, incensed that I am forced into this defensive position. *What did I do?* Turning to the staff physician, not even bothering to mask my ire, I ask, "Have you even examined her? Have you even looked at all those self-inflicted wounds, all those cuts and burns covering her torso and abdomen? Have you even looked?"

Somewhat abashed, she replies, "Well, no, I hadn't noticed," but agrees to examine the oozing abrasions as soon as the hearing is over. Scanning the room, I attempt to explain to this highly eclectic group that my client, their patient, has Multiple Personality Disorder. While I admit to having no idea which alter has created all the chaos, I emphasize that Grace Ann is manipulating them all, as she has simply switched to a different state of consciousness in an effort to avoid hospitalization. My vigorous explanation has a solid start, but dwindles to a halting, feeble plea as I sense there is no one in the room sympathetic to my plight. My intuition is right on target, for my description of the disorder, and the day's events, is met with quizzical stares, a shuffling of feet, and silence.

"You are free to go, Ms. Hughes. I have no reason to hold you. But you'd better behave yourself! I don't want to see you in here again!"

"Thank you, Your Honor. I promise, I won't cause trouble again."

It's now my turn to have a tantrum. Openly furious, I spin on my heels, stomp out of the room, through the corridor, and out into the deceptively sunny day. *I've never been so angry!* Upon reaching my office, an equally furious secretary meets me. "Deborah, what the hell happened today? I can't believe this! The hospital just called. They wanted to be sure Grace Ann has an appointment scheduled with you before she is released. I told them you would call back—I certainly wasn't going to set one up! They let her out? Didn't they hear anything you said?"

Enraged, I shake from head to toe as I dial the number. Grace Ann has held this office hostage long enough! Someone, I don't know who (*unfortunately*) answers the phone.

"You can tell whoever called this office that I have no intention of ever seeing Grace Ann Hughes again. There will be *no more* appointments! You let her out! She's *your* problem now! *You* take care of her!"

I do not ask, but am told, that Grace Ann is rocking…rocking… rocking, while chanting, over and over, "Dr. Debbie told us no one would ever hurt us again! She lied. Why does Dr. Debbie hate us so?"

The Color Grey

I've had it! I cannot, will not, continue this merciless work. I feel like the Little Red Hen. No one is willing to plant the wheat, or harvest the grain, or bake the bread! But everyone is willing, without a shred of remorse, to come to the table! I have tried and tried to keep Grace Ann out of the hospital! I have *always* worked to meet her needs! What about *my* needs? No one seems to be particularly concerned about *my* mental health! Maybe *I* should have asked to be committed! I do good work! I don't ask for help! Why couldn't they hear me? Why didn't they believe *me*? I *know* she needed to be admitted! If someone had been willing to help, even for a few days, *just for a little while,* I would still be able to work with her. All she needs is time! She needs time to realize that she's not alone. She needs time to gather her ego strength. She needs time to hear Strong Man's voice. Her answers lie *within*, yet she *refuses to hear.* I don't know if I am more angry *at* her, or *for* her. And, I don't know if I'm more disappointed for her, or in me....

———◦•✕•◦———

A bitter, bitter lesson has been learned from this thwarted hospitalization, a lesson that forces me to realize, once and for all, that I really have no choice but to terminate *(sorry, Jessica!)* with Grace Ann. I have asked for help time and time again, but a deaf ear has been turned and no help has been forthcoming. Should I continue with her, *were I able to continue with her*, I have no reason to believe an outstretched hand would be offered now.

Not surprisingly, no therapist will take the case. Social Services will not even continue with her, ostensibly due to her repeated boundary violations. Her primary care physician calls. She hears the silence beyond the words. She senses the unspoken desperation. Realizing I can no longer put out the fires, she steps in, and rescues us both—at least for a while. Scouting out the local community resources, she runs down a kindly Baptist minister with some sort of a counseling background, pleading with him to intercede. Grace Ann begrudgingly visits the willing, but ill-prepared pastor, once, twice, maybe even three times.

It doesn't matter. His intervention bought me time—time to discharge my anger, time to lick my wounds…time to grieve.

Recognizing that Grace Ann, just like any other client, deserves a proper and respectful termination, I agree to hold several closing sessions. Our meetings prove to be bittersweet, for I miss the client I know so well and had grown to admire. As if sensing a looming vacillation, my intuition, perhaps the product of my own inner-knower, speaks in a clear voice, a voice too unmistakable, too certain to be ignored. *My work with Grace Ann is through.* I can no longer meet her needs. Perhaps if I had been more experienced in establishing and enforcing boundaries, I would not be so "burned-out." It really doesn't matter, for it is far too late to repair that damage now. The transference is just too entrenched. The fatigue is all consuming. The dull, thudding headaches never seem to go away. I, like the "old" Grace Ann, have become hypervigilant, a ringing phone now causing every muscle to tense. A mild paranoia settles in. I *expect* to be harassed the moment I walk through the office door. Easily agitated, I find myself struggling to curb my jaded tongue. Grace Ann's antics invade my every waking hour. It is an exceedingly difficult time.

I liked you better as a teacher, Mom…

I told you to get rid of her—she's crazy…

I struggle to regain my emotional footing, climbing upward toward the light of understanding, its healing illumination almost in view, only to fall back into the darkness of indecision and doubt. A box is placed, undetected, at the office door. Cutting away layer after layer of packaging tape, I remove its top, part the crumpled paper, and lift out what appears to be a vase of silk roses. Pleased with someone's thoughtfulness, I examine the welcome visitor, hoping to discover the origin of my unexpected good fortune. Joy swiftly turns to disbelief! Startled, I clutch my tightening chest, for upon a closer look, I recognize the color palate, the all too familiar hues and shades. There, assembled within the florist's vase, is one rose for each alter. And something, some sort of clear substance, is dripping from the multicolored petals. It looks like raindrops, or maybe dew. I am wrong on both counts, for Grace Ann has sent me flowers studded with, not raindrops, but her tears.

Grace Ann, forlorn, yet stoic, presents for these final sessions clad, not in pink or green or blue or peach or red, or even in purple, but in grey. It is not until our last meeting that I jolt upright in recognition! The alters had, week in and week out, arrived for sessions clothed in one of their many colors! No one ever wore grey! *What does this mean? Is grey the color of fear, or uncertainty? Could it be yet another alter? I'm not even going to think about the possibility.*

Hesitantly, for I truly do not want to open this door, I ask, "I notice you are wearing a different color, one that I don't remember ever having seen. Can you tell me whose color is grey?"

My former client looks down, wrings her hands, and whispers a barely perceptible, "Mine...."

I've heard that voice—in the hospital!

"But who are you?"

"You don't know me, Dr. Debbie," is the feeble reply.

"No, I don't. Can you tell me something about yourself?"

The soft, halting voice continues. I strain to hear for, head down-turned, she, or he, speaks in a bare whisper. It seems that Grace Ann's hospital ordeal triggered memories of confinement and abuse, leading her to, once again, dissociate. Since all of her helpers have been integrated, everyone except Strong Man, this *new alter is created* so Grace Ann can once again escape to her "safe, free place."

"I haven't had a chance to tell you, Dr. Debbie," my old friend, Strong Man, chimes in. I pleaded with her to let me help. She just will not listen. She has shut me out of her life. She is still so very angry at God...I fear the worse, Dr. Debbie. I do not think her life will get much better until she is reunited with me. But, I have no choice but to respect her wishes. Perhaps she will see. Perhaps she will not. Time will tell. She has the right not to come to the light...."

"I guess you're right, Strong Man. I guess time will tell...."

It is with great sadness that I learn that this entity responsible for all the ruckus is not Grace Ann, but a newly created alter, appropriately named Job.

The story, however, is far from over....

———◆◆◆◆———

Within a year of Grace Ann's untimely termination, a second Dissociative Identity Disorder referral winds its way to my office at The
Madeline Center. The afternoon caller is none other than Dr. Sullivan,
Grace Ann's psychiatrist. I hold my breath and grip the receiver in
revulsion as the respected physician shares a now hauntingly familiar
story. Clearly frustrated, he offers an overview of a complex and laby-
rinthine case. I nod with a sickening awareness as I learn of multiple
therapists, resistant depressions, debilitating panic attacks, recurring
headaches, self-mutilating behaviors, suicidal ideation, repeated hos-
pitalizations, and not surprisingly, the presence of vague, seemingly
overlapping dissociative states.

Perhaps Dr. Sullivan senses my silent reluctance, for he quickly
assures me of this patient's relative mental stability, anxiously offering
that this individual is not nearly so fragmented and without boundaries
as our mutual client, Grace Ann. He enthusiastically volunteers that
this individual does have health insurance, then artfully delivers the
blow: "Would you, Deborah, be willing to accept this referral?"

Struggling with the rising nausea, yet strangely exhilarated, I hear
my own disembodied voice agree to provide, not therapy services, but
a single consultation.

The single consultation turned into eighteen months. I reflect upon
my hesitation at accepting this second dissociative client as I nervously
pace the office reception area. The hour of the National Public Radio
broadcast is rapidly approaching, and I find myself attempting to quell
my anxiety. My "consultation turned client," now fully integrated, has
been invited to discuss her diagnosis and healing. A bare three minutes
into the program, my labored breathing ceases. Fear subsides, pride
emerges, and an unsuspecting tear wells up as her strong and articulate
voice permeates the room. *She is obviously not nervous. Why should I
be?*

I listen with excited anticipation as, in a direct and matter-of-fact
manner, she addresses the potentially explosive issue of child abuse,
acknowledges it as a factor in her own DID, then firmly closes the
door to this non-productive line of questioning. Reframing the process, casting the discourse in a more positive light, she shares her gratitude *(yes, her gratitude!)* toward the dissociative process. She is ap-

preciative of her former inside family, and describes her joyful, creative life beyond recovery. Caller after caller congratulates her on her courage, determination to leave a painful past behind, and willingness to forgive.

Jane's presentation had been similar to Grace Ann's. "Little Jane and Janie*"* were the system's children. The adolescent (and persecutor) alter, originally known as "The Evil One," was renamed (in a stroke of genius) "Darling" by the client's unsuspecting husband. The "Inner-Knower" called herself, or Herself, "Guide." Having learned my lessons well, I didn't balk, but simply followed the procedure painstakingly hammered out in my previous, *seemingly* unsuccessful case. *Guide* directed. I did what I was told. The rest, as they say, is history....

—◆·※◆·◆—

And now, back to the saga of Grace Ann Hughes. The year after termination is dreadful at best. My colleague, Dr. JoAnn, recognizing how troubled I am, reluctantly agrees to take Grace Ann's case. I consult before each session, yet must remain out of sight, for every encounter with my former client is nothing less than disastrous. A chance meeting in the parking lot causes quite a stir, as a sulking and petulant Grace Ann shrieks, "Why, Deborah? Why? You liked my alters, but you can't stand me! What did I do to deserve this? You said no one would hurt us, ever again. You promised! Is this how you treat all your clients? Why did you send us away? Why?"

The depression worsens. Arriving early one chilly spring morning, I decide to help out our secretary by retrieving the overnight messages from the voice mail. Startled, I hear, "Is anybody up there? This lady is curled up on our front porch. She's barefoot...seems real confused— just keeps mumbling something over and over, something about George. Is she one of your patients? Somebody needs to call us back. We're going to have to call the police to pick her up."

Dear God, not the police!

I hurriedly dial the number, only to discover I'm too late. Grace Ann has been taken to the hospital—again.

Grabbing my jacket, I unlock the back door, intending to wander through the spring gardens, needing to clear my head. But, my plans quickly change, for there, neatly positioned on the top step, are a tooth-brush and a shoe, silent reminders of Grace Ann's pain.

My walk is cancelled. I sit on the step and cry.

Dr. JoAnn consults with Dr. Sullivan. Grace Ann's depression has deepened, taking on a psychotic-like quality. The night on the porch has convinced them she must be hospitalized—to protect her from her-self! Having long since exhausted her mental health allowance, Dr. Sullivan has no choice but to admit her in a state-run psychiatric facil-ity, some sixty miles away. Grace Ann is heavily medicated. She stays for $2^1/_2$ months.

A month or so after her release, and no longer on psychotropic medication, I find her sitting in The Madeline Center's waiting room, two indistinguishable items in plastic bags perched upon her still shrink-ing lap. Approaching cautiously, for it's been a long time and I have absolutely no idea what to expect, I offer, in what I hope is my most casual and upbeat voice, "Well, Grace Ann, imagine finding you here. I didn't know you had an appointment with JoAnn today!"

Her face turns upward to greet me, and instantly I know I am gaz-ing into the eyes of Strong Man Jesus. Caught off guard, *once again*, I question, "Who's here with me? With whom am I speaking?"

"It's me, Deborah, Grace Ann. I baked you and JoAnn some pound cakes. I don't know if they'll be as good as Judith's, but at least I tried."

The gentleness of the voice and the sparkle in the eyes really has me confused by now, for I have no doubt that Strong Man is here in the room. I can feel his presence.

"I'll bet you thought I was Strong Man, didn't you, Deborah?"

"Grace Ann, I must admit I did," I respond nervously, the confu-sion written all over my face. "I, I just don't know what to say! You look fantastic! There's such a glow about you. You look happy… contented, so…peaceful. Yes, that's it, peaceful."

Smiling that hauntingly familiar smile, all the while radiating "the peace that passes all understanding," she, my *all healed* friend offers,

"Deborah, it took me awhile, but Strong Man and I are one. I'll have to tell you about it sometime."

"Yes, Grace Ann, you certainly will!"

———◆◆◆◆◆———

Some time later, Grace Ann talked with me about her healing.

"Over and over you talked to me about letting go of the pain, the anger. Well, after all my fighting, it was really simple.

"I stopped blaming God.

"I remembered what you said all along. I guess you were right—I do have a hard head. Anyway, I realized that God didn't do those things to me, that He would never put me through such hell. You were right. I was never alone. He *did* hold my hand. He shielded me, protected me, was, and is, a part of me.

"If God hadn't fragmented my mind and cradled my heart, I wouldn't be sitting here with you today. I made up my mind that day that I would never again turn my back—would never again doubt God.

"I don't know why all that awful stuff happened. I don't need to know. It just did. I survived. I'm whole. That's all that matters, Deborah. That's all that really matters...."

"Thank you."

Thank you all....

Reaching To Be Free

I was alone, desperate, surrounded by a wall of fear
      then you came into my life

You saw my wall, but knew it was not impenetrable
      and you worked to break it down

Not all at once – painfully, like a woodcutter with
      his ax cutting swiftly and carelessly,
      leaving sharp, piercing splinters

But peacefully, like the ocean,
      with its fusion of strength and gentleness
      as it slowly makes of the rocks
      the warm, soft sand

Now my wall is thinner: cracks are beginning to
      appear, and light enters

I reach out toward the light
      with my soul in the shape of fingers

My fingers grope, and find yours,
      reaching out to me

I feel the warmth and softness of your touch
      and I am less afraid

Through your loving touch I am encouraged
      to reach further

Anxious to free my fingers – my soul –
      to encounter the many things outside my wall

The rocks, the sand, and the ocean I have seen
      through your love

The first poem written in therapy by Grace Ann Hughes

EPILOGUE

I can almost hear Jessica's lively banter as my eyes are drawn to the garden's majestic purple day lily.

"This bee's Strong Man's bootiful color, Dr. Debbie," I *hear* her say.

Judith's crimson coral bells are here, along with the little ones' barely pink phlox, its "face tenderly turned upward in an attempt to gather instructions from the Master Planner." Karl designed and planted this haven for me.

"Maybe it'll keep you from losing your mind! I don't know what else to do."

We all enjoy its sheltering bliss.

Trouble, the Norwegian Forest cat rescued from the local animal shelter, is lazily swinging a not-very-menacing paw into the kidney-shaped koi pond. Kady, our four-year-old Springer Spaniel, is sprawled upon her back, legs flung haphazardly into the air, apparently exhausted from her dawn walk and already in the throes of the first nap of the day.

Smiling, I gaze ahead, conscious of the particular blueness of the eastern mountains on this sleepy summer morning. Jacqueline would have burst into the office with, "Dr. Debbie, you have to come see. It's such a beautiful day! Did you watch the shadows move about the mountain? Did you see my color, Dr. Debbie? Did you see?"

As my awareness shifts back to the garden, a speckled peach and yellow lantana catches my eye, its furry foliage spilling recklessly from an oversized clay pot. The peach stirs memories of 'barrassed Janice, and I laugh aloud at the memory of her adolescent antics. The yellow, however, evokes a wistfulness. I sigh as I recall the day Jessica first announced, in quite a grown-up voice, that yellow was now a part of their internal spectrum. Confused, I had asked, "What's this all about, Jessica? Yellow isn't one of your colors!"

"We's gonna have sunshine in our lives, Dr. Debbie. Strong Man Jesus says so!"

Well, if Strong Man Jesus says so, it must be true! I stopped asking questions long ago, willingly surrendering the directorship to a force far greater than I. It still surprises me that Grace Ann, of all people, would put up such a fight! Oh well, it doesn't matter now, since all appears to be well.

Absently, my eyes wander to the garden gate, its burnished bronze plaque carefully selected many summers ago. I read, then re-read its inscription, as if *seeing*, or *hearing*, its words for the first time.

> *There is always music amongst the trees in the garden,*
> *but one must be very quiet to hear it.*

Grace Ann's unwillingness to hear the music caused her such unnecessary pain!

I am reminded of a phrase within the Big Lady's "alaxation" tape,

> *In the stillness of the garden, all that she needs to know will*
> *be revealed to her. She does not fret, nor does she worry.*
> *She is one with nature. She is at perfect peace. You, too,*
> *Grace Ann, can know that peace....*

I had chosen that plaque and penned those words long before I had heard the word *transpersonal*. Upon reflection, I recognize *I knew without knowing*. My own *understanding* had evolved from a doctrinal, historical, external context to an inner knowing, a mystical awakening to unbounded potentialities. I reluctantly concede that if I had been more experienced, or perhaps even more successful with a traditional treatment approach, I may, in all likelihood, have been disinclined to follow Strong Man's lead. If I had not felt bewildered and incompetent, I certainly would have been less willing to depart from my well-rehearsed psychoanalytic path. The struggle had weakened my confidence. My ego had been sorely bruised. I embraced my own inner-knower out of sheer desperation, and came to rely upon my internal source of wisdom, not due to a religious conviction, but because, quite simply, I had no other choice. I came to know the meaning of a "lived spirituality." I walked then, as now, hand in hand, with a *living* God.

———◆◈◆◈◆◆———

Dr. Charles O. Matthews, the Advanced Theories Professor who had kindly listened to my anxious babble about this perplexing case, had officially introduced me to Transpersonal Psychology. As I paused to take a break from my incessant dialogue, he turned, lifted a well-worn copy of *Paths Beyond Ego*, and offered, "Deborah, I think this might help. Why don't you order a copy? I expect it will shed some light on this circuitous journey you've been traveling."

I followed his advice, ordered my edition, and inhaled its contents. Bewilderment gave way to validation. Pathology turned to promise. Strong Man Jesus, Grace Ann's internal self- helper, had assumed the role of guide and director of this, the most unusual of all plays, be-cause I, as therapist, had embraced the experience of unbounded aware-ness.

Grace Ann is currently in recovery following her double knee re-placement surgery. Even though all debt to me was forgiven, month after month a small check arrives, marked "payment on old bill." All other creditors have either been paid in full or are nearly satisfied.

Dissociative symptoms have remained in remission. George is a permanent resident of my office, holding fort from his perch at the base of the mahogany plant stand—clothed in Judith's red bra.

Grace Ann's life remains a remarkable testament to the power of the light that is awaiting us all.

Over the years, I have met other inner-knowers, including *Guide, Wings, Joseph,* and most recently, *Master.* Although I now know that to access this enigmatic alter means we're well on our way to healing, I am still amazed at the room's ethereal calm when He, or She, ap-pears.

I am grateful beyond words for these experiences.

Deborah
March 2002

GLOSSARY

Abreaction: The discharge of energy involved in recalling an event that has been repressed because it was consciously intolerable. The experience is one of reliving the trauma as if it were happening in the present, complete with physical as well as emotional manifestations (Cohen, Giller, Lynn W., Eds., 1991).

Acting-Out: An expression of unconscious feeling in actions rather than words. Acting out can take many forms, such as self-inflicted violence or suicidal gestures (Cohen, Giller, Lynn W., Eds., 1991).

Alter Personality: "An entity with a firm, persistent, and well-founded sense of self and a characteristic and consistent pattern of behavior and feelings in response to a given stimuli. It must have a range of functions, a range of emotional responses, and a significant life history of its existence" (Kluft, R.P., "An Introduction to Multiple Personality Disorder," *Psychiatric Annals*. 14.23). "Alters are dissociated parts of the mind that the patient experiences as separate from each other" (ISSD Practice Guidelines Glossary, 1994).

Amnesia: "Pathologic loss of memory; a phenomenon in which an area of experience becomes inaccessible to 'conscious recall.' The loss in memory may be organic, emotional, dissociative, or of mixed origin, and may be permanent or limited to a sharply circumscribed period of time" *(American Psychiatric Glossary*, p 13).

Amnesia Barriers: A highly adaptive use of the human imagination that allows the abuse victim to survive. As the abuse continues year after year, the victim compartmentalizes the memories, reinforcing and entrenching the illusion that the alters are actually separate people (Ross, 1989).

Axis II Pathology: Axis II is one component of the diagnostic system as outlined in the DSM-IV. An Axis II diagnosis denotes the presence of a personality disorder, such as borderline, histrionic, avoidant, or borderline personality disorder.(A personality disorder is characterized by inflexible, maladaptive personality traits.) Often comorbid (occurring in conjunction) with the Axis I diagnosis of Dissociative Identity Disorder, its presence often complicates treatment, contributing additional chaos, impairment, and distress (*DSM-IV*, 1994).

BASK: The Behavior, Affect, Sensation, and Knowledge Model for the treatment of Dissociative Disorders developed by Braun. The long-range goal of treatment is the integration of the four BASK components (Braun, The BASK Model of Dissociation, 1985).

Borderline Personality Disorder: A chronic pattern of instability of mood, interpersonal relationships, and self-image, beginning in early childhood and present in a variety of contents, as indicated by at least five of the following:

1) a pattern of unstable and intense interpersonal relationships, characterized by alternating between extremes of over idealization and devaluation;

2) impulsiveness in at least two areas that are potentially self- damaging, e.g., spending, sex, substance abuse, shoplifting, reckless driving, binge eating;

3) affective instability: marked shifts from baseline mood to depression, irritability, or anxiety, usually lasting a few hours and only rarely more than a few days;

4) inappropriate, intense anger or lack of control of anger, e.g., frequent displays of temper, constant anger, recurrent physical fights;

5) recurrent suicidal threats, gestures, or self-mutilating behavior;

6) marked and persistent identity disturbance manifested by uncertainty about at least two of the following: self-image, sexual orientation, long-term goals or career choice, type of friends desired, preferred values;

7) chronic feelings of emptiness or boredom;

8) frantic efforts to avoid real of imagined abandonment (*DSM-IV*, pp. 650-654).

Bipolarity: The Bipolar conception of Washbum's Dynamic-Dialectical

Paradigm divides the psyche into the egoic (ego functions of reality testing and self-control, and personal experience) and nonegoic (numinous power or spirit) poles (Washburn, 1995, p. II).

Body Memory: The term frequently refers to "body sensations that symbolically or literally capture some aspect of the trauma.... A person who is raped may later experience pelvic pain similar to that experienced at the time of the event. This type of bodily sensation may occur in any sensory mode: tactile, taste, smell, kinesthetic, or sight" (Sidran Foundation, 1995). This concept is referred to as somatoform disorder or somatic memory in the DSM-IV. (Sidran Foundation, 1995).

Boundaries: Appropriate touch, number, and length of therapy sessions, number and length of phone calls, etc., are examples of the therapeutic boundaries often established for the protection of both client and therapist. Since the DID client has little or no knowledge of healthy boundaries, having had her personal space repeatedly violated throughout the abuse, it is imperative that well-defined boundaries, or expectations, be established (Sidran Foundation, 1995).

Confabulation: "This term originally referred to a neurological deficit in which a person who is unable to recall previous situations or events fabricates stories in response to questions about those situations or events. It is now used more broadly to refer to 'false memories' that are supposedly created in response to questions asked by a therapist or interviewer" (Sidran Foundation, 1995).

Copresence: Occurs when an alter personality in the background takes joint control of the body without displacing the primary personality, or when this alter influences the primary personality's affects or perceptions. Copresence may be also referenced as co-consciousness (Ross, 1989).

Countertransference: " A therapist's conscious or unconscious emotional reactions to a client. It is a therapist's job to monitor his or her reactions to a client and to minimize their impact on the therapeutic relationship and treatment" (Sidran Foundation, 1995).

Depersonalization Disorder: An alteration of the individual's sense of self so that the person feels unreal, as if in a dream. The individual may report memories of a dream-like quality, which at times can not be distinguished as fantasy. Individuals often report the experience of being outside of one's body, watching oneself or looking down from above (Putnam, p.15).

Derealization: Often occurring in conjunction with depersonalization, derealization, a surrealistic awareness, can be described as estrangement, detachment, and a sense that one's external world is strange or unreal (*DSM-IV*, 1994).

Diagnostic Axes: The Diagnostic and Statistical Manual of Mental Disorders—Fourth Edition (1994) uses a multiaxial system to assist the treating professional to plan the course of treatment and to some degree, predict outcome. The five diagnostic axes are:

Axis I   Clinical Disorders

Axis II   Personality Disorders/Mental Retardation

Axis III   General Medical Condition, i.e. endocrine disorders, diseases of the digestive system, congenital anomalies, complications of childbirth, etc.

Axis IV Psychosocial and Environmental Problems, i.e., problems with primary support group, educational problems, occupational problems, housing problems, economic problems, problems with access to health care services, problems relating to the legal system, etc.

Axis V   Global Assessment of Functioning, based on a 100 point scale (American Psychiatric Association (1994), pp. 25-31) .

Discrete State of Consciousness: A d-SoC is a unique pattern of psychological structures which, in spite of subsystem or environmental variation, is stabilized by a number of processes so that it retains its identity and function. "...an automobile remains an automobile whether on a road or in a garage (environmental change), whether you change the brand of spark plugs or the color of the seat covers (internal variation). Examples of d-SoC are the ordinary waking state, non-dreaming sleep, dreaming sleep, hypnosis, alcohol intoxication, marijuana intoxication, and meditative states" (Tart, In Walsh & Vaughan, p. 35).

Discrete Altered State of Consciousness: A d-ASC is a d-SoC that is different from the baseline state of consciousness (b-SoC). The d-ASC represents a new system, a restructuring of consciousness (Tart, In Walsh & Vaughan, 1993).

Dissociation: "A complex process of changes in a person's consciousness which causes an alteration in the normally integrative functions of identity, memory, thoughts, feelings, and experiences (Cohen, et al. p. 226).

Dissociative Identity Disorder: The existence within the person of two or more distinct personalities or personality fragments (each with its own relatively enduring patterns of perceiving and relating to the environment and self), with at least two of these personalities or personality states recurrently taking complete control of the individual's behavior (*DSM-IV*, 1994).

Diagnostic Statistical Manual: The DSM-IV (fourth edition) was published in 1994 by the American Psychiatric Association, and contains standard definitions of the recognized psychological disorders. (*DSM-IV*, 1994).

Dissociative Disorder Interview Scale: A structured interview developed by Ross, Heber, Norton, and Anderson for the purpose of standardization of the DID diagnosis. Utilized in both clinical and research settings, the DDIS has good clinical validity, and "has shown that DID is a valid diagnosis with a consistent set of features and that both dissociative experiences and dissociative disorders are common" (Ross, p. 135).

Dissociative Experiences Scale: The DES is a 28 item self-report instrument developed by Frank Putnam, M.D., and Eve B. Carlson, Ph.D. The respondent is asked to indicate the frequency with which certain dissociative or depersonalization experiences occur (Sidran Foundation, 1995).

False Memory Syndrome: "False Memory Syndrome is a term coined in the early 1990's by the False Memory Syndrome Foundation (FMSF). The FMSF defines the syndrome as 'a condition in which the person's personality and interpersonal relationships are oriented around a memory that is objectively false but strongly believed in to the detriment of the welfare of the person and others involved in the memory' (Goldstein, "Confabulations: Creating False Memories—Destroying Families," p. iv). This organization was founded by parents of adult children who reported delayed memories of child abuse usually uncovered in psychotherapy. These parents deny the abuse and believe false memories have been implanted by the therapists in the minds of their adult children. The term 'false memory syndrome' is popular in the media but is not based on clinical research or accepted theoretical formulations. It is not listed as a diagnosis or symptom in the DSM-IV" (Sidran Foundation, 1995).

Flashback: "A type of spontaneous abreaction common to victims of acute trauma. Also known as 'intrusive recall,' flashbacks can take the form of (a) dreams or nightmares, (b) dreams from which the dreamer awakens but has difficulty establishing contact with reality, (c) conscious flashbacks, in which the individual may not lose contact with reality but may experience auditory, visual, olfactory, and/or tactile hallucinations and, (d) unconscious flashbacks, in which the individual 'relives' a traumatic event while remaining anmestic of the event" (Cohen, et al. p. 226).

Fragment: A dissociated, split-off part of the personality state which, while consistent in emotional and behavioral response to specific situations, has a limited function and is not as well developed as an "alter" personality (Putnam, 1989).

Internal Self Helper: An altered state, generally a helper or protector who has a working knowledge of the personality system. "Experienced therapists disagree about the nature or the ISH personalities and whether they occur in all MPD [DID] patients. Typically they are physically passive and relatively emotionless personalities, who provide information and insight into the inner working of the system" (Putnam, p. 110).

Iatrogenesis: The belief (freqently held by skeptics of DID) that a therapist treating a dissociative client may, with or without hypnosis, unwittingly reinforce the client's behavior and contribute to the dissociative process (Putnam, 1989; Ross, 1989).

Losing Time: Unaccounted for periods of time (minutes, hours, days, weeks, years) of which the individual has no memory and no recollection of her activities. Frequently confusing and frightening to the individual, these "lost" periods often allow for re-victimization (Sidran Foundation, 1995).

Mapping: A drawing or outline prepared by a helper personality which diagrams the altered states and explains the inner world of the system. This "map" must be updated periodically as additional personality states are identified (Putnam, 1989).

Medical Model: "The view that abnormal behavior results from a physical/ biological cause and should be treated medically.... As non-medical disciplines have become more involved in the treatment of mental disorders, the conflict between the medical model and social/behavioral models has become heightened" (Sidran Foundation, 1995).

Medications:

Fluoxetine Hydrochloride, otherwise known as *Prozac*, selectively inhibits serotonin uptake, and is commonly used in the treatment of Major Depression.

Alprazolam, commonly known as *Xanax*, is classified as a benzodiazepine and is used in the treatment of anxiety disorders associated with depression.

Diclofenac Sodium, or *Voltaren*, is a nonsteroidal anti-inflammatory often used to treat acute and/or chronic rheumatoid arthritis, osteoarthritis, etc.

Mental Status Exam: A formal evaluation of a presenting client's current psychological, emotional, and behavioral functioning. The MSE includes orientation to time, place, and person, thought content, cognition, mood, affect, insight, and suicidallbomicidal ideation or intent. The MSE is often administered during the initial therapy session.

Panic Attack: An attack of uncontrollable anxiety, usually lasting several minutes though possibly continuing for hours (Bootzin & Acocella, 1988).

Posttraumatic Stress Disorder: An intense form of anxiety disorder that results from exposure to acutely traumatic events (natural disasters, assault, rape, wartime combat). The victims often re-experience the traumatic event in recollections and/or nightmares, may appear unaware of their present surroundings, and may suffer physical symptoms and/or intense irritability. The symptoms frequently last for six months, but may remain for years (Bootzin & Acocella, 1988).

Polyfragmentation: Another term for the layering of personality fragments within the dissociative client's system.

Psychogenic Amnesia: A sudden inability to recall important personal information that is too pervasive to be explained by ordinary forgetfulness and cannot be attributed to an organic mental disorder (Putnam, 1989).

Psychogenic Fugue: Involves a sudden, unexpected travel away from the individual's home or work place coupled with an inability to recall the past and a frequent assumption of a new identity (Putnam, 1989).

Regression: The return to an earlier psychological state. In DID, child alters are an example of trauma-based regression (Sidran Foundation, 1995).

Revivification: "The vivid remembering of past experiences. When remembering traumatic events the client may see, hear, taste, smell, and feel as though the event is happening in the present. This is common during an abreaction or flashback of previous trauma" (Sidran Foundation, 1995).

Screening: A healing technique utilized by therapists of dissociative clients in which the client is helped into a trance and asked to visualize a movie or television screen, and to project his experiences onto the screen so they can be viewed from afar. Screening serves to minimize painful revivification during an abreaction (Putnam, 1989).

Script Memory: A manufactured identity or memory purposefully implanted during ritual or cult abuse (Mungadze, "Scripts and Screen Memories in Victims of Ritual Abuse," November 1992 Conference, ISSMP&D).

Self-Mutilation: A form of self-harm that occurs in at least one third of all DID clients (Putnam, et al., 1986). Self-mutilation typically involves cutting with glass or razor blades, burning with cigarettes or matches, and "may also take bizarre forms, such as insertion of broken glass or other foreign objects into the vagina" (Putnam, p. 64).

Schneiderian First Rank (Order) Symptoms: The medical model criteria utilized in the diagnosis of Schizophrenia. Dissociative patients frequently
experience such Schneiderian symptoms as voices within the head and
control by outside forces.

Switching: The psychophysiological process of changing from one alter personality to another, often accompanied by affective, facial, motor, behavioral, voice and speech, and dress and grooming changes. Switching
may be the result of internal dynamics or may be triggered by external
events (Putnam, 1989).

Triphasic: The division of human development into three general phases—
the preegoic, egoic, and transegoic (Washburn, 1995).

NOTES

Chapter 1

1 (p. 16)   Doleski, *The Hurt*

Chapter 2

2 (p. 26)   Shel Silverstein, *Where the Sidewalk Ends.*

3 (p. 39)   Minirth, Meier, Henfelt, Snead. *Love Hunger* 1990.

4 (p. 43)   Assagioli, Roberto. Psychosynthesis, 1965 pg. 210.

5 (p. 72)   Sigmund Freud, "1897 Letter to Wilhelm Fleiss."

Chapter 3

6 (p. 74)   Machen, Nancy. *The Newsletter for the Society for the Investigation, Treatment and Prevention of Ritual and Cult Abuse*, 1, 3, Fall/Winter, 1993-1994.

7 (p. 74)   Greaves, G. (1992). *Alternative Hypotheses Regarding Claims of Satanic Cult Activity: A Critical Analysis.* In D. Sakheim & S. Devine (Ed.*), Out of darkness: Exploring Satanism and Ritual Abuse* pp. 45-69 New York: Lexington Books.

8 (p. 76)   Smith, M. & Pazder, L. (1980). *Michelle Remembers.* New York: Simon and Schuster, Inc.

9 (p. 76)   Finkelhor, David., Ph.D. *Paper presented to the Family Research Laboratory at the University of New Hampshire,* 1988, pg. 20.

10 (p. 76)   *Ritual Child Abuse: Definitions, Typology, and Prevalence, "Believe the Children" Newsletter,* X, Fall, 1993.

11 (p. 76)   Ibid.

12 (p. 77)   Illinois Public Act #87-1167, January 1993.

13 (p. 78)   Smith, M., *Ritual Abuse: What It Is, Why It Happens, How to Help*, 1993. pg. 3.

14 (p. 80)   StarDancer, Caryn, Shackles, Sibylline: *Mind Control in the Context of Ritual Abuse, Survivorship Newsletter*, 1992.

15 (p. 81)   Mayer, Robert, M.D. *Satan's Children.* 1992.

16 (p. 81)   Ibid.

17 (p. 84)   Mayer, Robert, M.D., *Satan's Children,* 1992.

18 (p. 85)   American Psychiatric Association (1994). *Diagnostic & Statistical Manual of Mental Disorders* (4th edition). Washington D.C.: American Psychiatric Association Press.

19 (p. 85)   *Ibid.* pp. 481-490.

20 (p. 85)   Cohen, B., Giller, E. & Lynn, W. (Ed.). (1991*). Multiple Personality from the Inside Out.* Lutherville, Md: Sidran Press. pg. 82.

21 (p. 85)   *Ibid.* pg. 199.

22 (p. 85)   Putnam, Frank. *Diagnosis and Treatment of Multiple Personality Disorder.* New York: The Guilford Press. 1989, pg. 49. (Putnam has been a premier researcher in the field of dissociative identity disorder. He devised the original categories of "personalities," later known as "altered stated of consciousness.")

23 (p. 86)   Kluft, R. (1984). *An Introduction to Multiple Personality Disorder.* Psychiatric Annals, 14, pp. 19-24.

24 (p. 86)   Putnam, Frank. *Diagnosis and Treatment of Multiple Personality Disorder.* New York: The Guilford Press. 1989.

25 (p. 87)   Gould, Catherine. *Torture Based Mind Control: What It Is and How to Treat It.* A lecture delivered at the 1995 Ritual abuse Conference in Los Angeles, CA.

26 (p. 88)   Smith, M., *Ritual Abuse: What It Is, Why It Happens, How to Help.* 1993.

27 (p. 88)   David Neswald, Ph.D., and Catherine Gould, Ph.D., and Vicki Costain-Graham. *Basic Treatment and Program Neutralization Strategies for Adult M.P.D. Survivors of Satanic Ritual Abuse, Treating Abuse Today*, 1992, pp. 2,3

28 (p. 88)   StarDancer. 1992 Newsletter.

29 (p. 88)   Gould, Catherine. 1995 Lecture in Los Angeles.

30 (p. 89)   Ibid.

31 (p. 89)   Ibid.

32 (p. 90)   Ibid.

33 (p. 90)   Putnam. *Diagnosis and Treatment of Multiple Personality Disorder*. New York. The Guilford Press. 1989.

34 (p. 91)   Ibid.

35 (p. 90)   Ibid. pp. 203-204.

36 (p. 91)   Katchen, Martin H. *The History of Satanic Religions*, in Sakheim and Devine's *Out of Darkness: Exploring Satanism and Ritual Abuse*, Lexington Books, New York.1992, p. 1.

37 (p. 91)   Ross, Colin A. (1995). *Satanic Ritual Abuse: Principles of Treatment*. Toronto, Canada: University Toronto Press.

38 (p. 91)   Katchen, Martin. pg. 2

39 (p. 91)   *The Encyclopedia of Mystical and Paranormal Experiences*, pg. 236.

40 (p. 91)   Ross, Colin. pg. 22.

41 (p. 91)   Katchen, pg. 3.

42 (p. 91)   Ross, Colin, pg. 23.

43 (p. 92)   Katchen, pg. 3.

44 (p. 92)   Ibid. pg. 3.

45 (p. 91)   Sally Hill, M.S.W., and Jean Goodwin, M.D., as quoted by Martin H. Katchen in Sakheim and Devine's, *Out of Darkness: Exploring Satanism and Ritual Abuse*, pg. 3.

46 (p. 92)   Smith, M. *Ritual Abuse: What It Is, Why It Happens, How to Help*. 1993. pg. 14.

47 (p. 92)   Katchen, pg. 41

48 (p. 93)   Ibid. pg. 6.

49 (p. 93)   Ross, Colin A. pg. 34.

50 (p. 93)   Smith, M. pg. 14.

51 (p. 93)   Ross, Colin A. pp. 37-38.

52 (p. 93)   Katchen, Martin H. pg. 7.

53 (p. 94)   Ibid. pg. 8.

54 (p. 94)   Ibid. pg. 8.

55 (p. 94)   Ross, Colin A. pg. 32.

56 (p. 94)   Katchen, Martin H. pp. 8-9.

57 (p. 94)   *Freemasonry and Satanism, Followers of Jesus Christ* (pamphlet) Evansville, IN 1994.

58 (p. 94)   John Symonds and Kenneth Grant, Eds. *The Confessions of Alliester Crowley.* London: Arkana, 1979 pg. 19.

59 (p. 94)   *The Encyclopedia of Mystical and Paranormal Experiences*, pg. 130.

60 (p. 95)   Katchen. pg. 13.

61 (p. 95)   Ibid. pg. 30.

62 (p. 95)   Smith, M. pp. 78-79.

63 (p. 95)   George B. Greaves, *Alternative Hypotheses Regarding Claims of Satanic Cult Activity: A Critical Analysis*, in Sakheim & Devine, *Out of Darkness: Exploring Satanism and Ritual Abuse*, 1992, pg. 48.

64 (p. 96)   Smith, M. pp. 78-79

Chapter 4

65 (p. 132)   Social Services Report

Chapter 5

66 (p. 136)   Williams, Margery. *The Velveteen Rabbit.*

67 (p. 157)   From the book *I Like Me.*

68 (p. 158)   Ann Adams. *The Silver Boat.* 1990.

69 (p. 177)   Wylie, D. *The Shadow of a Doubt.* The Family Therapy Networker, 3, pp. 32-41.

70 (p. 178)   Ibid.

Chapter 6

71 (p. 191)   Breur, J., & Freud, S. (1986). *Studies on Hysteria.* New York: Pelican Books. (Original work published 1895.)

72 (p. 193)   Barclay, William. (1954), *The Daily Study Bible: The Gospel of Mark.* Edinburgh: The Saint Andrew Press, p. 163.

73 (p. 194)   Philippians 4:6-7.

74 (p. 194)   Luke 11:9-10.

75 (p. 194)   John 8:32.

76 (p. 194)   Excerpt from The Confessions of St. Augustine.

77 (p. 194)   Quotes from Tolstoy, Jung and Dante etched along border of personal Bible.

78 (p. 198) Scheffer, M. *Bach Flower Therapy: Theory and Practice.* pg. 9.

79 (p. 198) Ibid. pg. 3.

80 (p. 199) Ibid. pg. 86.

81 (p. 199) Ibid. pg. 175.

82 (p. 200) Bucke, R. *Cosmic Consciousness.* New York. Penguin Books. 1901. pg. 5.

83 (p. 201) Ibid. pg. 10.

84 (p. 205) Flinders, Carol. *Enduring Grace: Living Portraits of Seven Women Mystics.* Harper Collins, San Francisco, CA. pg. 98.

85 (p. 205) Ibid. pg. 203.

86 (p. 206) Ibid. pg. 143.

87 (p. 206) Ibid. pg. 109.

88 (p. 206) Ibid.

89 (p. 207) Ibid. pg. 172.

90 (p. 208) Ibid. pg. 178.

91 (p. 208) Ibid.

92 (p. 209) Ibid.

93 (p. 210) Ibid. pg. 89.

94 (p. 210) In Flinders book: Poem by T. S. Elliott.

95 (p. 210) Ibid. pg. 92.

96 (p. 211) Ibid. pg. 93.

97 (p. 211) Ibid. pg. 100.

98 (p. 211) Ibid. pg. 96.

99 (p. 213) Ibid. pg. 100.

100 (p. 213) Ibid. pg. 51.

101 (p. 214) Ibid. pg. 53.

102 (p. 214) Ibid. pg. 59.

103 (p. 214) Ibid. pg. 58

104 (p. 215) Ibid. pg. 143.

Chapter Seven

105 (p. 218) *The Selfish Giant*, Oscar Wilde.

BIBLIOGRAPHY

A Course in Miracles: Manual for Teachers. Tiburon, CA: Foundation for Inner Peace, 1975.

Abraham, Scott. (1995). "Repressed Memory Syndrome"

Ackerman, N. (1956). *The Psychodynamics of Family Life.* New York: BasicBooks.

Adityanjee, R. & Khandelwal, S. K. (1989*). Current Status of Multiple Personality in India. American Journal of Psychiatry,* pp. 146, 1607-1610.

Adams, A. (1990). *The Silver Boat.* Cincinnati, OH: BSC.

Adler, A. (1917). *Study of Organ Inferiority and its Psychical Compensation.* New York: Nervous & Mental Disease Publishing Co.

———. (1928). On Teaching Courage. *Survey Graphic,* 61, pp. 241-242.

———. (1929). Position in Family Influences Lifestyle. *International Journal of Individual Psychology,* 3, pp. 211-227.

Aiaye, Swani. Psychotherapy – *East and West: A Unifying Paradigm, Pennsylvania: The Himalayan International Institute of Yoga Science and Philosophy of the U.S.A.* 1983.

Allison, R. (1974). A Guide to Parents: How to Raise Your Daughter to Have Multiple Personalities. *Family Therapy,* 1, pp. 83-88.

———. (1974). A New Treatment Approach for Multiple Personalities. *American Journal of Clinical Hypnosis*, 17, pp. 15-32.

Almaas, A. H. (1990). *The Pearl Beyond Price.* Berkeley, CA: Diamond Books/Almaas Publications.

American Psychiatric Association (1980). *American Psychiatric Glossary.* Washington, DC: American Psychiatric Association Press.

American Psychiatric Association (1994). *Diagnostic & Statistical Manual of Mental Disorders* (4th edition). Washington, DC: American Psychiatric Association Press.

Assagioli, R. (1965). *Psychosynthesis.* New York: Penguin Books.

———. (1973). *The Act of Will.* London: Penguin Books.

————. (1976). *Transpersonal Inspiration and Psychological Mountain Climbing*. New York: Psychosynthesis Research Foundation.

Bandura, A. (1977). *Principles of Behavior Modification*. New York: Holt, Rinehart, & Winston.

————. (1982). "Self-efficacy Program in Human Agency." *American Psychologist*, 37, pp. 122- 147.

Barach, Peter. (1993). "Draft of Recommendations for Treating Dissociative Identity Disorder." International Society for the Study of Multiple Personality and Dissociation.

Barclay, William. (1954). *The Daily Study Bible: The Gospel of Mark*. Edinburgh: The Saint Andrew Press.

Beck, A. (1972). *Depression: Causes and Treatment*. Philadelphia: University of Pennsylvania Press.

————. (1978). *Anxiety Checklist*. Philadelphia: Center for Cognitive Therapy.

Beere, D. (1989). "Satanic Programming Designed to Undercut Therapy." Sixth International Conference on Multiple Personality/Dissociation. (Report).

Beere, D. (1994). "The Experience of Shame and Traumatization in Mind Control." Williamsburg, VA: Second Annual Conference on Ritual Abuse/Mind control. (Report).

"Believe the Children Newsletter." P. O. Box 268462, Chicago, IL 60626.

Bernstein, E. & Putnam, F. (1986). "Development, Reliability, and Validity of a Dissociation Scale." *Journal of Nervous and Mental Disease*, 174, pp. 727-735.

Binet, A. (1977). *Alterations of Personality*. Washington: University Publications of America. (Original work published 1890.)

Bliss, E. (1984). "A Symptom Profile of Patients with Multiple Personalities, including MMPI Results." *Journal of Nervous and Mental Disease*, 172, pp. 197-202.

————. (1986). *Multiple Personalities: Allied Disorders and Hypnosis*. New York: Oxford University Press.

Bliss, E. & Bliss, J. (1985). *Prism: Andrea's World*. New York: Stein & Day.

Bohm, D. (1980). *Wholeness and the Implicate Order*. London: Routledge & Kegan Paul.

Boon, S., & Draijer, N. (1993). "Multiple personality in the Netherlands: A clinical investigation of 71 patients." *American Journal of Psychiatry*, 150, 489-494.

Boor, M. (1982). "Childhood Experiences of a Client With Multiple Personalities." *Psychological Reports*, 51, pp. 317-318.

———. (1982). "The Multiple Personality Epidemic: Additional Cases and Inferences Regarding Diagnosis, Etiology, Dynamics, and Treatment." *Journal of Nervous and Mental Disease, 170*, pp. 302- 304.

Boorstein, S. (Ed.). (1996). *Transpersonal Psychotherapy*. New York: State University of New York Press.

———. (Ed.). (1997). *Clinical Studies in Transpersonal Psychotherapy*. New York: State University of New York Press.

Bootzin, R. & Acocella, J. (1988). *Abnormal Psychology*. New York: Random House.

Borg, W. & Gall, M. (1989). *Educational Research*. New York: Longman.

Bowen, M. (1960). "A Family Concept of Schizophrenia." In D. Jackson. *The Etiology of Schizophrenia*. New York: BasicBooks.

———. (1978). *Family Therapy in Clinical Practice*. New York: Jason Aronson.

Brooke Medicine Eagle. (1990). "Open to the Great Mystery." In B. Shield & R. Carlson (Eds.), *For the Love of God* pp. 97-102. California: New World Library.

Braun, B. G. (1985). "Dissociation: Behavior, Affect, Sensation, Knowledge. Dissociative Disorders: Proceedings of the Second International Conference on Multiple Personality/Dissociative States." Rush University: Chicago, IL.

Braun, B. (1988). Bask Model. "Dissociation" pp. 1, 11-12.

———. (1989). Comments. *Ritual child abuse: A Professional Overview*. Ukia, CA: Cavalcade Productions (videotape).

Breur, J. & Freud, S. (1986). *Studies on Hysteria*. New York: Pelican Books. (Original work published 1895.)

Brewer, Connie. (1984). *Escaping the Shadows, Seeking the Light*. San Francisco, CA: Harper.

Broughton, J. (1975). "Development of Natural Epistemology in Adolescence and Early Adulthood." Doctoral dissertation: Harvard University.

Browne, Angela & Finkelhor, David. (1986). "Impact of Child Sexual Abuse: A Review of the Research." *Psychological Bulletin, 99, No. 1.*

Bucke, Richard Maurice. (1991). *Cosmic Consciousness*. New York: Arkanc Books.

California Institute of Integral Studies. (1996-1998). San Francisco, CA: Self Published.

Calof, D. (1993). "Facing the Truth About False Memory." *The Family Therapy Networker*, pp. 41, 43.

Carnes, Patrick J. (1993). "Addiction and Post-Traumatic Stress: The Convergence of Victim's Realities." *Treating Abuse Today*, 3, 3.

Cashdan, Sheldon. (1988). *Object Relations Therapy*. New York: W.W. Norton & Sons.

Casey, K. & Vanceburg, M. (1983). *The Promise of a New Day*. New York: Hazelden Foundation.

Caul, D. (1983). "On Relating to Multiple Personalities. New York." *Paper presented at the annual meeting of the American Psychiatric Association.*

————. (1984). "Group and videotape techniques for multiple personality disorder." *Psychiatric Annals*, pp. 14, 43-50.

"Characteristics of Female Incest victims: Survivors of Incest Anonymous." Baltimore, MD: World Service Office, 1994.

Chess, Jan, as quoted in "An Open Letter from Lauren Stratford" 1994.

"Child Sexual Abuse Survivors Vulnerable." *The Menninger Letter*, February, 1993.

Chinen, A. (1996). "The Emergence of Transpersonal Psychiatry." In B. Scotton, A. Chinen, & J. Battista (Ed.). *Textbook of Transpersonal Psychiatry and Psychology* pp. 9-20. New York: BasicBooks.

Chopra, Deepak. (1995) *The Higher Self*. Illinois: Nightengale-Conant Corp.

Cleary, T. & Shapiro, S. (1995). "The Plateau Experience and the Post-mortem Life: Abraham H. Maslow's Unfinished Theory." *Journal of Transpersonal Psychology*, 27, 1-23.

Cohen, B., Giller, E. & Lynn, W. (Ed.). (1991). *Multiple Personality From the Inside Out*. Lutherville, MD: Sidran Press.

Cohen, J. (1982). "Multiple Personality Shown to be a Distinct Clinical Entity." *Psychiatric News*, 10, 1.

Comstock, C. (1987). Internal Self-helpers or Centers. *Integration*, 3, pp. 3-12.

Constantine, A. (1995). "Government Uses of Torture Based Mind Control." Los Angeles, CA: A lecture delivered at the 1995 Ritual Abuse Conference.

Coons, P. (1986). "Child Abuse and Multiple Personality Disorder: Review of the Literature and Suggestions for Treatment." *Child Abuse and Neglect*, 10, pp. 455-462.

Copeland, C. & Kitching, E. (1937). A Case of Profound Dissociation of the Personality. *Journal of Mental Science*, 83, pp. 719-726.

Corey, G., Corey, M., & Callanan, P. (1993). *Issues and Ethics in the Helping Professions*. California: Brooks/Cole Publishing Company.

Carlson, N. (1984). *I Like Me*. New York: Penguin Books.

Corsini, R., & Wedding, D. (Ed.). (1995). *Current Psychotherapies*. Itasca, IL: F.E. Peacock Publishers, Inc.

Cortright, B. (1997). *Psychotherapy and Spirit*. New York: State University of New York Press.

Cowlan, D. (1978). *Piaget with Feeling*. New York: Holt Publishing Company.

Deikman, A. (1996). "Sufism and Psychiatry." In S. Boorstein (Ed.), *Transpersonal Psychotherapy,* pp. 241-260. New York: State University of New York Press.

Denzin, N. & Lincoln, Y. (Ed.). (1994). *Handbook of Qualitative Research*. California: Sage Publications, Inc.

Doleski, T. (1983). *The Hurt*. New Jersey: Paulist Press, Inc.

Don, N. (1996). "A Case Study in Multi-modality Therapy." In S. Boorstein (Ed.), *Transpersonal Psychotherapy,* pp. 343-375. New York: State University of New York Press.

Dreikers, R. & Mosak, H. (1967). "The tasks of life. II. The fourth life task." *Individual Psychologist*, 4, pp. 51-55.

Dubin, W. (1991). "The use of meditative techniques in psychotherapy supervision." *Journal of Transpersonal Psychology*, 23, pp. 65-80.

———. (1994). "The use of meditative techniques for teaching dynamic psychology." *Journal of Transpersonal psychology,* 26, pp. 19-36.

Duncan, C. W. (1994). *The Fractured Mirror*. Deerfield Beach, Florida: Health Communications, Inc.

Each Day a New Beginning. (1985). New York: The Hazelden Foundation.

Eisler, R. (1990). "The Long Journey Home". In B. Shield & R. Carlson (Ed.), *For the Love of God,* pp. 16-23. California: New World Library.

Engler, J. (1993). "Becoming Somebody and Nobody: Psychoanalysis and Buddhism." In R. Walsh & F. Vaughan (Eds.), *Paths Beyond Ego: The Transpersonal Vision,* pp. 118-129. New York: G.P. Putnam's Sons.

Erickson, Milton. (1992). *Healing in Hypnosis*. New York: Irvington Publishers, Inc.

Eyesnck, H. (1967). *The Biological Basis of Personality.* Springfield, IL: Charles C. Thomas.

Fadiman, J. & Speeth, K., "Transpersonal Psychotherapy." In R. Hendrik (Ed.), *Handbook of Psychotherapy.* New York: New American Press, In Press.

Fairbain, W. (1954). *An Object Relations Theory of Personality.* New York: BasicBooks.

Foote, W. (1996). "Guided-imagery Therapy." In B. Scotton, A. Chinen, & J. Battista (Ed.), *Textboook of Transpersonal Psychiatry and Psychology,* pp. 355-365. New York: BasicBooks.

Fehmi, L & Selzer, F. (1996). "Biofeedback and Attention Training." In S. Boorstein (Ed.), *Transpersonal Psychotherapy* pp. 377-404. New York: State University of New York Press.

Feldman, G. (1993). *Lessons in Evil, Lessons From the Light: A True Story of Satanic Abuse and Spiritual Healing,* New York: Crown Publishers.

Fidao, Wendy. (1995). "Shamanic Antecedents to Dissociation, Mind Control, and Healing in Ritually Abused Patients." Los Angeles, CA: 1995 Ritual Abuse Conference. (Report)

Flinders, C. (1993). *Enduring Grace: Living Portraits of Seven Women Mystics.* San Francisco: Harper Collins.

———. (1994). *Enduring Grace.* Audiotape # A247. Boulder, Co.: Sounds True Audio.

Frankel, F. (1990). "Hypnotizability and Dissociation." *American Journal of Psychiatry,* 147.

Frankl, V. (1963). *Man's Search for Meaning: An Introduction to Logotherapy.* New York: Pocket Books.

Frankl, V. (1969). *Will to Meaning.* New York: World Publishing.

Freemasonry and Satanism, Followers of Jesus Christ (Pamphlet) 5220 Ashley Drive, Evansville, IN 47711

Freeman, L. (1983). *It's My Body.* Charlotte, N.C.: Kids Rights.

Freud, S. (1894). "The Neuropsychosis of Defense."In J. Strachey (Ed.), *Complete Psychological Works of Sigmund Freud: Standard Edition.* London: Hogarth Press.

———. (1900). "The Interpretation of Dreams." In J. Strachey (Ed.), *Complete Psychological Works of Sigmund Freud: Standard Edition.* London: Hogarth Press.

———. (1914). "The History of the Psychoanalytic Movement." In J. Strachey (Ed.), *Complete Psychological Works of Sigmund Freud. Standard Edition.* London: Hogarth Press.

Freyd, Jennifer. (1993). "Theoretical and Personal Perspectives on the Delayed Memory Debate." Paper presented at the Center for Mental Health at Foote Hospital's Continuing Education Conference: Controversies Around Recovered Memories of Incest and Ritualistic Abuse, Ann Arbor, MI.

Friesen, J. (1997). *Uncovering the Mystery of MPD.* Eugene, Oregon: Wipf & Stock Publishers.

Gannaway, G. (1989). "Historical Truth Versus Narrative Truth: Clarifying the Role of Exogenous Trauma in the Etiology of Multiple Personality and its Variants." *Dissociation,* 2, pp. 205-220.

———. (1990). "A Psychodynamic Look at Alternative Explanations for Satanic Ritual Abuse in MPD Patients." Chicago, IL. Paper delivered at Seventh International Conference on Multiple Personality/Dissociative States.

Gardiner, G. (1974). "Hypnosis With Children and Adolescents." *International Journal of Clinical and Experimental Hypnosis,* 22, pp. 20-38.

Garmezy, N. (1983). "Stressors in Childhood." In N. Garmezy & M. Rutter (Ed.), *Stress, Coping and Development in Children.* New York: McGraw Hill.

Gawain, S. (1990). "God in Everyday Life." From B. Shield & R. Carlson (Ed.), *For the Love of God* pp. 145-151. California: New World Library.

Gil, Eliana. (1990). *United We Stand: A Book for People with Multiple Personalities.* Walnut Creek, CA: Launch Press.

Glass, James. (1993). *Shattered Selves: Multiple Personality in a Post Modern World.* New York: Cornell University.

Glesne, C. & Peshkin, A. (1992). *Becoming Qualitative Researchers: An Introduction.* New York: Longman.

Goettman, C., Greaves, G., & Coons, P.M. (Ed.). (1994). *Multiple Personality and Dissociation, 1791-1992: A Complete Bibliography.* Lutherville, MD: The Sidran Press.

Golston, Joan C. (1993). "Raising Hell in Psychotherapy," *Treating Abuse Today.*

Gonzalez, Shapiro and others. (1993). "Children's Patterns of Disclosures and Recantations of Sexual and Ritualistic Abuse Allegations in Psychotherapy." *Child Abuse and Neglect: The International Journal,* 17, 2, March/April.

Goodwin, J. (1990). "Sadistic Sexual Abuse." Illustration from the Marquis de Sade. Chicago, IL: Paper delivered at Seventh International Conference on Multiple Personality/Dissociative States.

Gould, Catherine. (1989). Comments. *Ritual Child Abuse: A Professional Overview.* Ukia, CA: Calvacade Productions (videotape).

———. (1995). "Torture-based Mind Control: What It Is and How to Treat It." Los Angeles, CA: 1995 Ritual Abuse Conference. (Report). September 29, 1995.

Gould, Catherine & Cozouno, Louis. (1992). "Ritual Abuse, Multiplicity, and Mind Control." *Journal of Psychology and Theology,* 20, pp. 194-196.

Greaves, G. (1989). A Cognitive-Behavioral Approach to the Treatment of MPD Ritually Abused Satanic Cult Survivors." Chicago, IL: Paper presented at the Sixth International Conference of Multiple Personality/Dissociative States.

Greaves, George B. (1992). "Alternative Hypotheses Regarding Claims of Satanic Cult Activity: A critical analysis." In D. Sakheim & S. Devine (Ed.), *Out of Darkness: Exploring Satanism and Ritual Abuse,* pp. 45-69, New York: Lexington Books.

Grof, Christine & Grof, S. (1993). "Spiritual Emergency : The Understanding and Treatment of Transpersonal Crises." In R. Walsh & F. Vaughan (Ed.), *Paths Beyond Ego: The Transpersonal Vision,* pp. 137-143. New York: J.G. Putnam's Sons.

———. (1993). Addiction as a Spiritual Emergency. In R. Walsh & F. Vaughan (Eds.), *Paths Beyond Ego: The Transpersonal Vision,* pp. 144-148. New York: J. G. Putnam's Sons.

Grof, C. (1994). *The Thirst for Wholeness.* San Francisco, CA: Harper.

Grof, S. (1988). *The Adventure of Self-discovery.* New York: State University of New York Press.

———. (1996). "Observations from Psychedelic Therapy and Holotropic Breathwork." In S.Boorstein (Ed.), *Transpersonal Psychotherapy*, pp. 485-519. New York: State University of New York Press.

Guiley, Rosemary Ellen. (1991). *Harper's Encyclopedia of Mystical and Paranormal Experience.* New York: Castle Books.

Haley, J. (1976). *Problem-solving Therapy.* San Francisco: Jossey-Bass.

Hamel, J., DuFour, S., & Fortin, D. (1993). *Case Study Methods*. California: Sage Publications, Inc.

Hergenhahn, B. (1994). *An Introduction to Theories of Personality*. Englewood Cliffs, NJ: Prentice-Hall.

Herman, J. (1986). "Recovery and Verification of Memories of Childhood Sexual Trauma." Washington, D.C. Paper presented at the annual meeting of the American Psychiatric Association.

————. (1990). "The Treatment of Trauma: Incest as a Paradigm." Cambridge, Mass.: Paper presented at *Psychological Trauma*. Sponsored by Harvard Medical School.

Herman, J. & Harvey, M. (1993). "The False Memory Debate: Social Science or Social Backlash. *The Harvard Mental Health Letter*, 9, 10.

Hertenstein, Mike and Truit, Jim. (1993) *Selling Satan*. Chicago, IL: Cornerstone Press.

Hicks, R. (1990). "Police Pursuit of Satanic Crime: I." *Skeptical Inquirer,* 14, pp. 276-286.

Hill, Sally & Goodwin, Jean. (1990). "Satanism: Similarities Between Patient Accounts and Pre-inquisition Historical Sources." *Dissociation*, 2, 39-44.

Hill, M. (1993). *Archival Strategies and Techniques*. Newberry Park, CA.: Sage Publications, Inc.

Hindas, A. (1981). "Psychotherapy and Surrender: A Psychospiritual Perspective." *The Journal of Transpersonal Psycholog.* pp. 13, 27-31.

Hochman, John. (1994). "Recovered Memory Therapy and False Memory Syndrome." *Skeptic,* Vol. 2, *No. 3*.

Hoffman, E. (1988). *The Right to be Human: A Biography of Abraham Maslow*. Los Angeles: Tarcher.

Hoffman, Wendy. (1994). *Ascent From Evil*. New York: Triumph Books.

Huxley, A. (1993). "The Perennial Philosophy." In R. Walsh & F. Vaughan (Ed*.), Paths Beyond Ego: The Transpersonal Vision,* pp. 212-213. New York: J.G. Putnam's Sons.

The Institute of Transpersonal Psychology. (1996-1997). Palo Alto, CA: Self-Published.

International Society of the Study of Dissociation. (1994). *Practice Guidelines Glossary*.

Jackson, D. (1965). Family rules: Marital Quid Pro Quo. *Archives of General Psychiatry,* 12, pp. 589-594.

James. W. (1961). *The Varieties of Religious Experience*. New York: Collier Books. (Original work published 1902.)

———. (1983). *The Principles of Psychology*. Cambridge: Harvard University Press. (Original work published 1890).

Johnson, Steve. (1995). *Past Imperfect*. Chicago: Chicago Tribune Company.

Jones, David. (1991). "Ritualism and Child Sexual Abuse. Child Abuse and Neglect:" *The International Journal,* 15, pg. 3.

Jonker, F. and Jonker-Bakker, P. "Experiences with Ritualistic Child Sexual Abuse: A Case Study from the Netherlands." *Child Abuse and Neglect: The International Journal*, 15, 3.

Jue, R. (1996). "Past-life Therapy." In B. Scotton, A. Chinen, & J. Battista (Ed.), *Textbook of Transpersonal Psychiatry and Psychology*, pp. 377-387. New York: BasicBooks.

Jung, C. (1958). Foreword to the *I Ching*, commentary on the *Tibetan Book of Great Liberation and The Tibetan Book of the Dead*, and foreword to *Introduction to Zen Buddhism*. In *Collected Works* (Vol. 11). Princeton, NJ.: Princeton University Press. Commentary on *The Golden Flower*. In *Collected Works* (Vol. 13). Princeton, NJ: Princeton University Press.

Jung, C. (1977). "On the Psychology and Pathology of So-called Occult Phenomena." In C. Jung, (Ed.), *Psychology and the Occult*, pp. 6-91. Princeton: Princeton University Press. (Original work published 1902.)

Kahner. (1988). *Cults That Kill*. Warner Books: New York.

Katchen, Martin H. (1992). "The History of Satanic Religions," in Sakheim and Devine, *Out of Darkness: Exploring Satanism and Ritual Abuse*. New York: Lexington Books.

Kavanaugh, K. (Trans.) (1991). *The Collected Works of Saint John of the Cross*. (Rev. Ed.), Washington: ICS Publications. As referenced in Steele, S. (1994). "The Multistate Paradigm and the Spiritual Path of John of the Cross." *The Journal of Transpersonal Psychology*, 26, 55-80.

Kernberg, O. (1975). *Borderline Conditions and Pathological Narcissism*. New York: Jason Aronson.

Kernberg, O. (1976). *Object Relations Theory and Clinical Psychoanalysis*. New York: Jason Aronson.

Kernberg, O. (1982). "Self, Ego, Affects, and Drives." *Journal of the American Psychoanalytic Association*, pp. 893-917.

Kernberg, O. (1984). *Severe Personality Disorders*. New Haven: Yale University Press.

Kierkegaard, S. (1954). *Fear and Trembling and the Sickness Unto Death.* Garden City, NJ: Doubleday.

Kinscherff, Robert and Barnum, Richard. (1992). "Child Forencis Evaluation and Claims of Ritual Abuse or Satanic Cult Activity: A Critical Analysis in Sakheim and Devine, *Out of Darkness: Exploring Satanism & Ritual Abuse.* New York: Lexington Books.

Klein, M. (1952). Some theoretical conclusions regarding the emotional life of the infant. In M. Klein (Ed.). (1975). E*nvy and gratitude and other works, 1946-1963.* New York: Delacorte Press.

Klein, M. & Tribich, D. (1981). "Kernberg's Object-relations Theory: A Critical Evaluation." *International Journal of Psychoanalysis,* pp. 27-43.

Kluft, Richard P. (1984). "An Introduction to Multiple Personality Disorder." *Psychiatric Annals,* 14, pp. 19- 24.

———. (1984). "Treatment of Multiple Personality Disorder: A study of 33 cases." *Psychiatric Clinics of North America.* 7, *pp* 9-29.

———. (1985). *Childhood Antecedents of Multiple Personality.* Washington, DC: American Psychiatric Press, Inc.

———. (1987). "First Rank Symptoms as a Diagnostic Clue to Multiple Personality Disorder." *American Journal of Psychiatry,* pp. 144, 293-298.

Laney, M. (1996). "Multiple Personality Disorder: Resilience and Creativity in the Preservation of the Self." *Psychoanalysis and Psychotherapy,* 13, pg. 1.

Langer, Lawrence. (1991). *Holocaust Testimonies: The Ruins of Memory.* New Haven, CT: Yale University Press.

Laning, Kenneth V. (1991). "Ritual Abuse: A Law Enforcement View or Perspective." *Child Abuse and Neglect: The International Journal,* 15, 3.

Larson, Bob. (1990). *In the Name of Satan: An In-depth Look at Satanism.* Denver, CO: Compassion Connection, Inc.

Lee, K. & Speier, P. (1996). "Breathwork: Theory and Technique." In B. Scotton, A. Chinen, and J. Battista, (Ed.), *Textbook of Transpersonal Psychiatry and Psychology,* pp. 366-376. New York: BasicBooks.

Lehrman, Fredric. (1995). *Prosperity Consciousness.* Illinois: Nightengale-Conant Corp.

Lincoln, Y. & Guba, E. (1985). *Naturalistic Inquiry.* Beverly Hills, CA: Sage Publications.

Lobby, T. (1990). *Jessica and the Wolf.* New York: Magination Press.

Loftus, Elizabeth F. (1993). The Reality of Repressed Memories. *American Psychologist.* 48, pp. 518-537.

Loftus, E. (1995). "Afterward" in C. Ross, *Satanic Ritual Abuse: Principles of Treatment,* pp. 203-209. Toronto, Canada: University of Toronto Press.

London, P. (1965). "Developmental experiments in hypnosis.*" Journal of Projective Techniques and Personality Assessments,* 29, pp. 189-199.

London, Perry & Cooper, Leslie M. (1969). "Norms of Hypnotic Susceptibility in Children." *Developmental Psychology,* 1, pp. 113-124.

Lowenstein, F. (1992). "President's Message." *ISSMP & D. News.*

Loewenstein, R. (1993). "Posttraumatic and Dissociative Aspects of Transference and Countertransference in the Treatment of Multiple Personality Disorder." In R. Kluft, and G. Fine (Eds.), *Clinical Perspectives on Multiple Personality Disorder,* pp. 51-85. Washington, D.C.: American Psychiatric Press.

Lukoff, Turner. (1993). "Transpersonal Psychology Research Review: Psychospiritual Dimensions of Reality." *The Journal of Transpersonal Psychology.* Vol. 25. Nov. 1.

Lynn, W. (Ed.). (1993). *Mending Ourselves.* Ohio: Many Voices Press.

Lyons, A. (1988). *Satan Wants You: The Cult of Devil Worship in America.* New York: Mysterious Press.

Mahen, Nancy. (1993-1994). As reported in *The Newsletter for the Society for the Investigation, Treatment, and Prevention of Ritual and Cult Abuse,* 1, 3, Fall/Winter.

Maddison, J. (1953). "A Case of Double Personality." *Medical Journal of Australia,* 1, pp. 814-816.

Madsen, D. (1983). "Successful Dissertations and Theses." San Francisco: Jossey-Bass Publishers.

MacDonald, M., Brown, K., & Mitsch, R. (1991). *Setting New Boundaries.* Nashville, TN: Thomas Nelson, Inc.

Mahler, M. (1952). "On Child Psychosis and Schizophrenia: Autistic and Symbiotic Infantile Psychoses." *Psychoanalytic Study of the Child,* 7, pp. 206-305.

Mahler, M., Pine, F., & Bergman, A. (1975). *The Psychological Birth of the Human Infant.* New York: BasicBooks.

Malenbaum, Roxanne and Russell, Andrew T. (1987). "Multiple Personality Disorder in an Eleven-Year-Old-Boy and His Mother." *Journal of the American Academy of Child and Adolescent Psychiatry.* Vol. 24, No. 3.

Many Voices: Words of Hope for People with MPD or a Dissociative Disorder. (1993). Cincinnati, OH: MV Co.

Maslow, A. (1964). *Religions, Values and Peak Experiences.* Columbus, OH: Ohio State University Press.

———. (1969). Theory Z. *Journal of Transpersonal Psychology,* pp. 31-47.

———. (1972). *The Farther Reaches of Human Nature.* New York: Viking Press.

Masson, J. (1984). *The Assault on Truth.* New York: Farrar, Strauss, & Giroux.

Marmer, S. (1991). "Multiple Personality Disorder: A Psychoanalytic Perspective." *Psychiatric Clinics of North America,* 14, pp. 377-693.

May, R. (1953). *Man's Search for Himself.* New York: Norton.

———. (1969). *Love and Will.* New York: Norton.

———. (1977). *The Meaning of Anxiety.* New York: Norton.

Mayer, Robert. (1992). *Satan's Children,* New York: Avon Books. October 1992.

———t. (1992). *Through Divided Minds.* New York: Avon Books.

Middleton-Moz, J. (1989). *Children of Trauma.* Deerfield Beach, FL: Health Communications, Inc.

Millon, T. (1981). *Disorders of Personality.* New York: John Wiley & Sons.

Minuchin, S. (1974). *Families and Family Therapy.* Cambridge, MA: Harvard University Press.

Mithers, Carol. (1994). *Silent Scream.* Buzz, Inc.

Moffatt, Bettyclaire. (1994). *Soulwork.* California: Wildcat Canyon Press.

Mollica, Richard F., Grace Wyshek, James Lavelle, Toan Trung, Svang Tor and Ter Yang. (1990). "Assessing Symptoms of Change in Southeast Asian Refugee Survivors of Mass Violence and Torture." *American Journal of Psychiatry.* Vol. 147. No. 1. January.

Money, J. (1974). "Two Names, Two Wardrobes, Two Personalities." *Journal of Homosexuality,* 1, pp. 5-70.

Modestin, J. (1992). "Multiple Personality in Switzerland." *American Journal of Psychiatry,* 149, pp. 88-92.

Moore, Thomas. (1994). *Care of the Soul.* New York: Harper Perennial.

Moriarty, Anthony R. (1991). "Adolescent Satanic Cult Dabblers: A Differential Diagnosis." *Journal of Mental Health Counseling*, 13, 3, July.

Mother Teresa. (1990). "Compassion in Action." In B. Shield, & R. Carlson (Ed.), *For the Love of God,* pp. 179-181. California: New World Library.

Mosak, H. & Lefevre, C. (1976). "The Resolution of 'Intrapersonal Conflict.'" *Journal of Individual Psychology,* 32, pp. 19-26.

Mungadze, J. (1992). "Scripts and Screen Memories in Victims of Ritual Abuse." 1992 ISSMP&D Conference. (Presentation).

————. (1995). "Christian Perspectives on Healing from Ritual Abuse and Mind Control." Los Angeles, CA: 1995 Ritual Abuse Conference. (Report).

Murphy, E. (1983). *God Cares for Me When I'm Thankful.* Elgin, IL. David C. Cook Publishing Co.

Murphy, M. and Donovan, S. (1989). *The Physical and Psychological Effects of Meditation.* San Rafael, CA: Esalen Institute.

Murphy, L.and Moriarty, A. (1976). *Vulnerability, Coping and Growth: From Infancy to Adolescence.* New Haven, CT: Yale University Press.

Nathan, Debbie and Snedeker, Michael. (1995). *Satan's Silence.* New York: Harper Collins Publishers, Inc.

Nelson, John E. (1994). *Healing the Split.* New York: State University of New York Press.

Neswald, D., and Gould, C. (1992). "Basic Treatment and Program Neutralization Strategies for Adult MPD Survivors of Satanic Ritual Abuse." *Treating Abuse Today,* pp. 2, 5-9.

Neswald, D., Gould, C., and Graham-Costain, V. (1991). "Common Programs Observed in Survivors of Satanic Ritual Abuse." *The California Therapist.*

Neswald, D. (1992). "Working with Primal Dissociative Experiences in Adult MPD Survivors of Satanic Ritualistic Abuse." Costa Mesa, CA: Fifth Annual Western Clinical Conference on Multiple Personality and Dissociation. (Report).

Noblett, Randy. (1993-94). "Multiple Choice: Which of the Following is the Most False: (A) The Memory (B) The Syndrome, or (C) The Foundation?" *The Society for the Investigation, Treatment, and Prevention of Ritual and Cult Abuse,* 1, 3, Fall/Winter.

Noll, R. (1990). *Bizarre Diseases of the Mind.* New York: Berkeley.

Pagans, Lonzo R. "Bo" (1995). *A Journey to the Me That I Can Be.* Desktop Publishing.

"Pain Produces Relief in Some Who Self-cut." *The Menninger Letter*, February, 1993.

Peters, L. (1981). *Ecstacy and Healing in Nepal.* Los Angeles: Undena Publications.

———. (1981). "An Experiential Study of Nepalese Shamanism." *The Journal of Transpersonal Psychology,* 13, pp. 1-26.

Prather, H. (1990). "Walking Home." In B. Shield & R. Carlson (Ed.), *For the Love of God.* pp. 172-178. California: New World Library.

Putnam, F. (1989). *Diagnosis and Treatment of Multiple Personality Disorder.* New York: The Guilford Press.

Putnam, Frank W. (1991). "The Satanic Ritual Abuse Controversy." *Child Abuse and Neglect: The International Journal,* 15, pg. 3.

Putman, F., Ganaway, G., Noel, R., Milhern, S. (1990). "Satanic Ritual Abuse, Critical Issues, and Alternative Hypothesis." Panel presentation at the Seventh International Conference on Multiple Personality/Dissociative States: Chicago, IL.

Putnam, F., Guroff, J., Silberman, E., Barban, L., and Post, R. (1986). "The Clinical Phenomenology of Multiple Personality Disorder: A review of 100 recent cases." *Journal of Clinical Psychiatry,* 47, pp. 285-293.

Pynoos, Robert S. (1994). *Post-traumatic Stress Disorder: A Clinical Review*, Lutherville, MD: Sidran Press.

Rasey, M. (1956). "Toward the End. In Moustakas," *The Self: Explorations in Personal Growth.* New York: Harper.

Reaching Out Newsletter, Woodland, CA, February, 1994.

"Report of the Ritual Abuse Task Force, Los Angeles County Commission for Women." *Ritual Abuse*, 1991.

Riggall, R. (1931). "A Case of Multiple Personality." *Lancet.* ii.

"Ritual Child Abuse: Definitions Typology and Prevalence." *Believe The Children Newsletter,* X, Fall, 1993.

Robertson, L., Flinders, C., & Ruppenthal, B. (1986). *Laurel's Kitchen.* Berkeley, CA: Ten Speed Press.

Rodgers, R. (1982). Multiple Personality and Channeling. *Jefferson Journal of Psychiatry,* 9, pp. 3- 13.

Rogers, C. (1942). *Counseling and Psychotherapy*. Boston: Houghton Mifflin.

———. (1957). "The Necessary and Sufficient Conditions of Therapeutic Personality Change." *Journal of Counseling Psychology,* 21, pp. 95-103.

———. (1980). *A Way of Being*. Boston: Houghton Mifflin.

Ross, Colin A. (1989). *Multiple Personality Disorder*. New York: John Wiley and Sons.

———. (1995). *Satanic Ritual Abuse: Principles of Treatment*. Toronto, Canada: University Toronto Press.

———. (1994). *The Osiris Complex*. Toronto, Canada: University of Toronto Press.

Ross, Colin A. & Heber, S. (1989). *The Dissociative Disorders Interview Schedule*.

Ross, C., Miller, D., Reagor, P., Bjornson, L., Fraser, G., & Anderson, G. (1990). "Schneiderian Symptoms in Multiple Personality Disorder and Schizophrenia." *Comprehensive Psychiatry,* 31, pp. 111-118.

Ross, C., Miller, S., Reagor, P., Bjornson, L., Fraser, G., Anderson, G. (1990). "Structured Interview Data on 102 Cases of Multiple Personality Disorders From Four Centers" *American Journal of Psychiatry,* 147, pp. 596-600.

Ross, C., Norton, G., Wozney, K. (1989). "Multiple Personality Disorder: An analysis of 236 cases." *Canadian Journal of Psychiatry,* 34, pp. 413-418.

Rudhyar, D. (1983). *Rythmn of Wholeness*. Wheaton, Il.:Theosophical Publishing Co.

Russell, L. (1966). *Love*. Swannanoa, Waynesboro, Virginia: University of Science and Philosophy.

Rutter, M. (1983). "Stress, Coping, and Development: Some Issues and Some Questions." In Garmezy, N. & Rutter, M.(Ed.), *Stress, Coping and Development in Children*. New York: McGraw-Hill.

Ryder, Daniel. (1992). *Breaking the Circle of Satanic Ritual Abuse*. Minnesota: Comp Care Publishing.

Sakheim, D. and Devine, S. (Ed.). (1992*). Out of Darkness: Exploring Satanism and Ritual Abuse*. New York: Lexington Books.

Saltman, D. vs. Soloman, R. (1982). "Incest and the Multiple Personality." *Psychological Reports,* 50, pp. 1127-1141.

Sarte, J. (1956). *Being and Nothingness*. New York: Philosophical Library.

"Satanic Ritual Abuse" on Ontario Center for Religious Tolerance Homepage.

Schatzow, Heman, J. L. (1987). "Recovery and Verification of Memories of Childhood Sexual Trauma." *Psychoanalytic Psychology.* Vol. 4.

Schwartz, Tony. (1995). *What Really Matters: Searching for Wisdom in America.* New York: Bantam Books.

Scheffer, M. (1984). *Bach T: Theory and Practice.* Rochester, Vermont: Healing Arts Press.

Scotton, B., Chinen, A., & Battista, J. (Ed.). (1996). *Textbook of transpersonal psychiatry and psychology.* New York: BasicBooks.

Shield, B. & Carlson, R. (Ed.). (1990). *For the Love of God.* California: New World Library.

Sidran Foundation (1995). Lutherville, MD: Sidran Press.

Siegel, Bernie. (1988). *Peace, Love, Medicine, and Healing.* New York: Harper and Row.

———— (1989). *Love, Medicine, and Miracles.* New York: Harper and Row.

Skinner, B. (1953). *Science and Human Behavior.* New York: Macmillan.

Smith, Michelle and Pazder, Lawrence. (1980). *Michelle Remembers.* New York: Simon and Schuster, Inc.

Smith, Michelle. (1993). *Ritual Abuse: What It Is, Why It Happens, How To Help.* San Francisco: Harper.

Socarides, D. and Stolorow, R. (1984-85). "Affects of self objects." *The Annual of Psychoanalysis.* 12/13.

StarDancer, Caryn. (1992). "Sibylline Shackles: Mind Control in the Context of Ritual Abuse." *Survivorship.* San Francisco, CA.

State of Illinois Public Act #87-1167, January 1, 1993.

Steindl-Rast D. (1990). "Encounter With God Through the Senses." In B.Shield, & R. Carlson (Ed.), *For the Love of God,* pp. 91-96. California: New World Library.

Stoop, D., & Arterburn, S. (1991). *The Twelve Step Life Recovery Devotional.* Wheaton, IL: Tyndale House Publishers.

Sratford, Lauren. (1993). *Stripped Naked.* Gretna, LA: Pelican Publishing Company.

Survivorship Newsletter, #3181, Mission #139, San Francisco, CA.

Sutich, A. (1969). "Some considerations regarding transpersonal psychology." *The Journal of Transpersonal Psychology,* pp. 11-26.

Symonds, John and Grant, Kenneth. (1979). *The Confessions of Alliester Crowley*. London: Arkana.

Taped Material – The Madeline Center.

Tart, C. (1991). "Multiple Personality, Altered States of Consciousness and Virtual Reality: The World Simulation Process Approach." *Dissociation,* pp. 222-233.

Tart, C. (1993). "The Systems Approach to Consciousness." In R. Walsh, and F. Vaughan, (Ed.), *Paths Beyond Ego: The Transpersonal Vision,* pp. 34-37. New York: J.G. Putnam's Sons.

Terry, M. (1987). *The Ultimate Evil: An Investigation of America's Most Dangerous Satanic Cult*. Garden City, NY: Doubleday.

Thompson, Richard. (1995). *Alien Identities*. Govardhon Hill Publishing. ghi@nerdc. ufl.edu.

Ulman, R. and Brothers, J. (1988). *A Psychoanalytic Study of Trauma: The Shattered Self*. Hillsdale, NJ. Analytic Press.

Van der Kolk, Bessel A., Perry, Christopher; Herman, Judith Lewis (1991). "Childhood Origins of Self-destructive Behavior." *American Journal of Psychiatry*. Vol. 148, No. 7, July.

Vaughan, F. (1993). "Healing and Wholeness: Transpersonal Psychotherapy." In R. Walsh, and F. Vaughan (Ed.), *Paths Beyond Ego: The Transpersonal Vision,* pp. 160-164. New York: J.G. Putnam's Sons.

———. (1995). *The Inward Arc: Healing in Psychotherapy and Spirituality*. Nevada City, CA: Blue Dolphin Publishing, Inc.

Victor, B. (1996). "Psychopharmacology and Transpersonal Psychology." In B. Scotton, A. Chinen, and J. Battista (Ed.), *Textbook of Transpersonal Psychiatry and Psychology,* pp. 227-234. New York: BasicBooks.

Wade, Janelle. (1993). *Out of Darkness*. Pennsylvania: Destiny Image.

Wade, J. (1996). *Changes of Mind: A Holonomic Theory of the Evolution of Consciousness*. New York: The State University of New York Press.

Waldschmidt, Carol, Graham-Costain, Vicki, and Gould, Catherine. (1991). "Memory Association in Play Therapy with Children with Multiple Personality Disorder." *Eighth International Conference on Multiple/Dissociative States*. (Report).

Wallis, L. (1985). *Stories for the Third Ear: Using Hypnotic Fables in Psychotherapy*. New York: W.W. Norton & Company, Inc.

Walsh, Roger, & Vaughan, Frances (Ed.). (1993). *Paths Beyond Ego: The Transpersonal Vision*. New York: G. P. Putnam Sons.

Warnke, Mike. (1972). *The Satan Seller.* New Jersey: Bridge Publishing, Inc.

Washburn, M. (1994). *Transpersonal Psychology in Psychoanalytic Perspective.* New York: State University of New York.

———. (1995). *The Ego and the Dynamic Ground.* New York: State University of New York.

Weiss, Morris; Sutton, Patricia; and Utecht, A.J. "Multiple Personality in a Ten-Year-Old- Girl." *Journal of the Academy of Child Psychiatry,* Vol. 24, No. 4.

West, Carol. (1993). *A Rainbow for Patti.* Ohio: Behavioral Science Center, Inc., Publications.

West, Kenneth. (1986). Lecture notes. Lynchburg College.

Wilbur, K., Engler, J., & Brown, D. (Ed.). (1986). *Transformations of Consciousness.* London: Shambhala Publishing.

Wilber, Ken. (1977). *Spectrum of Consciousness.* Wheaton, IL: Quest Publishing.

———. (1979). *No Boundary: Eastern and Western Approaches to Personal Growth.* Boston, MA: Shambhala Publishing.

———. (1980). *Atman Project: A Transpersonal View of Development.* Wheaton, IL: Quest Publishing.

———. (1993). The Great Chain of Being. In R. Walsh, and F.Vaughan (Ed.), *Paths Beyond Ego: The Transpersonal Vision,* pp. 214-222. New York: J.G. Putnam's Sons.

———. (1995). *Sex, Ecology, Spirituality: The Spirit of Evolution.* Boston, MA: Shambhala Publishing.

———. (1996). Transpersonal Art and Literary Theory. *The Journal of Transpersonal Psychology,* 28, pp. 63-91.

Wilde, Stuart. (1993). *Whispering Winds of Change.* Carson, CA: Hag House, Inc.

"Witchcraft in America" (video) produced by Hex Productions in association with A & E Networks, 1993.

Williams-Heller, Ann. (1990). *Kabbalah-Your Path of Inner Freedom.* London: The Theosophical Publishing House.

Wittine, B. (1993). "Assumptions of Transpersonal Psychotherapy." In R. Walsh, and F. Vaughan (Ed.), *Paths Beyond Ego: The Transpersonal Vision,* pp. 165-170. New York: J. G. Putnam's Sons.

Wolcott, H. (1990). *Writing Up Qualitative Research*. Newberry Park, CA.: Sage Publications, Inc.

Wylie, D. (1993). "The Shadow of Doubt." *The Family Therapy Networker,* 3, pp. 23-31.

Yalom, I. (1981). *Existential Psychotherapy*. New York: BasicBooks.

Yapko, J. (1993). "The Seductions of Memory." *The Family Therapy Networker,* 3, pp. 32-41.

Yensen, R. & Dryer, D. (1996). "The Consciousness Research of Stanislav Grof." In B. Scotton, A. Chinen, & J. Battista (Ed.), *Textbook of Transpersonal Psychiatry and Psychology,* pp. 75-84. New York: BasicBooks.

Yin, R. (1994). *Case Study Research: Design and Methods*. California: Sage Publications, Inc.

Young, Walter and others. (1991). "Patients Reporting Ritual Abuse C: A Clinical Syndrome. Report of 37 Cases." *Child Abuse and Neglect: The International Journal,* 15, pp. 181-189.

Young, W. (1992). "Recognition and Treatment of Survivors Reporting Ritual Abuse." In D. Sakheim & S. Devine (Ed.), *Out of Darkness: Exploring Satanism & Ritual Abuse,* pp. 249-278. New York: Lexington Books/ Macmillan.

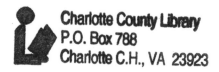